Cruising Utopia

Cruising Utopia

The Then and There of Queer Futurity

José Esteban Muñoz

NEW YORK UNIVERSITY PRESS
New York and London

NEW YORK UNIVERSITY PRESS
New York and London
www.nyupress.org

"For Freddy, Fucking Again," poem by Diane di Prima, from *Freddie Poems* (Point Reyes, CA: Eidolon Editions, 1974). Courtesy of the author.

"Having a Coke with You," from *The Collected Poems of Frank O'Hara*, by Frank O'Hara, edited by Donald Allen. Copyright © 1971 by Maureen Granville-Smith, Administratrix of The Estate of Frank O'Hara. Reprinted by permission of Alfred A. Knopf, a division of Random House, Inc.

"A photograph," *Collected Poems*, by James Schuyler. Copyright © 1993 by the Estate of James Schuyler. Reprinted by permission of Farrar, Straus and Giroux, LLC.

"One Art," from *The Complete Poems, 1927–1979*, by Elizabeth Bishop. Copyright © 1979, 1983 by Alice Helen Methfessel. Reprinted by permission of Farrar, Straus and Giroux, LLC.

Library of Congress Cataloging-in-Publication Data

Muñoz, José Esteban
Cruising utopia : the then and there of queer futurity / José Esteban Muñoz.
p. cm. — (Sexual cultures)
Includes bibliographical references and index.
ISBN-13: 978-0-8147-5727-7 (cl : alk. paper)
ISBN-10: 0-8147-5727-8 (cl : alk. paper)
ISBN-13: 978-0-8147-5728-4 (pb : alk. paper)
ISBN-10: 0-8147-5728-6 (pb : alk. paper)
1. Queer theory. 2. Utopias. 3. Homosexuality and art. 4. Performance art. I. Title.
HQ76.25.M86   2009
306.7601—dc22   2009021714

New York University Press books are printed on acid-free paper,
and their binding materials are chosen for strength and durability.
We strive to use environmentally responsible suppliers and materials
to the greatest extent possible in publishing our books.

Manufactured in the United States of America

c 10 9 8 7 6 5 4 3 2 1
p 10 9 8 7 6 5 4 3 2 1

Contents

Acknowledgments

THIS BOOK HAS been in the works for over ten years. I cannot hope to properly acknowledge all the people who have been supportive of the writing and research that went into these pages. I have presented the writing that became these chapters at seemingly countless universities, museums, performance spaces, and conferences. At these various institutions many audiences listened to this work and engaged in beneficial ways. Queer friendship has proven to be the condition of possibility for imagining what queerness can and should mean. The actual relational circuits I am lucky enough to find myself belonging to whet my desire for future collectivity.

I have had the gift of extraordinary research assistance. Joshua Chambers-Letson has invested so much of his own energy and intelligence in this book. Sujay Pandit has been indispensable in my completing this project. The manuscript benefited from the attention of Julia Steinmetz and Chelsea Adewunmi. So many excellent students have proven to be such great interlocutors for this book as it emerged. This list will be woefully incomplete: Hypatia Vourloumis, Jeanne Vacarro, Frank Leon Roberts, Sandra Ruiz, Katie Brewer-Ball, Eser Selen, Tina Majkowski, Karen Jamie, Ellen Cleghorne, Beth Stinson, Alex Pittman, Lydia Brawner, Roy Perez, Albert Laguna, Andre Carrington, Leticia Alvarado, Anna Fischer, Jonathan Mullins, Ronak Kapadia, Stephanie Weiss, and Justin Leroy. One of the greatest rewards in teaching is when your former students become your colleagues and friends: there are no better examples of this in my life than Christine Balance, Ricardo Montez, and Alexandra Vazquez. Also in that category is Shane Vogel, who also gave me great feedback on this volume. I teach in a relatively small department that I have chaired for the past few years, and I am grateful for the climate of mutual support and respect achieved in the Department of Performance Studies, Tisch School of the Arts at NYU. Colleagues like Barbara Browning, Karen Shimakawa, Richard Schenchner, Andre Lepcki, Diana Taylor, Barbara Kirshenblatt-Gimblet, Allen Weiss, Anna Deavere Smith, Deborah Kapchan, Tavia Nyong'o, and Ann Pellegrini make institutional life rewarding. Ann has been a co-editor of the series this book appears in, and I could never have anticipated enjoying such a fun and harmonious working relationship. I cannot begin to express properly my gratitude to the staff at Performance Studies who enable my work as a chair, a faculty member, and a scholar. Thank you Noel Rodriguez, Patty Jang, and Laura Elena Fortes for your extreme competence and good humor. Many friends outside of Performance Studies at NYU need to be thanked for their contributions to the texture of my life and thinking. The first to be mentioned is Lisa Duggan, who has been a staunch ally, loving friend, and brilliant interlocutor. Other friends include Anna McCarthy, Josefina Saldana-Portillo, Gayatri Gopinath, Ana Dopico, Phillip Brian Harper, and Carolyn Dinshaw.

The three scholars who have read this book for the press in different drafts offered me welcomed engagement. Elizabeth Freeman and I met each other as precocious graduate students on the conference circuit, and I see in her work some of the best thinking of my second-generation queer theory cohort. Judith Halberstam has simply been an ideal colleague and reader. She is also an amazing friend. I feel privileged to have the brilliant Fred Moten as a friend, comrade, and interlocutor. My editor, Eric Zinner, read this book with great care and skill. Ciara McLaughlin and Emily Park have been also been extremely helpful. A grant from the Tisch Dean's Faculty Development Award has helped me include color images in this book. I am especially grateful to Marvin Taylor and Ann Butler at the Fales Library, New York University.

John Andrews showed up in the middle of this writing project. He has responded to my work with equal parts enthusiasm and skepticism. He has been a perfect reader and the very best company I could have asked for. My other great companions during the writing of this book have been my princess bulldogs. The late great Lady Bully showed me the grandeur of companion-species utopias, and Dulce Maria is herself the sturdy embodiment of the good life. My family are amazingly supportive. My brother Alex's support is very touching. My cousin Albert strolled into my everyday life quite unexpectedly and has become a lovely presence, helping me watch the Northern Front. Sam Green is my kindred utopian spirit; his work and our bond inspire me. I am fortunate to know Jennifer Doyle, who has responded to my life and work with so much love, generosity, and intelligence. I owe a great debt to Kevin McCarty for helping me glimpse utopia. Luke Dowd has been my friend forever, and I continue to learn from his work and find beauty there. Tony Just's images have also provided necessary aesthetic pleasure. Nao Bustamante is simply awesome. Her friendship and art mean the world to me. Time spent over the years with Jonathan Flatley has been extremely rewarding. Nick Terry's friendship is treasured. I have enjoyed getting to know and write about My Barbarian (Malik Gaines, Jade Gordon, and Alex Segade), Kalup Linzy, and Dynasty Handbag (Jibz Cameron). An incomplete list of scholars, artists, and collaborators who have read this work, pushed these ideas, or generally engaged me include Lauren Berlant, Ann Cvetkovich, Ricardo Ortiz, Carla Freccero, Licia Fiol-Mata, Rebecca Schneider, Henry Abelove, Michael Moon, Jose Quiroga, Jorge Ignacio Cortinas, Alina Troyano/Carmelita Tropicana, Ela Troyano, Ana Margaret Sanchez, Karen Tongson, Carlos Carujo, David Román, Anjali Arondekar, Patricia Clough, Jasbir Puar, Michael Cobb, Josh Kun, Heather Lukes, Molly McGarry, George Haggerty, Gavin Butt, Dominic Johnson, Vaginal Davis, Janet Jacobsen, Kathleen McHugh, Chon Noriega, Eric Lott, Cindy Katz, Donald Pease, Michael Wang, Juana Maria Rodriguez, Rebecca Sumner Burgos, Coco Fusco, Abe Weintraub, and Shari Frilot. My foundational friendship with Antonio Viego makes this work and so much more possible. Guinevere Turner has kept things real in the most hallucinatory ways. Eve Kosofsky Sedgwick passed as I finished this book. She has been my great friend and mentor. Her gentle touch and luminous inspiration is everywhere for me.

Introduction

Feeling Utopia

A map of the world that does not include utopia is not worth glancing at.
—Oscar Wilde

QUEERNESS IS NOT yet here. Queerness is an ideality. Put another way, we are not yet queer. We may never touch queerness, but we can feel it as the warm illumination of a horizon imbued with potentiality. We have never been queer, yet queerness exists for us as an ideality that can be distilled from the past and used to imagine a future. The future is queerness's domain. Queerness is a structuring and educated mode of desiring that allows us to see and feel beyond the quagmire of the present. The here and now is a prison house. We must strive, in the face of the here and now's totalizing rendering of reality, to think and feel a *then and there*. Some will say that all we have are the pleasures of this moment, but we must never settle for that minimal transport; we must dream and enact new and better pleasures, other ways of being in the world, and ultimately new worlds. Queerness is a longing that propels us onward, beyond romances of the negative and toiling in the present. Queerness is that thing that lets us feel that this world is not enough, that indeed something is missing. Often we can glimpse the worlds proposed and promised by queerness in the realm of the aesthetic. The aesthetic, especially the queer aesthetic, frequently contains blueprints and schemata of a forward-dawning futurity. Both the ornamental and the quotidian can contain a map of the utopia that is queerness. Turning to the aesthetic in the case of queerness is nothing like an escape from the social realm, insofar as queer aesthetics map future social relations. Queerness is also a performative because it is not simply a being but a doing for and toward the future. Queerness is essentially about the rejection of a here and now and an insistence on potentiality or concrete possibility for another world.

1

That is the argument I make in *Cruising Utopia*, significantly influenced by the thinking and language of the German idealist tradition emanating from the work of Immanuel Kant and Georg Wilhelm Friedrich Hegel. An aspect of that line of thought is concretized in the critical philosophy associated with the Frankfurt School, most notably in the work of Theodor Adorno, Walter Benjamin, and Herbert Marcuse. Those three thinkers within the Marxist tradition have all grappled with the complexities of the utopian. Yet the voice and logic that most touches me, most animates my thinking, is that of the philosopher Ernst Bloch.

More loosely associated with the Frankfurt School than the aforementioned philosophers, Bloch's work was taken up by both liberation theology and the Parisian student movements of 1968. He was born in 1885 to an assimilated Jewish railway employee in Ludwigshafen, Germany. During World War II, Bloch fled Nazi Germany, eventually settling for a time in Cambridge, Massachusetts. After the war Bloch returned to East Germany, where his Marxian philosophy was seen as too revisionary. At the same time he was derided for his various defenses of Stalinism by left commentators throughout Europe and the United States. He participated in the intellectual circles of Georg Simmel and, later, Max Weber. His friendship and sometime rivalries with Adorno, Benjamin, and Georg Lukács are noted in European left intellectual history.[1] Bloch's political inconsistencies and style, which has been described as both elliptical and lyrical, have led Bloch to an odd and uneven reception. Using Bloch for a project that understands itself as part of queer critique is also a risky move because it has been rumored that Bloch did not hold very progressive opinions on issues of gender and sexuality.[2] These biographical facts are beside the point because I am using Bloch's theory not as orthodoxy but instead to create an opening in queer thought. I am using the occasion and example of Bloch's thought, along with that of Adorno, Marcuse, and other philosophers, as a portal to another mode of queer critique that deviates from dominant practices of thought existing within queer critique today. In my estimation a turn to a certain critical idealism can be an especially useful hermeneutic.

For some time now I have been working with Bloch's three-volume philosophical treatise *The Principle of Hope*.[3] In his exhaustive book Bloch considers an expanded idea of the utopian that surpasses Thomas More's formulation of utopias based in fantasy. *The Principle of Hope* offers an encyclopedic approach to the phenomenon of utopia. In that text he discusses all manner of utopia including, but not limited to, social, literary, technological, medical, and geographic utopias. Bloch has had a shakier reception in the U.S. academy than have some of his friends and acquaintances—such as Benjamin. For me, Bloch's utility has much to do with the way he theorizes utopia. He makes a critical distinction between abstract utopias and concrete utopias, valuing abstract utopias only insofar as they pose a critique function that fuels a critical and potentially transformative political imagination.[4] Abstract utopias falter for Bloch because they are untethered from any historical consciousness. Concrete utopias are relational to historically situated struggles, a collectivity that is actualized or potential. In our everyday life abstract utopias are akin to banal optimism. (Recent calls for gay or queer optimism seem too close to elite homosexual evasion of politics.) Concrete utopias can also be daydreamlike, but they are the hopes of a collective, an emergent group, or even the solitary oddball who is the one who dreams for many. Concrete utopias are the realm of educated hope. In a 1961 lecture titled "Can Hope Be Disappointed?" Bloch describes different aspects of educated hope: "Not only hope's affect (with its pendant, fear) but even more so, hope's methodology (with its pendant, memory) dwells in the region of the not-yet, a place where entrance and, above all, final content are marked by an enduring indeterminacy."[5] This idea of indeterminacy in both affect and methodology speaks to a critical process that is attuned to what Italian philosopher Giorgio Agamben describes as potentiality.[6] Hope along with its other, fear, are affective structures that can be described as anticipatory.

Cruising Utopia's first move is to describe a modality of queer utopianism that I locate within a historically specific nexus of cultural production before, around, and slightly after the Stonewall rebellion of 1969. A Blochian approach to aesthetic theory is invested in describing the anticipatory illumination of art, which can be characterized as the process of identifying certain properties that can be detected in representational practices helping us to see the not-yet-conscious.[7] This not-yet-conscious is knowable, to some extent, as a utopian feeling. When Bloch describes the anticipatory illumination of art, one can understand this illumination as a surplus of both affect and meaning within the aesthetic. I track utopian feelings throughout the work of that Stonewall period. I attempt to counteract the logic of the historical case study by following an associative mode of analysis that leaps between one historical site and the present. To that end my writing brings in my own personal experience as another way to ground historical queer sites with lived queer experience. My intention in this aspect of the writing is not simply to wax anecdotally but, instead, to reach for other modes of associative argumentation and evidencing. Thus, when considering the work of a contemporary club performer such as Kevin Aviance, I engage a poem by Elizabeth Bishop and a personal recollection about movement and gender identity. When looking at Kevin McCarty's photographs of contemporary queer and punk bars, I consider accounts about pre-Stonewall gay bars in Ohio and my personal story about growing up queer and punk in suburban Miami. Most of this book is fixated on a cluster of sites in the New York City of the fifties and sixties that include the New York School of poetry, the Judson Memorial Church's dance theater, and Andy Warhol's Factory. *Cruising Utopia* looks to figures from those temporal maps that have been less attended to than O'Hara and Warhol have been. Yet it seems useful to open this book by briefly discussing moments in the work of both the poet and the pop artist for the purposes of illustrating the project's primary approach to the cultural and theoretical material it traverses. At the center of *Cruising Utopia* there is the idea of hope, which is both a critical affect and a methodology.

Bloch offers us hope as a hermeneutic, and from the point of view of political struggles today, such a critical optic is nothing short of necessary in order to combat the force of political pessimism. It is certainly difficult to argue for hope or critical utopianism at a moment when cultural analysis is dominated by an antiutopianism often functioning as a poor substitute for actual critical intervention. But before addressing the question of antiutopianism, it is worthwhile to sketch a portrait of a critical mode of hope that represents the concrete utopianism discussed here.

Jill Dolan offers her own partially Blochian-derived mode of performance studies critique in *Utopia in Performance: Finding Hope at the Theater*.[8] Dolan's admirable book focuses on live theater as a site for "finding hope." My approach to hope as a critical methodology can be best described as a backward glance that enacts a future vision. I see my project as resonating alongside a group of recent texts that have strategically displaced the live object of performance. Some texts that represent this aspect of the performance studies project include Gavin Butt's excellent analysis of the queer performative force of gossip in the prewar New York art world,[9] Jennifer Doyle's powerful treatise on the formative and deforming force of "sex objects" in performance and visual studies,[10] and Fred Moten's beautiful *In the Break*, with its emphasis on providing a soaring description of the resistance of the object.[11] I invoke those three texts in an effort to locate my own analysis in relation to the larger interdisciplinary project of performance studies.

The modern world is a thing of wonder for Bloch, who considers astonishment to be an important philosophical mode of contemplation.[12] In a way, we can see this sense of astonishment in the work of both Warhol and O'Hara. Warhol was fond of making speech acts such as "wow" and "gee." Although this aspect of Warhol's performance of self is often described as an insincere performance of naiveté, I instead argue that it is a manifestation of the utopian feeling that is integral to much of Warhol's art, speech, and writing. O'Hara, as even his casual readers know, was irrepressibly upbeat. What if we think of these modes of being in the world—Warhol's liking of things, his "wows" and "gees," and O'Hara's poetry being saturated with feelings of fun and appreciation—as a mode of utopian feeling but also as hope's methodology? This methodology is manifest in what Bloch described as a form of "astonished contemplation."[13] Perhaps we can understand the campy fascination that both men had with celebrity as being akin to this sense of astonishment. Warhol's blue Liz Taylors or O'Hara's perfect tribute to another starlet, in the poem "Lana Turner Has Collapsed," offer, through glamour and astonishment, a kind of transport or a reprieve from what Bloch called the "darkness of the lived instant."[14] Astonishment helps one surpass the limitations of an alienating presentness and allows one to see a different time and place. Much of each artist's work performs this astonishment in the world. O'Hara is constantly astonished by the city. He celebrates the city's beauty and vastness, and in his work one often finds this sense of astonishment in quotidian things. O'Hara's poems display urban landscapes of astonishment. The quotidian object has this same affective charge in Warhol's visual work. Bloch theorized that one could detect wish-landscapes in painting and poetry.[15] Such landscapes extend into the territory of futurity.

Let us begin by considering Warhol's *Coke Bottle* alongside O'Hara's poem "Having a Coke with You":

Having a Coke with You
is even more fun than going to San Sebastian, Irún, Hendaye, Biarritz,
    Bayonne
or being sick to my stomach on the Travesera de Gracia in Barcelona
partly because in your orange shirt you look like a better happier St.
    Sebastian
partly because of my love for you, partly because of your love for
    yoghurt
partly because of the fluorescent orange tulips around the birches

partly because of the secrecy our smiles take on before people and
    statuary
it is hard to believe when I'm with you that there can be anything as
    still
as solemn as unpleasantly definitive as statuary when right in front of it
in the warm New York 4 o'clock light we are drifting back and forth
between each other like a tree breathing through its spectacles

and the portrait show seems to have no faces in it at all, just paint
you suddenly wonder why in the world anyone ever did them
I look
at you and I would rather look at you than all the portraits in the
    world
except possibly for the *Polish Rider* occasionally and anyway it's in the
    Frick
which thank heavens you haven't gone to yet so we can go together
    the first time
and the fact that you move so beautifully more or less takes care of
    Futurism
just as at home I never think of the *Nude Descending a Staircase* or
at a rehearsal a single drawing of Leonardo or Michelangelo that used
    to wow me
and what good does all the research of the Impressionists do them
when they never got the right person to stand near the tree when the
    sun sank
or for that matter Marino Marini when he didn't pick the rider as
    carefully
as the horse
    it seems they were all cheated of some marvellous experience
which is not going to go wasted on me which is why I'm telling you
    about it[16]

This poem tells us of a quotidian act, having a Coke with somebody, that signifies a vast lifeworld of queer relationality, an encrypted sociality, and a utopian potentiality. The quotidian act of sharing a Coke, consuming a common commodity with a beloved with whom one shares secret smiles, trumps fantastic moments in the history of art. Though the poem is clearly about the present, it is a present that is now squarely the past and in its queer relationality promises a future. The fun of having a Coke is a mode of exhilaration in which one views a restructured sociality. The poem tells us that mere beauty is insufficient for the aesthete speaker, which echoes Bloch's own aesthetic theories concerning the utopian function of art. If art's limit were beauty—according to Bloch—it is simply not enough.[17] The utopian function is enacted by a certain surplus in the work that promises a futurity, something that is not quite here. O'Hara first mentions being wowed by a high-art object before he describes being wowed by the lover with whom he shares a Coke. Here, through queer-aesthete art consumption and queer relationality the writer describes moments imbued with a feeling of forward-dawning futurity.

The anticipatory illumination of certain objects is a kind of potentiality that is open, indeterminate, like the affective contours of hope itself. This illumination seems to radiate from Warhol's own depiction of Coke bottles. Those silk screens, which I discuss in chapter 7, emphasize the product's stylish design line. Potentiality for Bloch is often located in the ornamental. The ornament can be seen as a proto-pop phenomenon. Bloch warns us that mechanical reproduction, at first glance, voids the ornamental. But he then suggests that the ornamental and the potentiality he associates with it cannot be seen as directly oppositional to technology or mass production.[18] The philosopher proposes the example of a modern bathroom as this age's exemplary site to see a utopian potentiality, the site where nonfunctionality and total functionality merge.[19] Part of what Warhol's study of the Coke bottle and other mass-produced objects helps one to see is this particular tension between functionality and nonfunctionality, the promise and potentiality of the ornament. In the *Philosophy of Andy Warhol* the artist muses on the radically democratic potentiality he detects in Coca-Cola.

> What's great about this country is that America started the tradition where the richest consumers buy essentially the same things as the poorest. You can be watching TV and see Coca-Cola, and you know that the President drinks Coke, Liz Taylor drinks Coke, and just think, you can drink Coke, too. A Coke is a Coke and no amount of money can get you a better Coke than the one the bum on the corner is drinking. All the Cokes are the same and all the Cokes are good. Liz Taylor knows it, the President knows it, the bum knows it, and you know it.[20]

This is the point where Warhol's particular version of the queer utopian impulse crosses over with O'Hara's. The Coke bottle is the everyday

Drawings, 1950s, *Still-Life (Flowers)*, ballpoint ink on Manila paper, 16 3/4 × 13 7/8 in. (42.5 × 35.2 cm), Andy Warhol (artist), The Andy Warhol Museum, Pittsburgh; Founding Collection, Contribution, The Andy Warhol Foundation for the Visual Arts, Inc., © 2008 The Andy Warhol Foundation for the Visual Arts/ARS, New York.

material that is represented in a different frame, laying bare its aesthetic dimension and the potentiality that it represents. In its everyday manifestation such an object would represent alienated production and consumption. But Warhol and O'Hara both detect something else in the object of a Coke bottle and in the act of drinking a Coke with someone. What we glean from Warhol's philosophy is the understanding that utopia exists in the quotidian. Both queer cultural workers are able to detect an opening and indeterminacy in what for many people is a locked-down dead commodity.

Agamben's reading of Aristotle's *De Anima* makes the crucial point that the opposition between potentiality and actuality is a structuring binarism in Western metaphysics.[21] Unlike a possibility, a thing that simply might happen, a potentiality is a certain mode of nonbeing that is eminent, a thing that is present but not actually existing in the present tense. Looking at a poem written in the 1960s, I see a certain potentiality, which at that point had not been fully manifested, a relational field where men could love each other outside the institutions of heterosexuality and share a world through the act of drinking a beverage with each other. Using Warhol's musing on Coca-Cola in tandem with O'Hara's words, I see the past and the potentiality imbued within an object, the ways it might represent a mode of being and feeling that was then not quite there but nonetheless an opening. Bloch would posit that such utopian feelings can and regularly will be disappointed.[22] They are nonetheless indispensable to the act of imaging transformation.

This fear of both hope and utopia, as affective structures and approaches to challenges within the social, has been prone to disappointment, making this critical approach difficult. As Bloch would insist, hope can be disappointed. But such disappointment needs to be risked if certain impasses are to be resisted. A certain affective reanimation needs to transpire if a disabling political pessimism is to be displaced. Another way of understanding Bloch's notion of hope is briefly to invoke the work of J. L. Austin. In *How to Do Things with Words* Austin displaces the true/false dichotomy that structures Western metaphysics with the much more conceptually supple distinction between the felicitous and infelicitous.[23] Austin's terms are derived from understanding the everyday speech act. Felicitous speech acts are linguistic articulations that *do* something as well as say something. But as Austin maps out the life of the felicitous speech act we see all the things that eventually go wrong and the failure or infelicity that is built into the speech act. Bloch's hope resonates with Austin's notion of the felicitous insofar as it is always eventually disappointed. The eventual disappointment of hope is not a reason to forsake it as a critical thought process, in the same way that even though we can know in advance that felicity of language ultimately falters, it is nonetheless essential.

The moment in which I write this book the critical imagination is in peril. The dominant academic climate into which this book is attempting to intervene is dominated by a dismissal of political idealism. Shouting down utopia is an easy move. It is perhaps even easier than smearing psychoanalytic or deconstructive reading practices with the charge of nihilism. The antiutopian critic of today has a well-worn war chest of poststructuralism pieties at her or his disposal to shut down lines of thought that delineate the concept of critical utopianism. Social theory that invokes the concept of utopia has always been vulnerable to charges of naiveté, impracticality, or lack of rigor. While participating on the Modern Language Association panel titled "The Anti-Social Thesis in Queer Theory," I argued for replacing a faltering antirelational mode of queer theory with a queer utopianism that highlights a renewed investment in social theory (one that calls on not only relationality but also futurity). One of my co-panelists responded to my argument by exclaiming that there was nothing new or radical about utopia. To some degree that is true, insofar as I am calling on a well-established tradition of critical idealism. I am also not interested in a notion of the radical that merely connotes some notion of extremity, righteousness, or affirmation of newness. My investment in utopia and hope is my response to queer thinking that embraces a politics of the here and now that is underlined by what I consider to be today's hamstrung pragmatic gay agenda. Some critics would call this cryptopragmatic approach tarrying with the negative. I would not. To some degree this book's argument is a response to the polemic of the "antirelation." Although the antirelational approach assisted in dismantling an anticritical understanding of queer community, it nonetheless quickly replaced the romance of community with the romance of singularity and negativity. The version of queer social relations that this book attempts to envision is critical of the communitarian as an absolute value and of its negation as an alternative all-encompassing value. In this sense the work of contemporary French philosopher Jean-Luc Nancy and his notion of "being singular plural"[24] seems especially important. For Nancy the postphenomenological category of being singular plural addresses the way in which the singularity that marks a singular existence is always coterminously plural—which is to say that an entity registers as both particular in its difference but at the same time always relational to other singularities. Thus, if one attempts to render the ontological signature of queerness through Nancy's critical apparatus, it needs to be grasped as both antirelational and relational.

Antisocial queer theories are inspired by Leo Bersani's book *Homos*, in which he first theorized the so-called thesis of antirelationality.[25] I have long believed that the antirelational turn in queer studies was a partial response to critical approaches to a mode of queer studies that argued for the relational and contingent value of sexuality as a category. Many critics have followed Bersani's antirelational turn, but arguably none as successfully as Lee Edelman in his book *No Future*.[26] I have great respect for *No Future*, and Edelman's earlier book offers an adroit reading of James Baldwin's *Just Above My Head*.[27] *No Future* is a brilliant and nothing short of inspiring polemic. Edelman clearly announces his mode of argumentation as being in the realm of the ethical, and this introduction is an anticipation of a reanimated political critique and should be read as an idiosyncratic allegiance to the polemical force of his argument and nothing like an easy dismissal. His argument and the seductive sway of the antirelational thesis energizes my argument in key ways.

Yet I nonetheless contend that most of the work with which I disagree under the provisional title of "antirelational thesis" moves to imagine an escape or denouncement of relationality as first and foremost a distancing of queerness from what some theorists seem to think of as the contamination of race, gender, or other particularities that taint the purity of sexuality as a singular trope of difference. In other words, antirelational approaches to queer theory are romances of the negative, wishful thinking, and investments in deferring various dreams of difference.

To some extent *Cruising Utopia* is a polemic that argues against antirelationality by insisting on the essential need for an understanding of queerness as collectivity. I respond to Edelman's assertion that the future is the province of the child and therefore not for the queers by arguing that queerness is primarily about futurity and hope. That is to say that queerness is always in the horizon. I contend that if queerness is to have any value whatsoever, it must be viewed as being visible only in the horizon. My argument is therefore interested in critiquing the ontological certitude that I understand to be partnered with the politics of presentist and pragmatic contemporary gay identity. This mode of ontological certitude is often represented through a narration of disappearance and negativity that boils down to another game of fort-da.

What then does a Blochian approach offer instead of a powerful critical impulse toward negation? Bloch found solid grounds for a critique of a totalizing and naturalizing idea of the present in his concept of the no-longer-conscious.[28] A turn to the no-longer-conscious enabled a critical hermeneutics attuned to comprehending the not-yet-here. This temporal calculus performed and utilized the past and the future as armaments to combat the devastating logic of the world of the here and now, a notion of nothing existing outside the sphere of the current moment, a version of reality that naturalizes cultural logics such as capitalism and heteronormativity. Concomitantly, Bloch also sharpens our critical imagination with his emphasis on hope. An antiutopian might understand himself as being critical in rejecting hope, but in the rush to denounce it, he would be missing the point that hope is spawned of a critical investment in utopia, which is nothing like naive but, instead, profoundly resistant to the stultifying temporal logic of a broken-down present. My turn to Bloch, hope, and utopia is a challenge to theoretical insights that have been stunted by the lull of presentness and various romances of negativity and have thus become routine and resoundingly anticritical. This antiutopian theoretical faltering is often nothing more than rote invocation of poststructuralist pieties. The critical practices often summarized as poststructuralism inform my analysis as much as any other source from which I draw. The corrective I wish to make by turning to utopia is attuned to Eve Kosofsky Sedgwick's critique of the way in which paranoid reading practices have become so nearly automatic in queer studies that they have, in many ways, ceased to be critical.[29] Antiutopianism in queer studies, which is more often than not intertwined with antirelationality, has led many scholars to an impasse wherein they cannot see futurity for the life of them.[30] Utopian readings are aligned with what Sedgwick would call reparative hermeneutics.[31]

Although *Cruising Utopia* routinely rejects what I describe as a "certain romance of negativity," I do not want to dismiss the negative *tout court*. Indeed I find some theories of the negative to be important resources for the thinking of a critical utopianism. For example, Paolo Virno elegantly describes the negation of the negation in *Multitude: Between Innovation and Negation*. Virno resists an oppositional logic that clouds certain deployments of negativity[32] and instead speaks to what he calls a negation that functions as a "modality of the possible," "a regression to the infinite."[33] Virno sees a potentiality in negative affects that can be reshaped by negation and made to work in the service of enacting a mode of critical possibility. Virno's theory of the negation of negation productively lines up with Shoshana Felman's theory of radical negativity: "Radical negativity (or saying 'no') belongs neither to negation, nor to opposition nor to correction ('normalization'), nor to contradiction (of positive and negative, normal and abnormal, 'serious' and 'unserious,' 'clarity' and 'obscurity')— it belongs precisely to scandal: to the scandal of their nonopposition."[34] Again, my argument with the celebration of negation in antirelational queer critique is its participation in what can only be seen as a binary logic of opposition. Radical negativity, like the negation of negation, offers us a mode of understanding negativity that is starkly different from the version of the negative proposed by the queer antirelationist. Here the negative becomes the resource for a certain mode of queer utopianism.

Once again I turn to a literary example with the hope of describing the performative force of that particular queer utopian writing project. A paragraph from Eileen Myles's extraordinary memoir of coming into queer consciousness in the 1960s and '70s is especially salient for my purposes. *Chelsea Girls* is a ribald text full of fucking, drinking, and other modes of potentially lyrical self-destruction. Near the end of this testament to the aching madness of lesbian desire, a powerful yet diminished figure briefly enters the frame. At this point the young poet has become the part-time caretaker for the great queer voice of the New York School of poetry— James Schuyler. Myles attended to the old and infirmed Schuyler in his residential room at the legendary Chelsea Hotel.

> From his bed he ran the show. It's a talent a few people I know have, mostly Scorpios which he was. You'd be hesitatingly starting your story, or like a cartoon character running right in when you realized the long wharf you were taking a short run on, his attention was not there. It was hopeless. The yellow in his room became brighter, the air became crinkly your throat became parched—you felt you had simply become a jerk. The presence of his attention was so strong, so deeply passive—such a thing to bathe your tiny desperate words in that when it was gone you had to stop and hover in silence again. Then he might begin, or perhaps you could come up with something else once the brittleness, the void passed. You had to stay silent for a very long time somedays. He was like music, Jimmy was, and you had to be like music too to be with him, but understand in his room he was conductor. He directed the yellow air in room 625. It was marvelous to be around. It was huge and impassive. What emerged in the silence was a strong picture, more akin to a child or a beautiful animal.[35]

In the spirit of the counterpolemical swerve that this introduction has been taking I want to suggest that this passage could be seen as representing an anti-antirelationality that is both weirdly reparative and a prime example of the queer utopianism for which I am arguing. Anti-antiutopianism is a phrase that I borrow from Fredric Jameson and index when marking this passage in Myles as anti-antirelational.[36] Anti-antiutopianism is not about a merely affirmative or positive investment in utopia. Gay and lesbian studies can too easily snap into the basically reactionary posture of denouncing a critical imagination that is not locked down by a short-sighted denial of anything but the here and now of this moment. This is the antiutopian stance that characterizes the antirelational turn. The prime examples of queer antirelationality in Bersani's *Homos*, Edelman's *No Future,* and all the other proponents of this turn in queer criticism are scenes of jouissance, which are always described as shattering orgasmic ruptures often associated with gay male sexual abandon or self-styled risky behavior. Maybe the best example of an anti-antirelational scene that I could invoke would be another spectacular instance of sexual transgression. The moments of pornographic communal rapture in Samuel Delany's work come most immediately to mind.[37] But instead I choose to focus on this relational line between a young white lesbian and an older gay white man because it does the kind of crossing that antirelational theorists are so keen on eschewing or ignoring.

Myles is paid to take care of Schuyler. On the level of political economy this relationship is easy to account for. But if we think of Delany's championing of interclass contact within a service economy and the affective surplus it offers, the passage opens up quite beautifully.[38] The younger poet notes a sense of "hopelessness" and feeling like a jerk as she works to take care of the older man, whose attention waxes and wanes. The relationality is not about simple positivity or affirmation. It is filled with all sorts of bad feelings, moments of silence and brittleness. But beyond the void that stands between the two poets, there is something else, a surplus that is manifest in the complexity of their moments of contact. Through quotidian service-economy interactions of care and simple conversation the solitary scene of an old man and his young assistant is transformed. A rhythm that is not simple relationality or routine antirelationality is established. This is the music that is Jimmy, this is the music of Eileen, this is the hum of their contact. This is Jimmy directing "the yellow air in room 625." It is Eileen watching, listening. It is the sense of contemplative awe that I have identified in Warhol's "wows" and O'Hara manic upbeat poetic cadence.

It is the mood of reception in which Bloch asks us to participate. It is the being singular plural of queerness. It is like the radical negativity that Shoshana Felman invokes when trying to describe the failure that is intrinsic in J. L. Austin's mapping of the performative. There is a becoming both animal and child that Myles ultimately glimpses in an infirmed Schuyler. In this passage we see the anticipatory illumination of the utopian canceling the relentless shadow play of absence and presence on which the antirelational thesis rests. The affective tone of this passage lights the way to the reparative.

This book has been written in nothing like a vacuum. I have written beside many beloved collaborators, interlocutors, and comrades. And while these friends have been a source of propulsion for me, they have expressed qualms about some of the theoretical moves I make in *Cruising Utopia*. For example, some friends have asked me why I have chosen to work with the more eccentric corpus of Bloch and not Benjamin's more familiar takes on time, history, or loss. I have also been asked how I could turn to a text such as Marcuse's *Eros and Civilization* after Michel Foucault famously critiqued that work in *History of Sexuality, Volume 1*. One reader of an earlier draft expressed concern that I take time to talk about Bloch in the context of Marxian thought but do not contextualize Heidegger in relation to Nazism. I have not had any simple or direct answers for these thoughtful readers. Their concerns have made me aware of a need to further situate this project. I have resisted Foucault and Benjamin because their thought has been well mined in the field of queer critique, so much so that these two thinkers' paradigms now feel almost tailor-made for queer studies. I have wanted to look to other sites of theoretical traction. Bloch was noted as not being especially progressive about gender and sexuality, Heidegger's eventual political turn was of course horrific, and Marcuse's insistence on avowedly liberationist rhetoric may seem like something of a throwback. A fairly obvious reading of Foucault's writing on the repressive hypothesis[39] would perceive it as a direct response to *Eros and Civilization*. Although Marcuse's version of surplus repression may potentially make reprehension the basic constitutive element for thinking about sex, it nonetheless offers a liberationist and critically utopian take on subjugation. Marcuse and Heidegger were not radical homosexuals like Foucault or romantic melancholics like Benjamin, with whom queers today can easily identify, but my turn to a certain modality of Marxian and phenomenological thought is calibrated to offer new thought images for queer critique, different paths to queerness.

Let me momentarily leave Bloch aside and instead look to the problematic figures of Marcuse and his onetime mentor Heidegger. My interest in their work (and Bloch's, for that matter) pivots from their relationship to the tradition of German idealism. Marcuse's Marxism sought out a philosophical concreteness that, in a provisional fashion, resonated with phenomenology and specifically with the interest of the Heidegger of *Being and Time* in pursuing a concrete philosophy. Both strains of thought rejected German idealism's turn to abstraction and inwardness. Both craved a practical philosophy that described the world in historically salient fashion. Marcuse turned to Heidegger as a philosophical influence and a source during what was described as the crisis in Marxism in Germany during the 1920s. At that point a mode of scientism dominated Marxism and led to an antiphilosophical and mechanistic approach to Marx. Marcuse and Heidegger's relationship famously faltered as Marcuse joined the Frankfurt School and Heidegger eventually joined the Nazi Party on May 1, 1933. Although we can now look at 1928's *Being and Time* and locate philosophical models that were perhaps even then politically right-wing, it is precisely this relational and political failure on which I nonetheless want to dwell. Marcuse saw in Heidegger's ontology a new route to better describe human existence. He was taken with his mentor's notion of historicity and what it could potentially do for what was then a Marxism in duress. Much later, Marx's 1844 manuscripts were discovered, and the concrete philosophical approach understood as historical materialism became fully manifest. Marcuse looked back and realized that the phenomenological version of historicity was not necessary. Although I too have a great disdain for what Heidegger's writing became, I nonetheless look on it as failure worth knowing, a potential that faltered but can be nonetheless reworked in the service of a different politics and understanding of the world. The queer utopianism I am espousing would even look back on Heidegger's notion of futurity in *Being and Time* and attach itself to aspects of that theory of temporality. In Heidegger's version of historicity, historical existence in the past allowed for subjects to act with a mind toward "future possibilities." Thus, futurity becomes history's dominant principle. In a similar fashion I think of queerness as a temporal arrangement in which the past is a field of possibility in which subjects can act in the present in the service of a new futurity. Is my thesis ultimately corrupted because it finds some kind of historical resonance with the now politically reprehensible Heidegger? Readers can clearly glimpse the trace of Marcuse's renounced mentor in his later writing, and indeed that problematic influence is part of the theoretical force of his left philosophy. To draw from such sources and ultimately make them serve another project, one that the author himself would have quickly denounced, serves as a critical engagement—critique as willful disloyalty to the master. Heidegger is therefore not the theoretical protagonist of my argument; more nearly, he is an opportunity and occasion to think queerness or queerly. Heidegger is then philosophical master and abject political failure. Thus, we see the thematic of virtuosity and failure that I describe in chapter 10 as queerness's way.

Thinking beyond the moment and against static historicisms is a project that is deeply sympathetic to Judith Halberstam's work on queer temporality's relation to spatiality, most immediately the notion of straight time. It also draws on Carla Freccero's notion of fantasmatic historiography, Elizabeth Freeman's theory of temporal drag, Carolyn Dinshaw's approach to "touching the past," Gayatri Gopinath's theorizing of the time and place of queer diaspora as an "impossible desire," and Jill Dolan's work on the utopian in performance.[40] Along those lines, although this writing project is not always explicitly about race, it does share much political urgency with a vibrant list of scholars working on the particularities of queers of color and their politics.[41] I have spent some time arguing against the antirelational move in queer theory. Queer feminist and queer of color critiques are the powerful counterweight to the antirelational. I situate my work squarely in those quarters.

Certainly Lauren Berlant's work on the politics of affect in public life has had a structuring influence on this project. In a 1994 essay, titled "'68 or Something," Berlant explained the article's project in a way that resonates with much of the powerful writing that has followed it: "This essay is written in favor of refusing to learn the lessons of history, of refusing to relinquish utopian practice, of refusing the apparently inevitable movement from tragedy to farce that has marked so much of the analysis of social movements generated post '68."[42] The refusal of empiricist historiography and its denouncement of utopian longing has been an important cue for this project. Berlant's insistence on the refusal of normative affect reminds me of the Great Refusal for which Marcuse called years earlier. *Cruising Utopia* is a critical move that has been forged in relation to the work of Berlant and other scholars with whom I have had the luxury to work under the banner of the Public Feelings Group.[43] That theoretical project has had an important activist component thanks to the inspired work of the Chicago Feel Tank.[44] The very idea that we can even venture to feel utopian in the here and now has been nourished through my fortunate association with this collegial cohort.

Ultimately, this book offers a theory of queer futurity that is attentive to the past for the purposes of critiquing a present. This mode of queer critique depends on critical practices that stave off the failures of imagination that I understand as antirelationality and antiutopianism in queer critique. The mode of "cruising" for which this book calls is not only or even primarily "cruising for sex." I do see an unlimited potentiality in actual queer sex, but books of criticism that simply glamorize the ontology of gay male cruising are more often than not simply boring. In this book I do nonetheless distill some real theoretical energy from historical accounts of fucking and utopia, such as John Giorno's journals (chapter 2) and Samuel Delany's memoir, *The Motion of Light and Water* (chapter 3). That may have something to with the historical texture those texts provide. Indeed this book asks one to cruise the fields of the visual and not so visual in an effort to see in the anticipatory illumination of the utopian. If, as indicated by the famous quotation from Oscar Wilde that appears in the epigraph, "a map of the world that does not include Utopia is not worth glancing at," then affective and cognitive maps[45] of the world that a critically queer utopianism can create, maps that *do* include utopia, need to be attended to in a fashion that indeed resembles a kind of politicized cruising. In the place of various exhausted theoretical stances *Cruising Utopia* not only asks readers to reconsider ideas such as hope and utopia but also challenges them to feel hope and to feel utopia, which is to say challenges them to approach the queer critique from a renewed and newly animated sense of the social, carefully cruising for the varied potentialities that may abound within that field.

1

Queerness as Horizon

Utopian Hermeneutics in the Face of Gay Pragmatism

for John

I BEGIN THIS chapter on futurity and a desire that is utopian by turning to a text from the past—more specifically, to those words that emanate from the spatiotemporal coordinate Bloch referred to as the no-longer-conscious, a term that attempts to enact a more precise understanding of the work that the past does, what can be understood as the performative force of the past. A 1971 issue of the gay liberation journal *Gay Flames* included a manifesto by a group calling itself Third World Gay Revolution. The text, titled "What We Want, What We Believe," offered a detailed list of demands that included the abolition of capital punishment, the abolishment of institutional religion, and the end of the bourgeois family. The entire list of sixteen demands culminated with a request that was especially radical and poignant when compared to the anemic political agenda that dominates contemporary LGBT politics in North America today.

> 16.) We want a new society—a revolutionary socialist society. We want liberation of humanity, free food, free shelter, free clothing, free transportation, free health care, free utilities, free education, free art for all. We want a society where the needs of the people come first.
>
> We believe that all people should share the labor and products of society, according to each one's needs and abilities, regardless of race, sex, age or sexual preferences. We believe the land, technology and the means of production belong to the people, and must be shared by the people collectively for the liberation of all.[1]

When we consider the extremely pragmatic agenda that organizes LGBT activism in North America today, the demand "we want a new society" may seem naive by the present's standards. Many people would dismiss these demands as impractical or merely utopian. Yet I contend that there is great value in pulling these words from the no-longer-conscious to arm a critique of the present. The use of "we" in this manifesto can be mistakenly read as the "we" implicit in the identity politics that emerged after the Third World Gay Revolution group. Such a reading would miss the point. This "we" does not speak to a merely identitarian logic but instead to a logic of futurity. The "we" speaks to a "we" that is "not yet conscious," the future society that is being invoked and addressed at the same moment. The "we" is not content to describe who the collective is but more nearly describes what the collective and the larger social order could be, what it should be. The particularities that are listed—"race, sex, age or sexual preferences"—are not things in and of themselves that format this "we"; indeed the statement's "we" is "regardless" of these markers, which is not to say that it is beyond such distinctions or due to these differences but, instead, that it is *beside* them. This is to say that the field of utopian possibility is one in which multiple forms of belonging in difference adhere to a belonging in collectivity.

Such multiple forms of belonging-in-difference and expansive critiques of social asymmetries are absent in the dominant LGBT leadership community and in many aspects of queer critique. One manifesto from today's movement that seems especially representative of the anemic, shortsighted, and retrograde politics of the present is "All Together Now (A Blueprint for the Movement),"[2] a text written by pro-gay-marriage lawyer Evan Wolfson that appeared on his website, freedomtomarry.org. Wolfson's single-minded text identifies the social recognition and financial advantages offered by traditional marriage pacts as the key to what he calls "freedom." Freedom for Wolfson is mere inclusion in a corrupt and bankrupt social order. Wolfson cannot critique the larger ideological regime that represents marriage as something desirable, natural, and good. His assimilationist gay politics posits an "all" that is in fact a few: queers with enough access to capital to imagine a life integrated within North American capitalist culture. It goes almost without saying that the "all" invoked by the gay lawyer and his followers are normative citizen-subjects with a host of rights only afforded to some (and not all) queer people. Arguments against gay marriage have been articulated with great acumen by Lisa Duggan and Richard Kim.[3] But it is Wolfson's invocation of the term *freedom* that is most unsettling.

Wolfson and his website's rhetoric degrade the concept of freedom. Homonormative cultural and political lobbyists such as Wolfson have degraded the political and conceptual force of concepts such as freedom in the same way that the current political regime of the United States has degraded the term *liberation* in the case of recent Middle Eastern foreign policy. I invoke Wolfson here not so much as this chapter's problem or foil but merely as a recent symptom of the erosion of the gay and lesbian political imagination. Wolfson represents many homonormative interests leading the contemporary LGBT movement toward the goal of "naturalizing" the flawed and toxic ideological formation known as marriage. The aping of traditional straight relationality, especially marriage, for gays and lesbians announces itself as a pragmatic strategy when it is in fact a deeply ideological project that is hardly practical. In this way gay marriage's detractors are absolutely right: gay marriage is not natural—but then again, neither is marriage for any individual.

A similar but more nuanced form of what I am referring to as gay pragmatic thought can be seen in Biddy Martin's work, especially her psychoanalytically inspired diagnosis that queer critique suffers from an androcentric bias in which queerness presents itself as the "extraordinary" while at the same time fleeing the charge of being "ordinary." Being ordinary and being married are both antiutopian wishes, desires that automatically rein themselves in, never daring to see or imagine the not-yet-conscious. This line of thought that I am identifying as pragmatic is taken from its vernacular register. I am not referring to the actual philosophical tradition of American pragmatism of Charles Peirce, William James, or John Dewey. But the current gay political strategy I am describing does share an interest in empiricism with that school. Gay pragmatic organizing is in direct opposition to the idealist thought that I associate as endemic to a forward-dawning queerness that calls on a no-longer-conscious in the service of imagining a futurity.

The not-quite-conscious is the realm of potentiality that must be called on, and insisted on, if we are ever to look beyond the pragmatic sphere of the here and now, the hollow nature of the present. Thus, I wish to argue that queerness is not quite here; it is, in the language of Italian philosopher Giorgio Agamben, a potentiality.[4] Alain Badiou refers to that which follows the event as the thing-that-is-not-yet-imagined,[5] and in my estimation queerness too should be understood to have a similar valence. But my turn to this notion of the not-quite-conscious is again indebted to Bloch and his massive three-volume text *The Principle of Hope*.[6] That treatise, both a continuation and an amplification of German idealist practices of thought, is a critical discourse—which is to say that it does not avert or turn away from the present. Rather, it critiques an autonatural-izing temporality that we might call *straight time*. Straight time tells us that there is no future but the here and now of our everyday life.[7] The only futurity promised is that of reproductive majoritarian heterosexuality, the spectacle of the state refurbishing its ranks through overt and subsidized acts of reproduction. In *No Future*, Lee Edelman advises queers that the future is "kid stuff."[8] Although I believe that there is a lot to like about Edelman's polemic—mostly its disdain for the culture of the child—I ul-timately want to speak for a notion of queer futurity by turning to Bloch's critical notion of utopia.

It is equally polemical to argue that we are not quite queer yet, that queerness, what we will really know as queerness, does not yet exist. I sug-gest that holding queerness in a sort of ontologically humble state, under a conceptual grid in which we do not claim to always already know queer-ness in the world, potentially staves off the ossifying effects of neoliberal ideology and the degradation of politics brought about by representations of queerness in contemporary popular culture.

A posterior glance at different moments, objects, and spaces might of-fer us an anticipatory illumination of queerness. We cannot trust in the manifestations of what some people would call queerness in the present, especially as embodied in the pragmatic debates that dominate contem-porary gay and lesbian politics. (Here, again, I most pointedly mean U.S. queers clamoring for their right to participate in the suspect institution of marriage and, maybe worse, to serve in the military.) None of this is to say that there are not avatars of a queer futurity, both in the past and the present, especially in sites of cultural production. What I am suggesting is that we gain a greater conceptual and theoretical leverage if we see queer-ness as something that is not yet here. In this sense it is useful to consider Edmund Husserl, phenomenology's founder, and his invitation to look to horizons of being.[9] Indeed to access queer visuality we may need to squint, to strain our vision and force it to see otherwise, beyond the limited vista of the here and now.

To critique an overarching "here and now" is not to turn one's face away from the everyday. Roland Barthes wrote that the mark of the uto-pian is the quotidian.[10] Such an argument would stress that the utopian is an impulse that we see in everyday life. This impulse is to be glimpsed as something that is extra to the everyday transaction of heteronormative capitalism. This quotidian example of the utopian can be glimpsed in uto-pian bonds, affiliations, designs, and gestures that exist within the present moment. Turning to the New York School of poetry, a moment that is one of the cultural touchstones for my research, we can consider a poem by James Schuyler that speaks of a hope and desire that is clearly utopian. The poem, like most of Schuyler's body of work, is clearly rooted in an observation of the affective realm of the present. Yet there is an excess that the poet also conveys, a type of affective excess that presents the enabling force of a forward-dawning futurity that is queerness. In the poem "A photograph," published in 1974 in the collection *Hymn to Life*, a picture that resides on the speaker's desk sparks a recollection of domestic bliss.

> *A photograph*
> Shows you in a London
> room; books, a painting,
> your smile, a silky
> tie, a suit. And more.
> It looks so like you
> and I see it every day
> (here, on my desk)
> which I don't you. Last
> Friday was grand.
> We went out, we came
> back, we went wild. You
> slept. Me too. The pup
> woke you and you dressed
> and walked him. When
> you left, I was sleeping.
> When I woke there was
> just time to make the
> train to a country dinner
> and talk about ecstasy.
> Which I think comes in
> two sorts: that which you
> Know "Now I am ecstatic"
> Like my strange scream
> last Friday night. And
> another kind, that you
> know only in retrospect:
> "Why, that joy I felt
> and didn't think about

when his feet were in
my lap, or when I looked
down and saw his slanty
eyes shut, that too was
ecstasy. Nor is there
necessarily a downer from
it." Do I believe in
the perfectibility of
man? Strangely enough,
(I've known un-
happiness enough) I
do. I mean it.
I really do believe
future generations can
live without the in-
tervals of anxious
fear we know between our
bouts and strolls of
ecstasy. The struck ball
finds the pocket. You
smile some years back
in London, I have
known ecstasy and calm:
haven't you too? Let's
try to understand, my
handsome friend who
wears his nose awry.[11]

The speaker remembers the grandness of an unspectacular Friday in which he and his addressee slept in and then scrambled to catch a train to a dinner out in the country. He attempts to explain the ecstasy he felt that night, indicating that one moment of ecstasy, a moment he identifies as being marked both by self-consciousness and obliviousness, possesses a potentially transformative charge. He then considers another moment of ecstasy in retrospect, a looking back at a no-longer-conscious that provides an affective enclave in the present that staves off the sense of "bad feelings" that mark the affective disjuncture of being queer in straight time.

The moment in the poem of deeper introspection—beginning "Do I believe in / the perfectibility of /man?"—is an example of a utopian desire inspired by queer relationality. Moments of queer relational bliss, what the poet names as ecstasies, are viewed as having the ability to rewrite a larger map of everyday life. When "future generations" are invoked, the poet is signaling a queerness to come, a way of being in the world that is glimpsed through reveries in a quotidian life that challenges the dominance of an affective world, a present, full of anxiousness and fear. These future generations are, like the "we" invoked in the manifesto by the Third World Gay Revolution group, not an identitarian formulation but, instead, the invocation of a future collectivity, a queerness that registers as the illumination of a horizon of existence.

The poem speaks of multiple temporalities and the affective mode known as ecstasy, which resonates alongside the work of Martin Heidegger. In *Being and Time* Heidegger reflects on the activity of timeliness and its relation to *ekstatisch* (ecstasy), signaling for Heidegger the ecstatic unity of temporality—Past, Present, and Future.[12] The ecstasy the speaker feels and remembers in "A photograph" is not consigned to one moment. It steps out from the past and remarks on the unity of an expansive version of temporality; hence, future generations are invoked. To know ecstasy in the way in which the poem's speaker does is to have a sense of timeliness's motion, to understand a temporal unity that is important to what I attempt to describe as the time of queerness. Queerness's time is a stepping out of the linearity of straight time. Straight time is a self-naturalizing temporality. Straight time's "presentness" needs to be phenomenologically questioned, and this is the fundamental value of a queer utopian hermeneutics. Queerness's ecstatic and horizonal temporality is a path and a movement to a greater openness to the world.

It would be difficult to mistake Schuyler's poem for one of Frank O'Hara's upbeat reveries. O'Hara's optimism is a contagious happiness within the quotidian that I would also describe as having a utopian quality. Schuyler's poetry is not so much about optimism but instead about a hope that is distinctly utopian and distinctly queer. The poem imagines another collective belonging, an enclave in the future where readers will not be beset with feelings of nervousness and fear. These feelings are the affective results of being outside of straight time. He writes from a depressive position, "(I've known un- / happiness enough)," but reaches beyond the affective force-field of the present.

Hope for Bloch is an essential characteristic of not only the utopian but also the human condition. Thus, I talk about the human as a relatively stable category. But queerness in its utopian connotations promises a human that is not yet here, thus disrupting any ossified understanding of the human. The point is to stave off a gay and lesbian antiutopianism that is very much tainted with a polemics of the pragmatic rights discourse that in and of itself hamstrings not only politics but also desire. Queerness as utopian formation is a formation based on an economy of desire and desiring. This desire is always directed at that thing that is not yet here, objects and moments that burn with anticipation and promise. The desire that propels Schuyler's "A photograph" is born of the no-longer-conscious, the rich resonance of remembrance, distinct pleasures felt in the past. And thus past pleasures stave off the affective perils of the present while they enable a desire that is queer futurity's core.

Queerness is utopian, and there is something queer about the utopian. Fredric Jameson described the utopian as the oddball or the maniac.[13] Indeed, to live inside straight time and ask for, desire, and imagine another time and place is to represent and perform a desire that is both utopian and queer. To participate in such an endeavor is not to imagine an isolated future for the individual but instead to participate in a hermeneutic that wishes to describe a collective futurity, a notion of futurity that functions as a historical materialist critique. In the two textual examples I have employed we see an overt utopianism that is explicit in the Third World Gay Revolution manifesto, and what I am identifying as a *utopian impulse* is perceivable in Schuyler's poetry. One requires a utopian hermeneutic to see an already operative principle of hope that hums in the poet's work. The other text, the manifesto, does another type of performative work; it *does* utopia.

To "read" the performative, along the lines of thought first inaugurated by J. L. Austin, is implicitly to critique the epistemological.[14] Performativity and utopia both call into question what is epistemologically there and signal a highly ephemeral ontological field that can be characterized as a *doing in futurity*. Thus, a manifesto is a call to a doing in and for the future. The utopian impulse to be gleaned from the poem is a call for "doing" that is a becoming: the becoming of and for "future generations." This rejection of the here and now, the ontologically static, is indeed, by the measure of homonormative codes, a maniacal and oddball endeavor. The queer utopian project addressed here turns to the fringe of political and cultural production to offset the tyranny of the homonormative. It is drawn to tastes, ideologies, and aesthetics that can only seem odd, strange, or indeed queer next to the muted striving of the practical and normalcy-desiring homosexual.

The turn to the call of the no-longer-conscious is not a turn to norma-tive historical analysis. Indeed it is important to complicate queer his-tory and understand it as doing more than the flawed process of merely evidencing. Evidencing protocols often fail to enact real hermeneutical inquiry and instead opt to reinstate that which is known in advance. Thus, practices of knowledge production that are content merely to cull selec-tively from the past, while striking a pose of positivist undertaking or em-pirical knowledge retrieval, often nullify the political imagination. Jame-son's Marxian dictate "always historicize"[15] is not a methodological call for empirical data collection. Instead, it is a dialectical injunction, suggesting we animate our critical faculties by bringing the past to bear on the pres-ent and the future. Utopian hermeneutics offer us a refined lens to view queerness, insofar as queerness, if it is indeed not quite here, is nonethe-less intensely relational with the past.

The present is not enough. It is impoverished and toxic for queers and other people who do not feel the privilege of majoritarian belonging, nor-mative tastes, and "rational" expectations. (I address the question of ratio-nalism shortly). Let me be clear that the idea is not simply to turn away from the present. One cannot afford such a maneuver, and if one thinks one can, one has resisted the present in favor of folly. The present must be known in relation to the alternative temporal and spatial maps provided by a perception of past and future affective worlds.

Utopian thinking gets maligned for being naively romantic. Of course, much of it has been naive. We know that any history of actualized utopian communities would be replete with failures. No one, other than perhaps Marx himself, has been more cognizant about this fact than Bloch. But it is through this Marxian tradition, not beside or against it, that the prob-lem of the present is addressed. In the following quotation we begin to glimpse the importance of the Marxian tradition for the here and now.

> Marxism, above all, was first to bring a concept of knowledge into the world that essentially refers to Becomeness, but to the tendency of what is coming up; thus for the first time it brings future into our con-ceptual and theoretical grasp. Such recognition of tendency is neces-sary to remember, and to open up the No-Longer-Conscious.[16]

Thus we see Bloch's model for approaching the past. The idea is not to at-tempt merely to represent it with simplistic strokes. More nearly, it is im-portant to call on the past, to animate it, understanding that the past has a performative nature, which is to say that rather than being static and fixed, the past does things. It is in this very way that the past is performative. Following a Blochian thread, it seems important to put the past into play with the present, calling into view the tautological nature of the present. The present, which is almost exclusively conceived through the parameters of straight time, is a self-naturalizing endeavor. Opening up a queer past is enabled by Marxian ideological tactics. Bloch explains that

> Marxism thus rescued the rational core of utopia and made it concrete as well as the core of the still idealistic tendency of dialectics. Romanticism does not understand utopia, not even its own, but utopia that has become concrete understands Romanticism and makes inroads into it, in so far as archaic material in its archetypes and work, contain a not yet voiced, undischarged element.[17]

Bloch invites us to look to this no-longer-conscious, a past that is akin to what Derrida described as the trace. These ephemeral traces, flickering illuminations from other times and places, are sites that may indeed appear merely romantic, even to themselves. Nonetheless they assist those of us who wish to follow queerness's promise, its still unrealized potential, to see something else, a component that the German aesthetician would call *cultural surplus*. I build on this idea to suggest that the surplus is both cultural and *affective*. More distinctly, I point to a queer feeling of hope in the face of hopeless heteronormative maps of the present where futurity is indeed the province of normative reproduction. This hope takes on the philosophical contours of idealism.

A queer utopian hermeneutic would thus be queer in its aim to look for queer relational formations within the social. It is also about this temporal project that I align with queerness, a work shaped by its idealist trajectory; indeed it is the work of not settling for the present, of asking and looking beyond the here and now. Such a hermeneutic would then be *epistemologically and ontologically humble* in that it would not claim the epistemological certitude of a queerness that we simply "know" but, instead, strain to activate the no-longer-conscious and to extend a glance toward that which is forward-dawning, anticipatory illuminations of the not-yet-conscious. The purpose of such temporal maneuvers is to wrest ourselves from the present's stultifying hold, to know our queerness as a belonging in particularity that is not dictated or organized around the spirit of political impasse that characterizes the present.

Jameson has suggested that for Bloch the present is provincial.[18] This spatialization of time makes sense in relation to the history of utopian thought, most famously described as an island by Thomas More. To mark the present as provincial is not to ridicule or demean the spots on queerness's map that do not signify as metropolitan. The here and now has an opposite number, and that would be the then and there. I have argued that the *then* that disrupts the tyranny of the *now* is both past and future. Along those lines, the here that is unnamed yet always implicit in the metropolitan hub requires the challenge of a there that can be regional or global. The transregional or the global as modes of spatial organization potentially displace the hegemony of an unnamed here that is always dominated by the shadow of the nation-state and its mutable and multiple corporate interests. While *globalization* is a term that mostly defines a worldwide system of manufactured asymmetry and ravenous exploitation, it also signals the encroaching of the there on the here in ways that are worth considering.

The Third World Gay Revolution group was an organization that grew out of the larger Gay Liberation Front at roughly the same time that the Radicalesbians also spun off from the larger group in the spring/summer of 1970. Although they took the name Third World Gay Revolution, the group's members have been described by a recent historian as people of color.[19] Their own usage of the term "Third World" clearly connotes their deep identification with the global phenomenon that was decolonization. It is therefore imperative to remember this moment from the no-longer-conscious that transcended a gay and lesbian activist nationalist imaginary. For Heidegger "time and space are not co-ordinate. Time is prior to space."[20] If time is prior to space, then we can view both the force of the no-longer-conscious and the not-yet-here as potentially bearing on the *here* of naturalized space and time. Thus, at the center of cultural texts such as the manifesto "All Together Now (A Blueprint for the Movement)" we find an ideological document, and its claim to the pragmatic is the product of a short-sighted here that fails to include anything but an entitled and privileged world. The there of queer utopia cannot simply be that of the faltering yet still influential nation-state.

This is then to say that the distinctions between here and there, and the world that the here and now organizes, are not fixed—they are already becoming undone in relation to a forward-dawning futurity. It is important to understand that a critique of our homosexual present is not an attack on what many people routinely name as lesbian or gay but, instead, an appraisal of how queerness is still forming, or in many crucial ways formless.

Queerness's form is utopian. Ultimately, we must insist on a queer futurity because the present is so poisonous and insolvent. A resource that cannot be discounted to know the future is indeed the no-longer-conscious, that thing or place that may be extinguished but not yet discharged in its utopian potentiality.

Bloch explains the Kantian nature of his project as the "saving" of a "rationalist core." It is worth remarking that Kant's rationalism is not merely held up in this instance; indeed *rationalism itself is refunctioned*. No longer is rationalism the ruler used by universalism to measure time and space. In Bloch's work rationalism is transformed via a political urgency. Rationalism is not dismissed but is instead unyoked from a politics of the pragmatic. Herbert Marcuse discussed the "irrational element in rationality" as an important component of industrial society's nature. Irrationality flourishes in "established institutions"—marriage is perhaps one of the very best examples of an institution that hampers rational advancement and the not-yet-imagined versions of freedom that heteronormative and homonormative culture proscribe.[21] In Marcuse's analysis the advancements in rationality made by technological innovations were counteracted by gay pragmatic political strategies that tell us not to dream of other spatial/temporal coordinates but instead to dwell in a broken-down present. This homosexual pragmatism takes on the practical contours of the homonormativity so powerfully described by Lisa Duggan in her treatise on neoliberalism, *The Twilight of Equality?*[22] Within the hermeneutical scope of a queer utopian inquiry rationalism is reignited with an affective spark of idealist thought.

Abstract utopias are indeed dead ends, too often vectoring into the escapist disavowal of our current moment. But a turn to what Bloch calls the no-longer-conscious is an essential route for the purpose of arriving at the not-yet-here. This maneuver, a turn to the past for the purpose of critiquing the present, is propelled by a desire for futurity. Queer futurity does not underplay desire. In fact it is all about desire, desire for both larger semiabstractions such as a better world or freedom but also, more immediately, better relations within the social that include better sex and more pleasure. Some theorists of postmodernity, such as David Harvey, have narrated sex radicalism as a turning away from a politics of the collectivity toward the individualistic and the petty.[23] In his *A Brief History of Neoliberalism* Harvey plots what he views as the condition of neoliberalism. In his account, "The narcissistic exploration of self, sexuality and identity became the leitmotif of bourgeois urban culture." In this account, the hard-fought struggles for sexual liberation are reduced to a "demand for lifestyle diversification." Harvey's critique pits the "working-class and ethnic immigrant New York" against elites who pursue "lifestyle diversification."[24] The experiences of working-class or ethnic-racial queers are beyond his notice or interest. Harvey's failing is a too-common error for some, but not all, members of a recalcitrant, unreconstructed North American left. The rejection of queer and feminist politics represented by Harvey and other reductive left thinkers is a deviation away from the Frankfurt School's interest in the transformative force of *eros* and its implicit relationship to political desire. The failings and limits of commentators such as Harvey have certainly made queer and utopian thinkers alike wary of left thought. Thus, I suggest a turn to previous modes of Marxian philosophy, such as the work of Marcuse or Bloch. The point is not to succumb to the phobic panic that muddles left thinking or to unimaginative invocations of the rationalism cited by neoliberal gays and lesbians. The point is once again to pull from the past, the no-longer-conscious, described and represented by Bloch today, to push beyond the impasse of the present.

I swerve away from my critique of the failures of imagination in the LGBT activist enterprises to Harvey for a very specific purpose. Harvey represented a fairly more expansive and nuanced critique in his previous work on postmodernity, writing that was thoughtfully critiqued by queer theorists such as Judith Halberstam.[25] But Harvey's work has become, like that of many Marxist scholars, all too ready to dismiss or sacrifice questions of sexuality and gender. Furthermore, these mostly white writers have, as in the example I cited in the preceding paragraph, been quick to posit race and class as real antagonisms within a larger socioeconomic struggle and sexuality and gender as merely "lifestyle diversification." In many ways they are performing a function that is the direct opposite of white neoliberal queers who studiously avoid the question of ethnic, racial, class, ability, or gender difference. This correspondence is representative of a larger political impasse that I understand as being the toll of pragmatic politics and antiutopian thought.

Concrete utopias remake rationalism, unlinking it from the provincial and pragmatic politics of the present. Taking back a rationalist core, in the way in which Bloch suggests we do in relation to romanticism, is to insist on an ordering of life that is not dictated by the spatial/temporal coordinates of straight time, a time and space matrix in which, unfortunately, far too many gays, lesbians, and other purportedly "queer" people reside.

To see queerness as horizon is to perceive it as a modality of ecstatic time in which the temporal stranglehold that I describe as straight time is interrupted or stepped out of. Ecstatic time is signaled at the moment one feels ecstasy, announced perhaps in a scream or grunt of pleasure, and more importantly during moments of contemplation when one looks back at a scene from one's past, present, or future. Opening oneself up to such a perception of queerness as manifestation in and of ecstatic time offers queers much more than the meager offerings of pragmatic gay and lesbian politics. Seeing queerness as horizon rescues and emboldens concepts such as freedom that have been withered by the touch of neoliberal thought and gay assimilationist politics. Pragmatic gay politics present themselves as rational and ultimately more doable. Such politics and their proponents often attempt to describe themselves as not being ideological, yet they are extremely ideological and, more precisely, are representative of a decayed ideological institution known as marriage. Rationalism need not be given over to gay neoliberals who attempt to sell a cheapened and degraded version of freedom. The freedom that is offered by an LGBT position that does not bend to straight time's gravitational pull is akin to one of Heidegger's descriptions of freedom as unboundness. And more often than not the "rhetorical" deployment of the pragmatic leads to a *not-doing*, an antiperformativity. Doing, performing, engaging the performative as force of and for futurity is queerness's bent and ideally the way to queerness.[26]

2

Ghosts of Public Sex

Utopian Longings, Queer Memories

Witnessing Queer Sex Utopia

In 1989 I saw Douglas Crimp give a rousing and moving talk titled "Mourning and Militancy" at the second national Lesbian and Gay Studies conference, held at Yale University.[1] Crimp explained the workings of mourning in queer culture as he cataloged a vast, lost gay male lifeworld that was seemingly devastated by the HIV/AIDS pandemic. I want to call attention here to a specific moment in Crimp's talk in which an idea of Freud's is put in conversation with queer spaces and practices from a historically specific gay male lifeworld:

> Freud tells us that mourning is the reaction not only to the death of a loved person, but also "to the loss of some abstraction which has taken the place of one, such as a fatherland, liberty, and ideal . . ." Can we be allowed to include, in this "civilized" list, the ideal of perverse sexual pleasure itself rather than one stemming from its sublimation? Alongside the dismal toll of death, what many of us have lost is a culture of sexual possibility: back rooms, tea rooms, movie houses, and baths; the trucks, the piers, the ramble, the dunes. Sex was everywhere for us, and everything we wanted to venture: Golden showers and water sports, cocksucking and rimming, fucking and fist fucking. Now our untamed impulses are either proscribed once again or shielded from us by latex. Even Crisco, the lube we used because it was edible, is now forbidden because it breaks down rubber. Sex toys are no longer added enhancements; they're safer substitutes.[2]

It has been seven years since the zenith of AIDS cultural criticism when Crimp wrote these words. One thing that has become clear at this moment in the epidemic is that the ideal spaces and practices that Crimp described never completely ceased to be. During the age of AIDS gay men have managed to maintain our queer sex, our spaces, and, to some lesser degree, the incredible sense of possibility that Crimp evokes. At this juncture, commercial sex spaces (backrooms, movie theaters, bathhouses) are weathering a new round of attacks from both the repressive state power apparatus and reactionary, sex-negative elements of the gay community. Despite these eruptions of antisex and homophobic policings, many gay men have managed to maintain the practices that Crimp lists, as they have been translated in the age of safer sex. Negotiated risks and other tactical decisions have somewhat modified these sexual impulses without entirely stripping them away. Although the moment that Crimp describes is a moment that is behind us, its memory, its ghosts, and the ritualized performances of transmitting its vision of utopia across generational divides still fuels and propels our political and erotic lives: it still nourishes the possibility of our current, actually existing gay lifeworld.

Crimp's writing stands as a testimony to a queer lifeworld in which the transformative potential of queer sex and public manifestations of such sexuality were both a respite from the abjection of homosexuality and a reformatting of that very abjection. The spaces and acts he lists represent signs, or ideals, that have been degraded and rendered abject within heteronormativity. Crimp's essay reclaims these terms, ideas, and remembrances and pushes them onto a list that includes such timeless values as fatherland and liberty. Crimp's essay thus bears witness to a queer sex utopia.

In a starkly dissimilar manner, Leo Bersani's own important essay in AIDS cultural criticism, "Is the Rectum a Grave?" debunks idealized notions of bathhouses as utopic queer space.[3] Bersani rightly brings to light the fact that those pre-AIDS days of glory were also elitist, exclusionary, and savagely hierarchized libidinal economies. Bersani's work does not allow itself to entertain utopian hopes and possibilities. His book of gay male cultural theory, Homos, further extends the lines of thought of "Is the Rectum a Grave?" in different directions.[4] Homos is even more concerned with dismantling and problematizing any simplistic, sentimental understanding of the gay community or gay politics. Through an especially powerful reading of Jean Genet, Bersani formulates a theory of antirelationality. The most interesting contribution of this theory is the way in which it puts pressure on previous queer theories and exposes the ways in which they theorize gay identity in terms that are always relational, such as gender subversion. But this lesson ultimately leads to a critique of coalition politics. Bersani considers coalitions between gay men and people of color or women as "bad faith" on the part of gays. The race, gender, and sexuality troubles in such a theory—all people of color are straight, all gay men are white—are also evident in his famous essay. The limits of his project are most obvious when one tries to imagine actual political interventions into the social realm, especially interventions that challenge the tedious white normativity that characterizes most of North American gay male culture.

Bersani's project does not need to see and believe in utopianism. Yet queer politics, in my understanding, needs a real dose of utopianism. Utopia lets us[5] imagine a space outside of heteronormativity. It permits us to conceptualize new worlds and realities that are not irrevocably constrained by the HIV/AIDS pandemic and institutionalized state homophobia. More important, utopia offers us a critique of the present, of what is, by casting a picture of what *can and perhaps will be*. In this chapter I look at moments in a few gay male cultural works that imagine utopia through what I call *queer utopian memory*.

Memory is most certainly constructed and, more important, always political. The case I make in this chapter posits our remembrances and their ritualized tellings—through film, video, performance, writing, and visual culture—as having world-making potentialities. Furthermore, I suggest that these queer memories of utopia and the longing that structures them, especially as they are embodied in work that I identify as public-sex-mimetic cultural production, help us carve out a space for actual, living sexual citizenship.[6] I single out moments, such as the passage from Crimp quoted earlier, that tell, remember, and reflect on public sex. I do not read these texts as nostalgic discourse but instead present them as moments in which queer utopian remembrance reenacts what Crimp has called a culture of sexual possibility. John Giorno's short autobiographical fiction and the visual work of conceptual artist Tony Just serve as the textual sites for this discussion of the workings of queer utopian memory and the structure of feeling that is adjacent to such a reconstructed notion of utopia and memory, a force field of affect and political desire that I call utopian longing.

Fucking Keith, Remembering Utopia

John Giorno's *You Got to Burn to Shine* is a rich mosaic of poetry, performance text, activist mission statements, and autobiographical prose. The book reflects on Giorno's life as a queer writer and performer over the past four decades in Manhattan's Lower East Side. Giorno's text is the uncanny testimony of a man who has survived various risky lifestyles. It is studded with fabulous star-fucking stories that sparkle like tawdry gems. The reader is, for example, treated to a tell-all account of the author's having sex with Andy Warhol, a tale that satisfactorily debunks popular myths that have circulated around Warhol to degay his sexuality.[7]

A section called "Great Anonymous Sex" recounts one of Giorno's encounters with another Pop Art superstar in 1982 at the Prince Street subway toilets. In this story Giorno fucks and sucks a young man who is later revealed to be Keith Haring. Giorno's sex narrative begins with his entrance to the Prince Street toilets, a space rife with anonymous public sex. Giorno writes about a plain-looking yet attractive boy with wire-rimmed glasses, a "kid" possessed of an "unusual passion":

> He was making love with great energy and focus, affection and delight, different than the routine going on around me. The guy's heart was pouring love and I went with the flow. I sucked the kid's cock (it was cut, not large but very hard). He sucked my cock, with his eyes looking up into mine. Two guys with poppers kept sticking them in our nostrils. We continued alternating sucking each other's cocks. He managed a few times to get my cock all the way down his throat and I fucked his face, moments of surrender for both of us. The onlookers jerked off watching us.[8]

Giorno's narrative rings of idealization and writerly hyperbole, which is not to doubt the "truth" of his account. In the passage, Giorno functions as a disseminator of public sex culture. The idealization that his prose enacts is, within the scope of my analysis, an example of the way in which a rich remembrance of sexual utopia feeds a transformative queer politics. The excess that Giorno's text produces is indeed more that simple sexual bravado. The space of the Prince Street toilets and the practices of public sex that are rendered in his narrative engender a certain transformative possibility.

The politics I understand as being enacted in Giorno's text are not immediately visible. In fact, the statement would seem to run counter to Giorno's assertions that "the great thing about anonymous sex is you don't bring your private life or personal world. No politics or inhibiting concepts, no closed rules or fixed responses. The great thing about anonymous sex is spontaneity."[9] Although Giorno understands this space as being one that is free of ideology, I think we can still read a powerful political impulse in Giorno's text, an impulse that is detectable in the acts that are being transcribed, the spaces that are being conceptually rendered, and the performance of writing that expresses his public sex history. I am most interested here in the latter of these.

The cataloging of public sex culture that Crimp performs in "Mourning and Militancy" can be read alongside Giorno's text as an act of queer world-making. More specifically, I see world-making here as functioning and coming into play through the performance of queer utopian memory, that is, a utopia that understands its time as reaching beyond some nostalgic past that perhaps never was or some future whose arrival is continuously belated—a utopia in the present.

I turn now to a 1964 printed dialogue between Frankfurt School social theorists Theodor W. Adorno and Ernst Bloch on "the utopian function of art."[10] At one point in the dialogue, Bloch turns to Adorno and confirms a basic truism about the politics of utopianism in spite of the climate of a mechanical age in which everything seems mechanically present and therefore cancels out the possibility of utopianism:

> Bloch: Thus, the fact that there is also utopia in this area where it has the most difficulty . . . [thus] *the essential function of utopia is a critique of what is present.* If we had not already gone beyond the barriers, we could not even perceive them as barriers. (Emphasis mine)[11]

The saliency of Bloch's point lies not merely in the fact that imagining any utopia offers us something that is more than another time but also, as in the case of Giorno and the gay male cultural workers I am considering here, in that what is made available first is a critique of the present and of its limits, its barriers. Adorno follows up his friend's point by casting his statement within the frame of the dialectic:

> Adorno: Yes, at any rate, utopia is essentially in the determined negation, in the determined negation of that which merely is, and by concretizing itself as something false, it always points, at the same time to what should be.
>
> Yesterday you quoted Spinoza in our discussion with the passage "Verum index sui et falsi" [the true is the sign of itself and the false]. I have varied this a little in the sense of the dialectical principle of the determined negation and have said Falsum—the false thing—index sui et veri [the false is the sign of itself and the correct]. That means that the true thing determines itself via the false thing, or via that

which makes itself falsely known. And insofar as we are not allowed to cast the picture of utopia, insofar as we do know what the correct thing will be, we know exactly, to be sure, what the false thing is.[12]

Dialectical thinking, especially what Adorno refers to as "the determined negation" enables us to read Giorno's text as something other than a nostalgic foreclosure on future political possibility. Instead, via the lens provided by these materialist philosophers, we can understand Giorno's text as pointing beyond the barriers of our current conditions of possibility, beyond the painful barriers of the AIDS pandemic; it lets us see, via a certain conjuring of "the past," and for many of us we see this past for the very first time. These pictures of utopia (a term that is used in later comments Adorno makes in the dialogue) do the work of letting us critique the present, to see beyond its "what is" to worlds of political possibility, of "what might be."

Here is another instance of Giorno doing what Adorno calls the casting of a picture:

> I unbuckled the kid's belt and he pulled down his pants. I turned him gently around, slowly eased in the wet head and slipped my cock into his ass, and he pushed to me and took it all. His ass was slightly lubricated with Vaseline, I wondered if it was from this morning or from last night, and if he had someone's cum in his ass. That thought made me hotter and the grease made my dick feel even better. Someone started rimming me, had his face buried in my ass, his tongue in my asshole, and was nibbling and sucking. This is also a great pleasure for me. I fucked the kid, gently at first, then gradually as hard as I could. Sweat poured off us in sheets. From the depth of the inebriating darkness of that underground cave, stretching my cock to the sky, I shot a big load of cum, straight and glorious. Perfectly arisen and accomplished, and perfectly dissolved back into primordially pure empty space.[13]

This, I want to suggest, is certainly a casting of a picture of sex, but, in the same instance, it is also a picture of utopian transport and a reconfiguration of the social, a reimaging of our actual conditions of possibility, all of this in the face of a global epidemic. The picture rendered through Giorno's performative writing is one of a good life that both was and never was, that has been lost and is still to come. It performs a desire for a perfect dissolution into a "primordially pure empty space."

After this scene in the Prince Street toilet, Giorno runs out and catches a train in the nick of time: "I said goodbye and I was out the door in a flash, onto the train going uptown." Once on the train he feels himself once again overwhelmed by the crushing presence and always expanding force field that is heteronormativity: "It always was a shock entering the straight world of a car full of grim people sitting dumbly with suffering on their faces and in their bodies, and their minds in their prisons."[14] This experience of being "shocked" by the prison that is heteronormativity, the straight world, is one that a reader, especially a queer reader, encounters after putting down a queer utopian memory text such as Giorno's. I think of my own experience of reading *You Got to Burn to Shine* at some predominantly straight coffee shop near where I live, looking up after the experience, and feeling a similar shock effect. I once again pick up the thread of Adorno's thinking from the same dialogue with Bloch:

> [Negation] is actually the only form in which utopia is given to us at all. But what I mean to say here . . . this matter has a very confounding aspect, for something terrible happens due to the fact that we are forbidden to cast a picture. To be precise, among that which should be definite, one imagines for it to begin with as less definite the more it is stated as something negative. But then—the commandment against a concrete example of Utopia tends to defame the Utopian consciousness and to engulf it. What is really important here is the will that it is different.[15]

In Giorno's work we can see the "will that is different." There are many reasons why these fantasies of rapturous unsafe sex might have a damaging effect on gay men living in the AIDS pandemic. But having said that, there is something noble and enabling about Giorno's storytelling. Adorno, in the passage just quoted, speaks out against a trend in socialism (and in humanism in general) in which utopianism becomes the bad object. Utopianism can only exist via a critique of the dominant order; it has no space to exist outside of the most theoretically safeguarded abstractions. In a roughly analogous way the pictures drawn by Giorno are also bad objects insofar as they expose gay men to acts, poses, and structures of desire that may be potentially disastrous. But, as Adorno teaches us, the importance of casting a picture is central to a critique of hegemony. Adorno explains, "If this is not said, if this picture cannot—I almost would like to say—appear within one's grasp, then one basically does not know at all what the actual reason for the totality is, why the entire apparatus has been set in motion."[16]

It might seem as though my oscillations between the worlds and sexual utopias produced in Giorno and the more theoretical utopian musing of Bloch and Adorno are something of a stretch. To that charge I answer, "of course." But, beyond that, I would point to the words with which Bloch ends the dialogue: "In conclusion, I would like to quote a phrase, a very simple one, strangely enough from Oscar Wilde: 'A map of the world that does not include utopia is not even worth glancing at.'"[17] Although it might be strange, from most vistas, that Bloch would be quoting Western culture's most famous convicted sodomite, it is certainly not so odd from the perspective of this queer inquiry. Wilde's sentence, when properly broken down and appreciated for its stylized precision, makes explicit the connection between queerness, utopia, and world-making. Queer world-making, then, hinges on the possibility to map a world where one is allowed to cast pictures of utopia and to include such pictures in any map of the social. For certainly, without this critical spot on the map we ourselves become the pained and imprisoned subjects on the fast-moving train Giorno describes.

Ghosts and Utopia

I turn now from the ghost of Oscar Wilde that haunts Bloch's thinking on utopia to the ghosts that circulate in the photography of Tony Just. In 1994 Just completed a project that attempted to capture precisely what I am calling the ghosts of public sex. The project began with just selecting run-down public men's rooms in New York City, the kind that were most certainly tea rooms before they, like the Prince Street toilets that Giorno describes, were shut down because of the AIDS/HIV public health crisis. Just then proceeded to do the labor of scrubbing and sanitizing sections of the public men's rooms. The preparation of the spaces is as central to the series as the photos I choose to focus on; the only evidence of this behind-the-scenes aspect of the larger project is the clean spaces themselves—Just's labor exists only as a ghostly trace in a sparkling men's room. He documented this project through color slides and photographs that focused on the bathrooms' immaculate state and the details of such spaces. The urinals, tiles, toilets, and fixtures that are the objects of these photo images take on what can only be described as a ghostly aura, an otherworldly glow. This aura, this circuit of luminous halos that surround the work, is one aspect of the ghosts of public sex that this chapter is interested in describing.

These ghosts of public sex are the queer specters whose substance Just's project and my own critical endeavor attempt to capture and render visible. In pan, I see the ghosted materiality of the work as having a primary relation to emotions, queer memories, and structures of feeling that haunt gay men on both sides of a generational divide that is formed by and through the catastrophe of AIDS. One of the things one risks when one talks of ghosts is the charge of ignoring the living, the real, and the material. I bolster my formulations against such potential reservations with the work of Raymond Williams. Williams's notion of a structure of feeling was a process of relating the continuity of social formations within a work of art. Williams explained structure of feeling as a hypothesis that

> has a special relevance to art and literature, where true social content is in a significant number of cases of this present and affective kind, that which cannot be reduced to belief systems, institutions, or explicit general relationships, though it may include all these as lived and experienced, with or without tension, as it also evidently includes elements of social and material (physical or natural) experience which may lie beyond or be uncovered or imperfectly covered by, the elsewhere recognizable systematic elements.

For Williams, the concept of structures of feeling accounts for

> the unmistakable presence of certain elements in art which are not covered by (though in one mode, might be reduced to) other formal systems. [This] is the true source of the specializing category of "the aesthetic", "the arts", and "imaginative literature". We need, on the one hand, to acknowledge (and welcome) the specificity of these elements—specific dealings, specific rhythms—and yet to find their specific kinds of sociality, thus preventing the extraction from social experience which is conceivable only when social experience itself has been categorically (and at root historically) reduced.[18]

The ghosts I detect in Just's project possess a materiality, a kind of substance, that does not easily appear within regimes of the visible and the tactile. These elements have their own specificity but are also relevant on a vaster map of social and political experience. To see these ghosts we must certainly read the "specific dealings, specific rhythms" that bring to life a lost experience, a temporally situated picture of social experience, that needs to be read in photo images, gaps, auras, residues, and negations. Due to the obstacles imposed by certain preconceptions of materiality—preconceptions that are often manifest as visual myopias—one cannot actually see the ghost of public sex in Just's project. But if the eye is sensitized in a certain way, if it can catch other visual frequencies that render specific distillations of lived experience and ground-level history accessible, it can potentially see the ghostly presence of a certain structure of feeling.

In the photos, the shine of porcelain and metal, the way in which light reflects around and off these surfaces and objects—be they a porcelain urinal or a slightly corroded chrome fixture—cast an effect that is strangely mimetic of the haunted structures of feeling that circulate around the sites of the project. The pictures interrogate the curves and arches of lifted toilet seats and the rounded edges of porcelain toilet frames. The emphasis on tile, in conjunction with the empty foreground of the rooms, makes one think of an echo chamber. The connotation becomes one of reverberation and resonance. The pictures, through the negative charge of absented bodies, instill in the spectator a sense of gathering emptiness. Such an emptiness is not the project's teleological objective; rather, that space of emptiness is meant to make room for other worlds of sexual possibility.

The deciphering enterprise at the center of this chapter accounts for these visual effects (which are also photographic effects) as a performance of a familiar yet otherworldly affective function that leaves a certain ephemeral trace, the appearance of which I am calling the production of ghosts. *Then ghosts.* Jacques Derrida, in his study of ghosts in Marx, employs a notion of *hauntology*, which he understands to be a conceptual tool for the understanding of being within the postmodern age of an electronic *res publica*: "neither living or dead, present or absent" and ultimately "not belong[ing] to ontology, to the discourse of the being of beings, or to the essence of life and death."[19] I suggest hauntology as a powerful mechanism for the work of situating semipublic phenomena such as public sex within queer history and politics.

Earlier in this chapter I discussed dialectics while conjuring Adorno. One reading of the absence of people and acts in Just's riffs on public sex would consider these representations of hollowed-out, mournful, and fetishistic spaces to be those of determined negations, the casting of pictures that represent utopia through the negative. Without casting out this dialectical optic, another critical vista, again found in Derrida's Marxian study, helps us to think about ghosts in terms that attempt to surpass the dialectic. Take, for instance, the moment in which Derrida ponders what he considers to be the logic of the ghosts:

> If we have been insisting so much since the beginning on the logic of the ghost, it is because it points toward a thinking of the event that necessarily exceeds a binary or dialectical logic, the logic that distinguishes or opposes effectivity or actuality (either present, empirical, living—or not) and ideality (regulating or absolute non-presence). The logic of effectivity or actuality seems to be of a limited pertinence. . . . [The limit] seems to be demonstrated better than ever by the fantastic, ghostly, "synthetic," "prosthetic," virtual happenings in the scientific domain and therefore in the domain of techno-media and therefore the public or political domain. It is also made more manifest by what inscribes the speed of a virtuality irreducible to the opposition of the act and the potential in the space of the event, in the event-ness of the event.[20]

Derrida is discussing a modality of techno-media that would include broadcast, videographic, and cybernetic communication, not the more established photographic technologies that Just works with and manipulates. Nonetheless, I continue to find an edifying understanding of what Derrida means by the surpassing of a binary between ideality and actuality when I consider these photographs. Within dialectical terms, Just weighs in on the side of determined negation, since, when one tries to unpack a dialectical opposition between "the act and the potential in the space of the event, in the event-ness of the event," we see with great clarity what Derrida has called the "eventness" of the space. Just's work represents the idealism of utopia while also representing the importance of effectivity and actuality. Its negation of physical players and its choice to represent absence permits a viewer, strangely enough, to occupy a space both inside and outside the predictability of such an established dialectical pattern.[21]

The negation that I am describing through my reading of this early work by Just is not one determined by a direct opposition between presence or absence; it does not signify a simple politics of lack. A quick consideration of Just's recent work helps to explicate this case further. A series of work from 2004 represents graffiti in a new and fascinating perspective. This series of pastel-on-paper renderings depicts, in something that is like

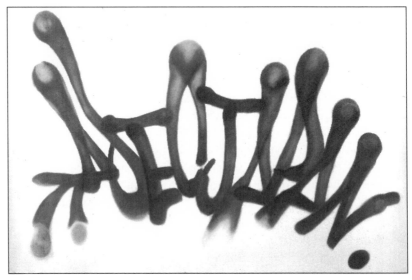

Tony Just, "London," 2004. Copyright Tony Just, Courtesy of the Gavin Brown Enterprise/ Gallery.

a modality of aesthetic surplus, graffiti "tags" and signs that are almost photo-realistically stylized. Yet although these pastels seem to be photos, they are powerfully attuned to questions of color. The images vividly resonate differently than most representations of graffiti, by not representing a world of urban decay associated with postindustrial decline. Electric blue scrawl on a pale blue background connotes something other than the negation we associate with lack or loss. Another image depicts yet another stark shade of blue that outlines blocks of silver paint. The entire piece resembles a section of a larger insignia in a larger urban landscape. Smaller letters circulate around the large block letters. If I were to hazard a guess as to what these letters connote, I would say that they seem to be initials— but that is in and of itself an interpretive stretch. Another graffiti image seems like freestyle squiggles over patches of soft pastel colors. Just's use of tagging through lush painterly practices makes the utopian in the quotidian manifest.

What are these tags showing us? Although they might affectively function very differently than urban realist representations of graffiti, these strange pastels do render something akin to the graffiti that marks city landscapes. In a Blochian parlance we can consider these urban markings as traces. Through the surplus they represent they seem to tell us something is missing or, in terms of the opening aphorisms in Bloch's text *Traces,* that what is here is "Not Enough." In *Traces,* three fairly concise sentences follow the title "Not Enough": "One is alone with oneself. Together with others, most are alone even without themselves. One has to get out of both."[22] This aphorism can be read as a brief instruction manual. This getting out of oneself with and without others is an insistence on another mode in which one feels the collective. This longing for collectivity, this movement away from the question of "the alone," is a line that runs through most of Just's work. In the same way that these Just paintings rehearse the potentially utopian aesthetics of the cityscape, two other canvases stylize past moments of political insurrectionist hope. One painting features what appear to be stenciled words over a half-green and half-pink background. The slogan reads, "Women of the World Take Over." Another image represents a circular swirl of vivid greens and other complementary hues connoting the wonders of the natural world. Thinly stenciled black

Tony Just, "Celebrate Trees." Copyright Tony Just, Courtesy of the Gavin Brown Enterprise/ Gallery.

letters spell out "Celebrate Trees." Both canvases speak politics of the past. They are the opposite of camp insofar as they are imbued a certain sincerity, a politics of sincerity that connote transformative political desire of the past that has become even more pressing. They are placards for the queer utopian imagination. They signal a need for a futurity, a moment of the not-yet-here that is as vivid as it is necessary.

Situating Ghosts

The double ontology of ghosts and ghostliness, the manner in which ghosts exist inside and out and traverse categorical distinctions, seems especially useful for a queer criticism that attempts to understand communal mourning, group psychologies, and the need for a politics that "carries" our dead with us into battles for the present and future. Ghosts have already been used by some queer scholars to explain the relationship of homosexuality to heteronormative culture. Mandy Merck, in a discussion that glosses ghost theory by Patricia White, Diana Fuss, and Terry Castle, explains the relational dynamic in this way: "The [homosexual] ghost that haunts heterosexuality is its uncanny double, the illicit desire needed to define legitimacy. The liminality of the figure, as Fuss and others have observed, reflects its ambiguity as a term of exclusion which nonetheless confers interiority."[23] If the terms and logic of Merck's analysis were to travel to other divides, beyond the homo/hetero split to splits that are currently being reified within queer cultures, in some branches of queer writing and in gay male communities, as well as between different generational and health status markers, we could begin to decipher the ways in which the specter of public sex—ostracized by many "legitimate" factions within the queer community—is still a foundational presence/antipresence that performs the illicit and helps these conservative factions formulate a "legitimate," sanitized gay world.

Ghost theory also worries the binary between HIV-positive and negative men, a binary that is currently being concretized in new gay male writing. Recently, there has been a shift away from the initial moment of AIDS cultural criticism that concentrated on people living with AIDS and the ways in which they are represented and "caught" within the dominant public sphere, to projects that figure the ontology of HIV-negative men. The aim of such projects is to make HIV-negativity a site of identity that can be inhabited despite the cultural morbidity that characterizes this historical moment. Although such interventions can be potentially valuable for activists who work on HIV prevention, the bolstering of HIV-negativity as an identification that men should be encouraged to "come out" into concomitantly puts a new set of pressures on people living with the HIV virus to be out also. The potential problem with cultural work and theory on and about HIV-negative men is that it does not resist and, in some ways, may inadvertently contribute to the stigmatization that surrounds AIDS and HIV in both mainstream North American culture and AIDS-phobic gay male regional and subcultural communities. In this chapter I have been considering what I call haunting and haunted cultural work that remembers and longs for a moment outside of this current state of siege. My critical move here, that of employing key words and thematics such as "ghosts," memory," "longing," and "utopia," has been to decipher the networks of commonality and the structures of feeling that link queers across different identity markers, including positive and negative antibody status as well as bodies separated along generational lines.

Such a strategy is born out of a partial skepticism toward projects such as Walt Odets's In The Shadow of the Epidemic: Being HIV-Negative in the Age of AIDS,[24] which bring to light the "psychological epidemic" that HIV-negative men face. The residual effects of such a project that focuses exclusively on negatives needs to be further interrogated. Some questions that linger include, Can we afford to redirect our critical energies away from bodies that are infected by a physical virus toward uninfected bodies that are caught within a psychological epidemic? How would the already stigmatized lives of infected people be affected by this work that bolsters HIV-negative identity? Does work on HIV-negativity produce a wedge between infected and uninfected sectors of the gay community, further solidifying a binary between negative and positive? In short, what might be the cost of work that affirms HIV-negative identity for those who are struggling with and attempting to manage illness? These questions cloud my reading of Odets and other writers attempting to delineate HIV-negativity. I do not want to foreclose the transformative and self-sustaining energies of such work—asking these questions is merely an attempt to bring the specters that haunt such theories into the light, out of the shadow.

Instead of focusing on the different ways—psychologically and physically—in which men suffer in the epidemic, I have been concerned with the ways in which the politics around queer memory, fueled by utopian longing, can help us reimagine the social. To this end I have suggested that viewing Just's photography in light of Giorno's writing, and vice versa,

affords the spectator a certain understanding of the world-making properties of queerness. We see, for instance, the imbrication of sex and utopias
across gay male generational rifts. We see the various circuits of narration
that gay men employ. The notion of a strategic and self-knowing modality of queer utopian memory, and, more important, the work that such
a memory does, becomes all the more possible. The utopian longing in
both artists' work is neither a nostalgic wish nor a passing fascination but,
rather, the impetus for a queerworld, for what Crimp has called a culture
of sexual possibility. The works I survey in this chapter, taken side by side,
tell us a story about the primary linkage between queer desire and queer
politics. Taken further, this work allows the spectator to understand her
or his desire for politics alongside the politics of desire. The lens of these
remembrances and the hazy mirages they produce not only allow us to
imagine utopia but, more important, whet our appetite for it.[25]

3

The Future Is in the Present

Sexual Avant-Gardes and the Performance of Utopia

FUTURITY CAN BE a problem. Heterosexual culture depends on a notion of the future: as the song goes, "the children are our future." But that is not the case for different cultures of sexual dissidence. Rather than invest in a deferred future, the queer citizen-subject labors to live in a present that is calibrated, through the protocols of state power, to sacrifice our liveness for what Lauren Berlant has called the "dead citizenship" of heterosexuality.[1] This dead citizenship is formatted, in part, through the sacrifice of the present for a fantasmatic future. On oil dance floors, sites of public sex, various theatrical stages, music festivals, and arenas both subterranean and aboveground, queers live, labor, and enact queer worlds in the present. But must the future and the present exist in this rigid binary? Can the future stop being a fantasy of heterosexual reproduction? In this chapter I argue for the disruption of this binarized logic and the enactment of what I call, following C. L. R. James, a future in the present.[2] To call for this notion of the future in the present is to summon a refunctioned notion of utopia in the service of subaltern politics. Certain performances of queer citizenship contain what I call an anticipatory illumination of a queer world, a sign of an actually existing queer reality, a kernel of political possibility within a stultifying heterosexual present. I gesture to sites of embodied and performed queer politics and describe them as outposts of actually existing queer worlds. The sites I consider are sites of mass gatherings, performances that can be understood as defiantly public and glimpses into an ensemble of social actors performing a queer world.

The Past for the Future: Queer Happenings

I begin this study of the future in the present by turning to the past. Samuel R. Delany's memoir *The Motion of Light in Water* periodizes the advent of postmodernity through the evidence provided by two modes of avant-garde performance. These performances do more than represent an epistemic shift; they enable the memoirist to procure a new vista on the world. The writer describes images from his then present (now squarely the past), and these pictures purchase a vision of the future. I want to suggest that these performances that are described by Delany announced and enacted a new formation within the social.

The first of these performances was held in a Second Avenue studio apartment in New York's East Village during the summer of 1960. Delany and a cousin had stumbled on a performance of Allan Kaprow's entitled "Eighteen Happenings in Six Parts." It was the first time the word *happening* had been used in a performance context. Delany explained that "many times now Kaprow's piece (today we would call it performance art) has been cited by historians as the equally arbitrary transition between the modern and the postmodern in cultural developments. But I don't believe I've read a firsthand account of it by any of its original audience."[3] However, the memoirist has missed some of the most interesting accounts of this performance genre, for there is in fact a fascinating literature chronicling and documenting this artistic movement.[4] Delany's account is nonetheless valuable. He remembers entering an apartment that was taken up by polyethylene walls on painted wood frames. These walls divided the performance space into six sections of about eight feet by eight feet. The sections were accessible from a door-wide space on the outside but were separated from one another by semitranslucent walls through which one could make out "the ghost" of what was happening in the adjoining section. There were half a dozen or so wooden folding chairs in each room. The remembered performance that Delany narrates consisted of a child's windup toy being set on the ground and let run and then wound up again and again over the twenty-minute running time of the performance. Through the plastic walls the sounds and sights of other happenings partially filtered into the writer's cubicle. He could make out the buttery glow of a candle in one room, while in another he heard the sounds of a drum.

The writer's expectations were severely challenged by this performance. He had assumed that the work would be "rich, Dionysian and colorful." He expected the happenings themselves to be "far more complex, denser and probably verbally boundable." He expected happenings that would crowd in on one another and form an interconnected tapestry of occurrences and associations rich in meanings and meaning fragments, full of resonance and overlapping associations, "playful, sentimental and reassuring." Yet the work he encountered was "spare, difficult, minimal, constituted largely by absence, isolation, even distraction."[5] Delany expected the six parts to be chronologically ordered, like acts in a play, but they were instead spatially organized. Delany writes that "it was precisely in this subversion of expectations about the proper aesthetic employment of time, space, presence, absence, wholeness and fragmentation, as well as the general locality of 'what happens,' that made Kaprow's work signify: his happenings—clicking toys, burning candles, pounded drums, or whatever—were organized in that initial work very much like historical events."[6] Delany admits that his expectations were formed by a modernist desire to see "meaningful plenitude," yet his disappointment waned once he had found the time to contemplate Kaprow's project, work that he found to be "more interesting, strenuous and aesthetically energetic." Delany concludes his recollection by claiming that "'Eighteen Happenings in Six Parts' was about as characteristic a work as one might choose in which to experience the clash that begins our reading of the hugely arbitrary postmodern."[7]

That avant-garde performance is intimately linked to another mode of "happening" that occurs later in the memoir. Delany was alerted to this particular performance venue by a painter friend in the East Village. His friend Simon had told him about the trucks parked by the river at the end of Christopher Street as a place to go at night for instant sex. Once the author passed the truck's threshold, he discovered that, on a regular basis, between 35 and 150 men slipped through the trailers, some to watch but most to participate in "numberless silent sexual acts." Delany describes these acts as rituals that reconstructed intimacy: "At those times, within those van-walled alleys, now between the trucks, now in the back of the open loaders, cock passed from mouth to mouth to hand to ass to mouth without ever breaking contact with other flesh for more than seconds; mouth, hand, ass passed over whatever you held out to them, sans interstice; when one cock left, finding a replacement—mouth, rectum, another cock—required moving the head, the hip, the hand no more than an inch, three inches."[8] This scene is described as "engrossing," "exhausting," "reassuring," and "very human." The writer explains how the men in this space took care of one another not only by offering flesh but by performing a care for the self that encompassed a vast care for others—a delicate and loving "being for others."[9]

Delany follows this description pages later with another retelling of public sex performances. On his first visit to the St. Mark's Baths, Delany encountered a well-lit mass of perverts. Lighting made a difference insofar as the piers operated under the cover of a protective darkness that also kept the massiveness of the crowd available. In this respect he compares the piers to Kaprow's "Eighteen Happenings in Six Parts." In the more formally theatrical happening, "no one ever got to see the whole" because institutions such as subway johns, the trucks parked on the Christopher Street pier, pornographic theaters, and other institutions of public sex accommodated these performances by cutting them up, by making sure that the whole was distorted. In the blue light of the St. Mark's Baths something was confirmed deeply for the then twenty-year-old budding science-fiction writer: "What this experience said was that there was a population—not of individual homosexuals, some of whom now and then encountered, or that those encounters could be human and fulfilling in their way—not of hundreds, not of thousands, but rather of millions of gay men, and that history had, actively and already, created for us whole galleries of institutions, good and bad, to accommodate our sex."[10]

This section of *Motion of Light in Water* is critiqued by historian Joan Wallach Scott, who oddly employs this memoir as an example of gay history's reliance on unreconstructed narratives of experience, fixed identity, and "the visual."[11] (Lisa Duggan has already pointed out the inappropriateness of making such an argument on gay and lesbian history based on a writer's nonfiction memoir.)[12] Scott attempts in her article to partially recant her reading of Delany, yet she ultimately fails to comprehend the author's project. The Kaprow piece taught Delany a valuable lesson about the way in which public culture is cut up through the institutions of the majoritarian public sphere. The happening thematized vision to show the ways in which vision is constantly compromised. Most of Delany's memoir narrates through a Kaprowian understanding of the alienation and segmentation that characterize the real. His moment of seeing the whole of public sex is a utopian break in the narrative—it is a deviation from the text's dominant mode of narration. Public sex culture revealed the existence of a queer world, and Kaprow's happening explained the ways in which such utopian visions were continuously distorted. Delany explains that "the first apprehension of massed bodies" signals a direct sense of political power. This apprehension debunks dominant ideology's characterization of antinormative subject-citizens as "isolated perverts."[13] Kaprow's performance and the piers were adjacent happenings that presented only shades of the whole; the blue light of the bathhouse offered a glimpse of utopia.

I turn to this memoir of the sixties at this particular moment because it echoes the ongoing attack on cultures of sexual dissidence that New

York City is currently weathering. The draconian rule of mayor Rudolph Giuliani saw the institution of a policy that rezoned the vast majority of public sex out of the city. New laws closed down most adult bookstores, bars, movie theaters, peep shows, and performance spaces that featured sexually oriented performance—not only female strippers at straight bars but go-go boys at queer clubs. The crackdown on public sex was part of Giuliani's notorious "quality of life campaign," now carried on under the mayorship of Michael Bloomberg. The venues Delany employed to see "the massed bodies" that signaled political power have become harder and harder to glimpse. In many ways the fragmentation that will characterize this New York City's culture of public sex will be far more alienating than that described in Delany's chronicle of pre-Stonewall New York. While normative middle-class subjects enjoy a porn-free Manhattan, citizen-subjects who participate in the service economy of the sex industry now experience a level of harassment that surpasses even that experienced by other wage workers such as street vendors and taxi drivers. Giuliani instituted a range of policies that clamped down on those professions as well, industries that, like that of sex workers, are heavily populated by people of color.

In the late 1990s Times Square entered its last phase of what I half jokingly call "late Disneyfication." Many local adult businesses were, and continue to be, replaced with more corporate representation, such as Disney stores and Starbucks franchises. Queers and other minoritarian subjects continue to be pushed further into the private sphere. Delany, in his now classic text *Times Square Red, Times Square Blue*, theorized what he calls "contact relations," as opposed to networking. Delany's thesis is a lucid and powerful one: "Given the mode of capitalism under which we live, life is at its most rewarding, productive, and pleasant when the greatest number of people understand, appreciate, and seek out interclass contact and communication conducted in a mode of good will."[14] Delany's work here uses his experience as a participant in Times Square's alternative erotic economy of public sex as the primary example of contact relations. Through anonymous and nonanonymous encounters, the writer experienced interactions that constituted powerful cross-race and interclass contact. The zoning of commercial sex culture will effectively replace these relations with basic networking. A salient example of networking and the new Times Square is the suburban tourists who are shuttled into the city in large tour buses. On the bus they interact exclusively with other tourists who have decided to venture into the big city. These tourists might then take in a show—let us just say it is Disney's *The Lion King* at a corporate-sponsored venue such as the American Airlines Theatre—and perhaps go out for dinner at chain restaurants such as Applebee's or Red Lobster. These tourists then hop on the bus and are safely deposited in their suburban homes. The only contact they have outside of their class strata is with representatives of the service industry who take their tickets or serve their meals. This is the new Times Square in post-Giuliani New York.

It is especially disturbing yet politically sobering to realize that the mayor's initiatives are supported by many gay voters. Lisa Duggan has recently described this phenomenon as *homonormativity*.[15] Duggan's term is meant to outline the retreat into the private sphere that conservative homosexuals have participated in, in an effort to assimilate and perhaps purchase a seat at the table that right-wing gay pundits such as Bruce Bawer and Andrew Sullivan long for.[16] Such writers are the major architects of the gay pragmatism I discuss in chapter 1. The larger point resonates with an earlier theorization of sexual assimilation. Theodor Adorno, in an essay recently translated as "Sexual Taboos and Law Today," debunks the mythology of what he called "sexual liberation." Adorno explains that sexual liberation is "mere illusion":

> This illusion arose together with the phenomenon sociology elsewhere describes with its favorite expression "integration": the same way in which bourgeois society overcame the proletarian threat by incorporating the proletariat. Rational society, which is founded upon the domination of inner and outer nature and disciplines the diffuse pleasure principle that is harmful to the work ethic and even the principle of domination itself, no longer needs the patriarchal commandment of abstinence, virginity, and chastity. On the contrary, sexuality, turned on and off, channeled and exploited in countless forms by the material and culture industry, cooperates with the process of manipulation insofar as it is absorbed, institutionalized and administered by society. As long as sexuality is bridled, it is tolerated.[17]

Both Giuliani's and Bloomberg's gay support has everything to do with the way in which assimilationist homosexuals are willing to "turn off and on" their sexuality. The contract that they have signed on to demands that sexuality be turned on only within the shelter of the private sphere, in a darkness that is far murkier than the shadows that enveloped the trucks on Christopher Street in a pre-Stonewall 1960. The assimilationist

homosexuals who backed Giuliani and back Bloomberg are a sexual pro-
letariat that has been swept into the conservative populism so powerfully
characterizing this moment, dominated as it is by neoliberalism and, more
specifically, gay pragmatism. The contract they have signed is one of fake
futurity. Rather than investing in children, they invest in an assimilation
that is forever over the rainbow.

During sex panics such as the current one, it seems especially important
to enact a criticism that accomplishes a few tasks. As Kaprow's happenings
and Delany's memoir did, we crucially need to map our repression, our
fragmentation, and our alienation—the ways in which the state does not
permit us to say "the whole" of our masses. It is also important to practice
a criticism that enables us to cut through the institutional and legislative
barriers that outlaw contact relations and obscure glimpses of the whole.
These glimpses and moments of contact have a decidedly utopian function that permits us to imagine and potentially make a queer world. Such
a criticism would work by allowing us to see "the future in the present."

C. L. R. James entitled his first volume of collected writing *The Future
in the Present*. This title riffs on an aspect of Hegelian dialectics suggesting
that the affirmation known as the future is contained within its negation,
the present. In James's coauthored *Facing Reality*, a document that has
been described as a classic of the American left, he argues that a socialist future could be glimpsed by observing worker interaction and sociality within the space of the industrialized factory. Furthermore, he explains
that the shop floor was an actually existing socialist reality in the present.
His most striking proof for this thesis considers the case of an anonymous
worker at an unnamed factory: "In one department of a certain plant in
the U.S. there is a worker who is physically incapable of carrying out his
duties. But he is a man with wife and children and his condition is due to
the strain of previous work in the plant. The workers have organized their
work so that for ten years he has had practically nothing to do."[18] James
looks to this situation and others like it throughout the world as examples
of an already existing socialist present outside of the bureaucracy that was
the Eastern Bloc. James argues that "the fundamental task is to recognize
the socialist society and record the facts of its existence"; thus, the scenes
he describes are to be read as "outposts of a new society."[19]

This idea in James, this notion of the future in the present, is manifested through his post-Trotskyist workerism, which has been critiqued
widely. Today it is easy to dismiss an intellectual romanticization of labor. Two of James's most famous collaborators denounced this notion as

delusional and naive. Cornelius Castoriadis (who contributed to the same book under one of his pen names, Pierre Chaulieu) has countered James's claims by explaining that "it is not difficult to understand that if socialist society already existed people would have noticed it." Raya Dunayevskaya, who founded the Johnson-Forest Tendency in American Marxism with James, stated that "the man who can write 'It is agreed that the socialist society exists' need never face reality."[20] These are harsh words from allies and friends. Yet, despite these damning critiques, I am still drawn to this idea in James and its emphasis on the factory worker, particularly its framing of the social performer as something more than a cog. I contend that James's dialectic utopianism is not useless insofar as it helps us imagine the future without abandoning the present. James's formulation works as a refunctioned utopianism that is predicated on a critique of the present. I suggest that the reading practice that James describes helps us read the world-making potentialities contained in the performances of minoritarian citizen-subjects who contest the majoritarian public sphere.[21]

I use the term *minoritarian* to index citizen-subjects who, due to antagonisms within the social such as race, class, and sex, are debased within the majoritarian public sphere. The remainder of this chapter considers performances that I describe as sexual avant-gardist acts whose ideological projects are both antinormative and critical of the state. Minoritarian performance—performances both theatrical and quotidian—transports us across symbolic space, inserting us in a coterminous time when we witness new formations within the present and the future. The coterminous temporality of such performance exists within the future and the present, surpassing relegation to one temporality (the present) and insisting on the minoritarian subject's status as world-historical entity. The stage and the street, like the shop floor, are venues for performances that allow the spectator access to minoritarian lifeworlds that exist, importantly and dialectically, within the future and the present. James's workerist theory allows us to think of the minoritarian performer as a worker and the performance of queer world-making as a mode of labor. These performances are thus outposts of an actually existing queer future existing in the present.

Magic Touches: Queers of Color and Alternative Economies

Research has taken me to Jackson Heights, Queens. There I visited and patronized the now-closed Magic Touch, a bar whose name signaled a mode of contact between sex workers and consumers that can potentially be described as interclass and interrace contact. As the clock ticks and the world of New York's culture of public sex faces extinction, I have made a point of soaking up as much of it as possible. This bar certainly did not compare to the illicit orgy on the piers that Delany chronicled. Yet it was very different from similar venues in the city, such as the Gaiety in Manhattan.

The Gaiety was one of the last surviving gay burlesque shows in New York City. A decade ago it was a hub of hustling and public sex activity. Patrons would not only interact with the performers, who were always available for private shows, but were equally interested in those sitting next to them. All sorts of sex would happen in this venue and others like it, including the similarly defunct Eros Theater and the Showpalace. The Gaiety managed to stay in business longer than its cohort by adopting many of the state's policies before the state actually instituted them. Patrons were not allowed anywhere near performers, performers were strictly forbidden from negotiating private shows, and security guards patrolled the aisles and made sure that patrons did not touch one another. The performers were almost exclusively white. All the dancers were conventionally attractive and extremely well muscled. Most were based in Canada, traveling to the Gaiety once a month to hustle on the side and strip on stage. These body types hold a powerful spot in the erotic imagination of mainstream homosexuality. I have described this phenomenon elsewhere as the "dominant imprint" that organizes mainstream desire in U.S. gay culture.[22] Later in this book I mention the way in which transgender performer Kevin Aviance figuratively and literally rises above this pervasive bodily mode. The dominant imprint is a blueprint of gay male desire and desirability that is unmarked and thus universally white. Patrons, like desiring subjects in mainstream gay culture, can never touch these boys unless they negotiate a private show in the adjacent lounge area. A private show averages about two hundred dollars. (Internet sites that discuss hustling from a consumer's perspective complain of the dancers' limited sexual repertoire. Two hundred dollars can generally buy a patron a "posing show," in which a flexing hustler offers mostly visual pleasure to the often frustrated sex consumer.)[23] The dancers' inaccessibility and desirability are a combination of contradictory attributes recognizable in the dominant imprint. Tall, blond white boys with pulsating muscles who barely dance are instead objects to be desired from afar and engaged only in private, thus conforming to a culture of sex work that can be characterized as primarily being about privatized networking relations.

There was no such policing at the Magic Touch. The show was run like a contest there: a raffle selected judges for a competition, and contestants were judged on a range of attributes, which included both dancing and physical appearance. Whereas the Gaiety's performers were mostly white, the Magic Touch's were mostly Latino and African American. Since the Magic Touch was one of only a few neighborhood gay bars in Queens, some lesbians and straight women would also show up. The bar's clientele stood in sharp contrast to the Gaiety's: the Gaiety was predominantly populated by white men and tourists from Europe and East Asia, whereas the racial diversity I encountered at the Magic Touch continues to surpass any I have seen at other gay clubs.

Filipino queens sat next to older white daddy types who were across the bar from beeper-wielding Latino hustlers who seemed to know the group of black men clustered around the jukebox. Some folks were Manhattanites braving the outer boroughs; others hailed from even deeper in Queens. The performers came out in uniforms—military garb, loose-fitting hip-hop fashions, snug-fitting gay club wear, blue-collar flannel drag—and stripped to a G-string. They were instantly disqualified if they showed anything that might be tucked inside the G-string. Their dancing styles varied: some let their bodies do all the work; other boys were quite acrobatic. Hip-hop dance moves dominated the performers' routines. The movements were often described as a highly sexualized break dancing. As soon as the contest was over and the winner was crowned, the boys would mingle with the audience for an hour or so. Tips were stuffed in bikinis and boots, deals were brokered, conversations ensued.

The dancers at the Gaiety did not seem to take as much pleasure in the dancing. Instead, most would strut around the stage. During any one show a dancer at the Gaiety would dance to two consecutive songs. The music was almost exclusively contemporary pop. During the first song the dancer would perform a striptease to his jock or underwear. He would then walk backstage, and there would be a minute or two when the audience anxiously awaited the dancer's next appearance. During this pause, the dancer was getting erect or, as it is known in the professional lexicon, "fluffed." The erect dancer was greeted by a round of applause when he reemerged from backstage. Sometimes the dancer would have tied a rubber band or a cock ring around the base of his penis to allow him to maintain his erection a little longer. But more often than not the erection had faded by the middle of this second number. A display of nudity would have closed down the Magic Touch. In fact, its dancers had to wear more than a G-string since the zoning laws prohibited female go-go dancers and male dancers from wearing anything as revealing as bikinis. A few topless dance bars throughout Manhattan survived by scrawling an *S* in front of the word *topless* on their signs, which now read "Stopless Dancing." The "stopless" dancers would pole dance while wearing T-shirts. Most of the male go-go dancers wore athletic shorts as they rehearsed their moves on stage. Although the strippers at the Magic Touch were unable to take it all off, the customer was able to achieve physical contact when tipping his dancer of choice. The Gaiety's antiseptic lounge had a rough equivalent in the Magic Touch's ironically titled VIP lounge. The VIP area was actually the bar's basement. It included a pool table and several pieces of rundown wicker furniture and white plastic picnic chairs. The contact enacted between dancer/stripper and spectator/john here was much more tactile and intense than what happened upstairs.

One of my friends, an anthropologist who works with gay Filipino men in New York City, would refer to the Magic Touch as the "Tragic Touch." This was a nickname given to the bar by some Jackson Heights locals. The tragic in this rewriting of the establishment's name was meant to poke fun at the pathos of the hustler-john relationship—the manner in which older men pay younger hustlers. From the vantage point of youth, we can clearly see the pathos of this relationship. Yet I want to suggest that it is a pathos that undergirds the ageism and, for lack of a better word, lookism of all gay male erotic economies. From yet another perspective, we can see this relationship as something else, another formation: this economy of hustler-john is an alternative economy in which flesh, pleasure, and money meet under outlaw circumstances. This economy eschews the standardized routes in which heteronormative late capitalism mandates networking relations of sex for money. This economy represents a selling of sex for money that does not conform to the corporate American sex trade always on display for us via media advertising culture and older institutions such as heterosexual marriage. The hustler-john relationship represents a threat to these other naturalized performances of sex for money, in part because it promotes contact between people of different class and racial backgrounds. At the Magic Touch I found men of all colors relating to one another, forming bonds, and I saw this in mass. I glimpsed a whole that is diverse and invigorating in its eclectic nature. Some men came for voyeuristic pleasure, some came to meet other men who were spectators, and others came to participate in the age-old economy of hustler and john—all were performing outlaw sexuality. The zoning legislation allows such establishments to function only in industrialized spaces far away from public transportation and other businesses, where men who brave these industrialized zones encounter far greater risks of gay bashing and robbery.

Stickering the Future

The phrase "Whose quality of life?" caught my eye. Someone had printed this line on a sticker attached to a street sign near my home. The rest of the text read, "It's a beautiful day. . . . 'Crime is down.' Police brutality is up. . . . What are you doing outside?" The sticker was signed by a Mickey Mouse head with the letters "f.t.m." superimposed over it. Text below the mouse insignia explained that the acronym stood for "fear the mayor." The main text is a takeoff of ABC network's ad campaign encouraging viewers to sit at home and watch TV despite a sunny day outside. I later encountered another sticker, this one showing an image of two white men in baseball caps with their arms around each other. The men represented the contemporary white gay male clone, the type that populates certain neighborhoods in major U.S. cities, such as New York's Chelsea or Los Angeles's West Hollywood. These images did not represent the dominant imprint but did resemble a look organized and formatted by the desire that is the dominant imprint. The text read, "Can we afford to be normal?" Below the photo I found what at first glance appeared to be the logo of corporate megachain store The Gap. But instead it spelled out G-A-Y. A slogan flanked the faux corporate insignia, reading, "Heteronormativity. Fall into the trap." I understood this sticker to be associated with the previous one when I located the same familiar mouse head in the corner. This time the acronym was different—it read "r.h.q.," which stood for "resist the heterosexualization of queerness." I began to inquire as to the authorship of these inspired little stickers and soon traced them to a group of young activists in New York City who had launched an impressive stickering/wheatpasting campaign against then-mayor Giuliani's directives. The group worked with the activist collective Sex Panic for a time but became disillusioned with that group's inability to incorporate questions of gender, race, and age into its critique of state censorship and homophobia. The group has refused to name itself, in an attempt to remain a working collective and sidestep the essentializing effects that occur when a group identity is adopted. At times the group employ the acronym "f.a.g.," which stands for "feminist action group." At other times it appropriates the name of the suburban high school group that all white, middle-class officials support, SADD (students against drunk driving), resignifying that acronym to mean "sex activists against demonization." The only constant graphic the group retains in its guerrilla posturing and stickering is the outline of a Mickey Mouse head, which is meant to represent New York's ominous Big Brother. In the group's activist statement—a zine titled *Swallow Your Pride*—members explain, "we choose to do a stickering/wheatpasting campaign because there are a lot of special perks to this kind of media. First, it's really cheap. Second, it reaches a different audience than the other options that are vaguely accessible: Internet, gay weeklies, and sometimes bigger newspapers, it's really local. People see the stuff on the street and in the city. It is not limited to people who have computers or read the newspaper regularly—which means younger people and poorer people."[24] This group has attempted not to replicate the mistakes of other important activists groups such as Sex Panic, Act-Up, and Queer Nation. Its guerrilla campaign has attempted to imagine and enact a mode of queer publicity that is calibrated to be responsive to modalities of difference that include race, class, gender, and sexuality. The young activists' insistence on an integrated and intersectional queer critique can be discerned if we consider a sticker that reads, "I Nushawn Williams." Williams is a young HIV-positive African American man who has been arrested for engaging in unprotected sex. He became a contemporary Typhoid Mary as sensationalized media reporting constructed him as the ultimate AIDS predator. The group's intervention in this case was a difficult and risky move. It is indeed a complex move to identify with someone who, though not behaving in a conventionally sexually responsible fashion, was, nonetheless, not the racialized monster constructed by the media's reporting.

The stickers function as performing objects inasmuch as they solicit a response from spectators. Sometimes people attempt to rip the stickers down; at other times people write directly on the stickers. The stickers themselves then become forums for public debate, where people work through pressing social issues in a space away from the corrupt mediatized majoritarian public sphere. The performances that the stickers demand from viewers open the possibility of critical thinking and intervention; they encourage lucidity and political action. They are calls that demand, in the tradition of African American vernacular culture, a response. The response is sometimes an outpouring of state ideology, yet at other times the responses are glimpses of an actually existing queer future in the present.[25]

One sticker in particular offers an important critique of the present that signals the coming of a new moment of queer activism and publicity. During Giuliani's mayoral reign, Washington Square was one of his pet projects. He first increased police presence at the park to truly militaristic proportions. The entire space of the park was and still is blanketed by at least a dozen or so police officers at any given moment. A large police trailer was parked next to the park, and it has become command central. I cannot count the times over the past six years that I have stood witness to three or four police officers jumping on one homeless drug dealer. (When I write "drug dealer" here, I mean homeless men who hustle tiny "dime bags" of marijuana.) This policing has a new technological dimension because the park is now completely covered by video cameras that record everything happening inside or near Washington Square. The park is currently the most surveilled public space in the city. A week or so after these cameras first appeared, I noticed the mouse head again. This time the acronym read "w.b.w.," which stood for "we are being watched." Another sticker soon followed. It had a great deal more text: "Smile!: You are on closed Circuit Television. The NYPD also installed surveillance cameras in Washington Square Park. In our public urban spaces we are watched and harassed by an increasingly brutal police force. The use of state-sanctioned violence against queers, youth, people of color and the homeless in an effort to 'clean-up' this city must stop. Giuliani's 'quality of life' campaign is driving us out of the places where we have always hung out." The sticker functions as a mode of political pedagogy that intends to publicize the state's machinations of power. While technologies of surveillance colonize symbolic space, the anonymous performance of stickering contests that reterritorialization and imagines another moment: a time and place outside the state's electronic eye. This working collective is watching the watcher and providing a much-needed counterpublicity to the state's power. In this work we also glimpse an avant-gardist sexual performance, which is to say a performance that enacts a critique of sexual normativities allowing us to bear witness to a new formation, a future in the present.

Mourning through Militancy: Matthew Shepard and Others

The point of seeing the whole of our masses did not become salient for me until I witnessed a theoretical formulation on the streets of New York, in the form of an uprising that was put down with brutal force by the

New York City Police Department. The policing of this uprising worked so that the masses would be unable to see the whole. Matthew Shepard was savagely beaten, bound to a fence, and left to die on a Wyoming road in the fall of 1998. The national attention this murder received was a surprise for many activists. Queer activists in New York City were very aware of the fact that, while crime was supposedly down under the Giuliani regime, violence against gays and lesbians was on the increase. In 1998 hate crime violence had increased by 8 percent.[26] Walking through the East or West Village, Chelsea, Brooklyn, or neighborhoods in Queens, queers have become very accustomed to seeing posters with the pictures of some queer person, often a queer person of color, who has been murdered or has "disappeared" in New York. We see similar posters warning us of other predators who prey on our community. It was Shepard's telegenic face that secured a lot of media attention. His "traditional" good looks echoed certain aspects of a dominant imprint, and that certainly helped him become a flag that many people could rally around. Many of the activists who showed up for the Matthew Shepard political funeral the next day understood that if Shepard had not been a pretty white boy, there would have been no such outcry. We nonetheless seized the moment and took to the streets, not only for Shepard but for the countless women and men of all colors who have survived and not survived queer violence on the streets of New York City and elsewhere.

The official advance estimate for this vigil was five hundred people; other estimates suggest that five thousand showed up. The New York City Police Department responded to the outpouring of activism by calling in the troops. Marchers during this rebellion attempted to take to the streets, but the police insisted that this massive group walk exclusively on the sidewalk. A rupture came, and people surged onto the streets. Violence ensued, horses were brought out, billy clubs were brandished, activists were pushed and knocked down. The protest's marshals, its leadership, were the first people arrested. I saw friends taken away, loaded on MTA buses commandeered by the police. Many people on antiviral drugs missed dosages and risked building up immunity to these precious drugs. My friend David was not planning to be arrested, but he was nonetheless randomly picked out of the crowd and taken to central booking. Another friend, Rebecca, avoided arrest but had a close call after she was shoved by a cop, her vigil candle spilling wax on another officer who turned angrily to her—in fear she apologized profusely, hoping not be taken in. Most people had not planned to be arrested; this was supposed to be a somber political vigil.

No one anticipated the horses, the bombardment of cops, the mass arrests, the force used against them. The peaceful vigil became something else. It became a moment when queer people, frustrated and sick of all the violence they had endured, saw our masses. The police responded by breaking up the group, factioning off segments of our groupings, obscuring our mass.

The state understands the need to keep us from knowing ourselves, knowing our masses. It is ready, at the drop of the proverbial dime, to transform public transportation into policing machines, to call out thousands of cops to match thousands of activists, to wield clubs and fists. The state, like Delany, understands the power of our masses, a power that can be realized only by surpassing the solitary pervert model and accessing group identity. Doing so entails resisting the privatization of queer culture for which the gay pragmatists such as Andrew Sullivan, Gabriel Rotello, and Bruce Bawer clamor. The next day the *New York Post* headline read, "Gay Riot." It was more nearly a queer riot, where queer energies manifested themselves and the state responded with calculated force and brutal protocols. The riot was sobering because the mechanisms of policing were partially displayed, revealed for an evening, and it became very clear to everyone present how the idea of queers making contact in a mass uprising scared the state. The utopian promise of our public performance was responded to with shattering force. Even though this impromptu rebellion was overcome easily by the state, the activist anger, a productive, generative anger, let those assembled in rage glean a queer future within a repressive heteronormative present.

Making Utopia

Adorno provided a succinct rendering of utopia when he described it as existing in "the determined negation of that which merely is." This negation points "to what should be."[27] The work I have considered in this chapter looks to what is and fashions important critiques of the present by insisting on the present's dialectical relation to the future. Our criticism should, like the cases I have surveyed, be infused with a utopian function that is attuned to the "anticipatory illumination" of art and culture. Such illumination cuts through fragmenting darkness and allow us to see the politically enabling whole. Such illumination will provide us with access to a world that should be, that could be, and that will be.

4

Gesture, Ephemera, and Queer Feeling

Approaching Kevin Aviance

THIS CHAPTER HAS two beginnings.[1] One is a story culled from personal memory, and the other is a poem by a prominent twentieth-century North American poet. Both openings function as queer evidence: an evidence that has been queered in relation to the laws of what counts as proof. Queerness has an especially vexed relationship to evidence. Historically, evidence of queerness has been used to penalize and discipline queer desires, connections, and acts. When the historian of queer experience attempts to document a queer past, there is often a gatekeeper, representing a straight present, who will labor to invalidate the historical fact of queer lives—present, past, and future. Queerness is rarely complemented by evidence, or at least by traditional understandings of the term. The key to queering evidence, and by that I mean the ways in which we prove queerness and read queerness, is by suturing it to the concept of ephemera. Think of ephemera as trace, the remains, the things that are left, hanging in the air like a rumor.

Jacques Derrida's idea of the trace is relevant here.[2] Ephemeral evidence is rarely obvious because it is needed to stand against the harsh lights of mainstream visibility and the potential tyranny of the fact. (Not that all facts are harmful, but the discourse of the fact has often cast antinormative desire as the bad object.) Ephemera are the remains that are often embedded in queer acts, in both stories we tell one another and communicative physical gestures such as the cool look of a street cruise, a lingering handshake between recent acquaintances, or the mannish strut of a particularly confident woman.

In this chapter I want to approach the idea of queerness and gesture. So much can be located in the gesture. Gesture, I argue throughout this book, signals a refusal of a certain kind of finitude. Dance is an especially valuable site for ruminations on queerness and gesture. This theoretical work is anchored to a case study, a living body, a performer who is a master of the pose. Kevin Aviance is a mainstay of New York City's club world. He is something of a deity in the cosmology of gay nightlife. He is paid to perform, to sing, and to move—at clubs in New York City and throughout the world. He has been flown all over North America, Europe, and Asia and has performed for devoted cognoscenti, men and women who share a global sphere of queer knowing, moving, and feeling. At the center of that international sphere of queer experience are gesture, Aviance's resonant poses, and the force of queer ephemera.

This chapter builds on and speaks to themes that animate at least three of the other contributions to the edited volume in which an earlier version of this chapter appeared.[3] Like Jonathan Bollen, I look at the dance floor as a stage for queer performativity that is integral to everyday life. I am on the same page as Bollen when he considers the dance floor as space where relations between memory and content, self and other, become inextricably intertwined. Furthermore, I also align my project with Bollen's Maurice Merleau-Ponty–inspired proposition that the dance floor increases our tolerance for embodied practices. It may do so because it demands, in the openness and closeness of relations to others, an exchange and alteration of kinesthetic experience through which we become, in a sense, less like ourselves and more like each other. In my analysis that does not mean that queers become one nation under a groove once we hit the dance floor. I am in fact interested in the persistent variables of difference and inequity that follow us from queer communities to the dance floor, but I am nonetheless interested in the ways in which a certain queer communal logic overwhelms practices of individual identity. I am also interested in the way in which the state responds to the communal becoming.

To this end I consider Paul Siegel's contribution to that aforementioned volume, "A Right to Boogie Queerly: The First Amendment on the Dance Floor," a valuable resource for students of queer dance who wish to understand not only the social significance of queer dance but the various ways in which a repressive state apparatus counters queer movements both literal and symbolic. Siegel's essay discusses the ways in which First Amendment discourse has ultimately served queer dance movements. Yet his chapter does not consider recent developments in New York City, such as the Giuliani administration's reanimation of archaic cabaret-license laws that have been used as a tool to shut down and harass various queer and racial-minority bars in New York City. Those bars that survive display large signs that read, "No Dancing—by Order of the New York City Department of Consumer Affairs."[4] This edict has not been repealed, and in this instance Siegel's optimistic appraisal of the juridical sphere does not hold. Nonetheless, the stories of queer legal victory that he recounts serve as a valuable resource for hope.

In a similar vein Paul Franklin's historical account of Charlie Chaplin's dance also stands as an incredible analysis of how queer movement, despite dominant biases against queer dance, can nonetheless provide us with a narrative of queer iconicity's force within popular culture. Although Kevin Aviance and Charlie Chaplin are an unlikely match, one a little white tramp and the other a big black queen, both are masters of the historically dense queer gesture.[5] Aviance, like Chaplin before him, calls on an expressive vocabulary beyond the spoken word. For both men, the body in motion is the foundation of a visual lexicon in which the gesture speaks loud and clear.

Dance studies has focused its attention on the idea of movement. Although a movement analysis of Kevin Aviance's work could certainly be elucidating, this chapter is instead a gesture analysis. I am not as interested in what the queer gesture means so much as I am interested in what such gestures perform. Such an analysis is inspired by what Elin Diamond has attempted to articulate, after Brecht's notion of *Gestus,* as gestic feminist criticism.[6] There is certainly something quite gestic about Aviance's performance practice, one that I argue does attempt to show its material conditions of (im)possibility and historical positionality. But although *Gestus* suggests a lot more than gesture, I wish to concentrate my focus on the precise and specific physical acts that are conventionally understood as gesture, such as the tilt of an ankle in very high heels, the swish of a hand that pats a face with imaginary makeup, and so many more precise acts. These acts are different, but certainly not independent, from movements that have more to do with the moving body's flow. Concentrating on gesture atomizes movement. These atomized and particular movements tell tales of historical becoming. Gestures transmit ephemeral knowledge of lost queer histories and possibilities within a phobic majoritarian public culture.

Beginning One: Memory

I am young, maybe five or six. Our house is crowded by relatives who have just arrived from Cuba via a brief stopover-exile in Spain. They arrived like my family did a few years earlier, without anything. Thus, the little South Florida house that barely held five is now occupied by eleven. The only television set is in the family room. The boy cousins, my brother, my father, and my uncle are watching boxing on television, perhaps one of those early matches between Cuba and the United States in which none of the recent refugees feels comfortable taking a side. I am bored. By this time it is clear that the culture of men and sports holds absolutely no allure for me. (Women's tennis is another matter altogether.) I walk across the red-brick floor and momentarily cross the screen. Then my oldest cousin calls out, "Look at the way he walks, how he shakes his ass. I wish I had a girlfriend who walked like that!" The other men and boys in the room erupt into laughter. I protest: "What is wrong with the way I walk? I don't understand." The taunts continue, and I am flushed with shame. I rush to my room to hide from this mockery, which I find amazingly painful.

My family has always been one that showed affection by mocking and joking. It is just our dysfunctional little way, and as those people with whom I live my emotional life today can attest, I am very much a child of that home. So it was odd, that reaction I had. I would usually have retorted by commenting on my cousin's newest and shiniest zit. This was a different wounding, one for which I had no defense, because I knew something was there, something I did not quite understand but felt at my core. This proto-homophobic attack made me sit down and think about my movement, to figure out what it was about the way I moved that elicited such mockery and such palpable contempt from a room full of males. I wanted to, needed to know: what was it about my body and the way I moved it through the world that was so off, so different? I studied movement from then on, watching the way in which women walked and the way in which men walked. I looked at the ways in which men steered a sidewalk and tried to understand how women did it so differently. I noticed a stiffness in the men around me and a lack of stiffness in the women next to them. I studied all this and applied it to my own body. I began a project of butching up, even though that is not what I understood it to be back then. I tried to avoid the fact that I was studying something that came very naturally to other boys. I avoided the fact that heterogender was a space I was strangely on the outside of—I was a spy in the house of gender normativity, and like any spy, I was extremely careful and worried that my cover would be blown. I did not understand that as long as I tried to ape the movements of heterosexuality, hardly anyone would even try to see through the facade because those around me did not want to believe in fairies. As long as I played the game, I was relatively safe. That strategy is not universal; other boys cannot or will not straighten their gesture, and for them childhood is often a degraded zone of random violence and constant policing.

Sometimes I would slip and be called out. I remember a fey boy who was part of my mother's car-pool system. He took me aside in junior high and told me that I pulled my books too close to my chest like a girl. I started carrying my books to the side, just like a little man. Every so often a boy would tell me my slip was showing, would caution me to straighten up, as though my gesture could ruin it for everyone. Part of me wants to encounter him again, now in a gay space, a march, a club, a bathhouse, and embrace him like a fellow survivor, somebody else who made it through. Yet I imagine him at home, in Miami, with a wife who might remind him every once in a while how he should position his legs when he sits down while visiting his in-laws.

That butching-up practice had a serious effect on me. Today I am not often accused of flaming. I am considered mildly butch for a gay man of my age. Yet the older I get, the more I enjoy camping it up with my nellier friends. And now I can only enjoy performing masculinity in the company of my butch female friends because something about being boys with them feels weirdly liberating. I take further pleasure in talking about being a guy with one of my friends, who is currently crossing and becoming a man. As I notice his voice deepen, his body bulk up, and his already butch mannerisms continue to evolve, I feel some kind of sweet revenge on gender.

When I encounter accomplished drag, I feel this revenge again. I am drawn to Justin Bond's Kiki, a strung-out, aging showbiz personality who is really a young white man in his thirties but plays a grizzled show-business veteran in her late sixties.[7] She is accompanied by Herb, who is actually Kenny Mellman, an attractive gay Jewish man in his thirties, who plays her homosexual accompanist, a gray little old man. Kiki cavorts and staggers as she does loungy-punk hybrids of contemporary pop songs and old standards. The drink in her hand is ever present as she stumbles from table to table. Often, she will mount the table of an unsuspecting guest, throw his cocktail to the floor, and demand that the patron sitting at the table lick her fishnet stocking because she is on fire, as intimated by the song she is singing, P. J. Harvey's "Rid of Me." The fishnets cover a dancer's set of gams, muscles that get exercised when Kiki does a fast and frantic tap number, competent and exaggerated at exactly the same time. She is visibly winded after finishing this self-consciously old-school number. She closes that component of the cabaret act with the line "Ladies and

Gentlemen! I started as a burlesque dancer in Baltimore in the fifties, and I still got it!" This line conjures a lot of showbiz divas on the decline.

That tap-dance number itself indexes a sick camp aesthetic that the fans of Kiki and Herb love. Their camp celebrates virtuosity while reveling in an antinormative degeneracy. In this instance camp works as an index to a shared aesthetic and a communal structure of feeling. The dance is over and seemingly gone, but it lives as an ephemeral happening that we remember, something that fuels anecdotes we tell one another. Because the show was weekly, the devoted went week after week, and it all took on the feel of a ritual. It lives, then, after its dematerializations as a transformed materiality, circulating in queer realms of loving and becoming. The story with which I began this section functions that way too. It is an ephemeral proof. It does not count as evidence in some systems of reading and understanding proper documentation and loving. Making a case for queer evidence in theory seems to beg the use of such "unreliable" proofs.

Here is one of my favorite poems, Elizabeth Bishop's "One Art," and a second opening:

> One Art
> The art of losing isn't hard to master;
> so many things seem filled with the intent
> to be lost that their loss is no disaster.
>
> Lose something every day. Accept the fluster
> of lost door keys, the hour badly spent.
> The art of losing isn't hard to master
>
> Then practice farther, losing faster:
> places, and names, and where it was you meant
> to travel. None of this will bring disaster.
>
> I lost my mother's watch. And look! my last, or
> next-to-last, of three loved houses went.
> The art of losing isn't hard to master.
>
> I lost two cities, lovely ones. And, vaster,
> some realms I owned, two rivers, a continent,
> I miss them, but it wasn't a disaster.

Even losing you (the joking voice, a gesture
I love) I shan't have lied. It's evident
the art of losing's not too hard to master
though it may look like (*Write* it!) like disaster.[8]

The parenthetical remarks within the poem are most interesting for my purposes. I suggest that these remarks are graphically differentiated through grammatical devices so that they might connote a different register than the majority of the poem. The parenthetical remarks communicate a queer trace, an ephemeral evidence. I read these remarks, words that evoke the idea of gesture, as gestures. Interest in these specific lines should not derail interest in the poem in its entirety. "One Art" offers the attentive reader a theory of the materiality of performance and ephemera. It has become somewhat axiomatic within the field of performance studies that the act exists only during its actual duration. I have been making a case for a hermeneutics of residue that looks to understand the wake of performance. What is left? What remains? Ephemera remain. They are absent and they are present, disrupting a predictable metaphysics of presence. The actual act is only a stage in the game; it is a moment, pure and simple. There is a deductive element to performance that has everything to do with its conditions of possibility, and there is much that follows.

In "One Art," the poet, Elizabeth Bishop, asks the forgetful person not to become upset about the loss of certain objects because they seem filled with the intent to be lost—their loss is no disaster.[9] She asks us to accept the fluster of loss and understand that it is not a disaster. Something is embedded within those acts, traces that have an indelible materiality. The poet is inviting us to do more than simply accept this loss but to embrace it and perhaps even to understand it not as loss but as something else. She is, within a parenthetical phrase in the poem's last line, asking us to "Write it!" The word "write" is not only in parentheses but italicized, more than doubling its emphasis. This command to write is a command to save the ephemeral thing by committing it to memory, to word, to language. The poet instructs us to retain the last thing through a documentation of our loss, a retelling of our relationship to it. Thus, her mother's watch now exists, or perhaps has found an afterlife, in its transformation and current status as residue, as ephemera. It partially (re)lives in its documentation.

And although we cannot simply conserve a person or a performance through documentation, we can perhaps begin to summon up, through the auspices of memory, the acts and gestures that meant so much to us. The poem clearly has an addressee, who is a "you." Now, we ask, who is that "you"? If we were to lean on biography—something I always caution my students against—it would be Lota de Macedo Soares, Bishop's estranged Brazilian lover who committed suicide. Much would suggest that identification ("the joking voice, a gesture I love"). The parenthetical remark contains queer content, queer memory, a certain residue of lesbian love.

One temptation is to say that Bishop was in the closet and, furthermore, that she gives frightened and furtive little signs of her lesbian desire. But that is a mistake and not what I mean by traces of queer desire. As the North American poetry scholar Katie Kent has suggested to me in a correspondence, calling Bishop's work closeted is a mistake: I am wary of calling her work more or less closeted. I think doing so reinforces this trajectory to her life that only right before she died did she claim her sexuality in her poetry and in any other way, whereas if you read her poems expecting to read about queerness, it is there throughout. A lot of the biographers and critics impose the closet on her as a way, I think, of not having to talk about the role of queer identity and queer sex play throughout her work.

Kent's suggestion, that we read with queerness as an expectation, challenges the reader to approach the poet with a different optic, one that is attuned to the ways in which, through small gestures, particular intonations, and other ephemeral traces, queer energies and lives are laid bare. The parenthetical remark in Bishop's "One Art" is a queer gesture, one that accesses the force of queer ephemera. It is utterly legible to an optic of feeling, a queer optic that permits us to take in the queerness that is embedded in gesture. The poem's narrative instructs us as to the transience of things filled with the intent to be lost, and as it does so, it retains a queer trace that lingers, tragically and lovingly, within the hold of parentheses. This poetic gesture in Bishop's masterful text is not unlike the moves that a queer artist can conjure on a dance floor or a stage. The gesture summons the resources of queer experience and collective identity that have been lost to us because of the demand for official evidence and facts.

We can understand queerness itself as being filled with the intention to be lost. Queerness is illegible and therefore lost in relation to the straight minds' mapping of space. Queerness is lost in space or lost in relation to the space of heteronormativity. Bishop's poem should be read as a primer for queer self-enactment or queer becoming. To accept loss is to accept the way in which one's queerness will always render one lost to a world of heterosexual imperatives, codes, and laws. To accept loss is to accept queerness—or more accurately, to accept the loss of heteronormativity, authorization, and entitlement. To be lost is not to hide in a closet or to perform a simple (ontological) disappearing act; it is to veer away from heterosexuality's path. Freedmen escaping slavery got lost too, and this is a salient reverberation between queerness and racialization. At this historical moment, one that can be described as being characterized by encroaching assimilationist ideology in the mainstream gay and lesbian movement, some gays and lesbians want to be found on a normative map of the world. Being lost, in this particular queer sense, is to relinquish one's role (and subsequent privilege) in the heteronormative order. The dispossessed are appropriately adept at critiquing possession as illogical. To accept the way in which one is lost is to be also found and not found in a particularly queer fashion.

A Body: Approaching Aviance

This section's subtitle is meant to connote a few things. I invoke the phrase "approaching Aviance" because I want to cast a picture from life, the scene of Aviance's being approached. To travel through the gay world of New York City with Kevin Aviance is certainly to call attention to oneself. Aviance is six foot two, bald, black, and effeminate. In or out of his unique drag he is immediately recognizable to anyone who has seen his show. To walk the cityscape with him is to watch as strangers approach him and remark on one of his performances. They often gush enthusiastically and convey how much a particular performance or his body of performances means to them. One will hear such things as "I'll always remember that one show you did before they shut the Palladium down" or "You turned it out at Roxy last week." Kevin will be gracious and give back the love he has just received.

His work, his singing and his movement, is not the high art of Bill T. Jones or Mark Morris, but I would venture to say that more queer people see Aviance move than have witnessed Jones's masterful productions. I do not mean to undermine the value of Jones's work. I only want to properly frame the way in which Aviance's nightlife performances matter. The gestures he performs matter worlds to the children who compose his audiences. Aviance is something of a beacon that displays and channels worlds of queer pain and pleasure. In his moves we see the suffering of being a gender outlaw, one who lives outside the dictates of heteronormativity. Furthermore, another story about being black in a predominantly white-supremacist gay world ruminates beneath his gestures. Some of his other gestures transmit and amplify the pleasures of queerness, the joys of gender dissidence, of willfully making one's own way against the stream of a crushing heteronormative tide.

The strong influence of vogueing practice in his moves affirms the racialized ontology of the pier queen, a personage who is degraded in New York City's aboveground gay culture. Often, one gesture will contain both positive and negative polarities simultaneously, because the pleasure and pain of queerness are not a strict binary. The conversations that ensue after his performances, the friends and strangers that approach him on the street, the ads in bar rags, the reviews in local papers, the occasional home-video documentation, and the hazy and often drug-tinged memories that remain after the actual live performances are the queer ephemera, that transmutation of the performance energy, that also function as a beacon for queer possibility and survival.

To understand the lure of Aviance's performance it is useful to describe a performance from Montreal's Red and Blue party. The Red and Blue is part of the circuit-party system. The circuit is just that, a loosely aligned social circuit of dance parties that happen throughout the year in major cities throughout North America. Aviance was invited to perform at Montreal. Another drag performer, a black queen in traditional illusionist drag, appears on stage and introduces the fierce and legendary Kevin Aviance. Aviance emerges from behind an ornate red curtain with gold trim. He is wearing a fantastical suit that features puffy, exaggerated purple shoulders that rise to the length of his ears.

As he sings his first club hit, his microphone emerges from his lapel, permitting his hands total freedom to move in gestures that are familiar to those conversant with vogueing and break-dancing styles. In the middle of the song his entire body becomes involved as he feigns cold robotic motions. The monster walks. He then sings his club hit "Cunty."[10] He sings, "Feeling like a lily / Feeling like a rose," and as he stands in place, his body quivers with extravagant emotion. He stands center stage, and as he screams, he quivers with an emotional force that connotes the stigma of gender ostracism. His gender freakishness speaks to the audiences that surround him. His is an amplified and extreme queer body, a body in motion that rapidly deploys the signs, the gestures, of queer communication, survival, and self-making. Spectators connect his trembling with the ways in which he flips his wrist and regains composure by applying imaginary pancake makeup.

By this juncture in the performance, the jacket is removed and the silly pants are removed. He is revealed in a body-embracing prismatic body stocking. He begins to bounce around the stage, offering the audience a particular version of runway—the vogueing practice of walking as though one were a supermodel. One particular Aviance gesture worth noting is the way in which his ankles fold or crack as he walks, or rather stomps, the runway. This gesture permits him to be quicker and more determined in his steps than most high-heeled walkers. This gesture connotes a tradition of queenly identification with the sadism of female beauty rituals. The move—walking with heels in such an unorthodox fashion—constitutes a disidentification with these traditions of gay male performances of female embodiment.[11] Aviance's refusal to wear wigs is a further example of this disidentificatory dynamic. The determined walking is replaced by a particular sway-back walk in which his buttocks and chest are both outstretched, exaggerating the features of a racialized body. To do so, I want to argue, is not to play the Venus Hottentot for a predominantly white Canadian audience; it is, instead, to insist on the fact of blackness in this overwhelmingly white space. Aviance then throws himself into the audience and is held aloft by it. He is lost in a sea of white hands; this being lost can be understood as a particularly queer mode of performing the self. That is how the performance ends. This amazing counterfetish is absorbed by the desiring masses. He has opened in them a desire or a mode of desiring that is uneasy and utterly important if he is to surpass the new gender symmetry of the gay world.

Aviance's biography is, in and of itself, a testament to queer survival. He grew up as Eric Snead in a large family in Richmond, Virginia. His first experience in drag was in the seventh grade. As a youth he escaped the narrow confines of the small town and moved to the nearest gay metropolis, Washington, D.C., where he worked as a hairdresser, did drag as an amateur, and developed a disabling drug habit. He eventually overcame crack with the help of the House of Aviance. The House of Aviance is not exactly like the vogueing houses of Jennie Livingston's film *Paris Is Burning*, since it does not compete. The House of Aviance is something of a queer kinship network in which members serve as extended, pretended, and—some would argue—improved family that supports and enables its members. Kevin Aviance was the name he took after initiation.

Aviance eventually landed in New York City, where he first made a name for himself at the now legendary Sound Factory, a queer club that began as a predominantly Latino and black space. He distinguished himself on the dance floor, grabbing the attention of major DJs and nightlife promoters, and soon became a professional performer. Today he is one of a handful of New York drag performers who can distinguish himself as living solely off his performance. He forsook traditional drag and the world of wigs early in his career. His look is reminiscent of the legendary group of black soul divas called LaBelle, the group that wrote the almost perfect disco hit "Lady Marmalade."[12] I think of Aviance's look when I study the album cover for LaBelle's phenomenal 1974 album *Nightbirds*. All three women, dressed in metallic outfits, are portrayed as swirls of space-age Afro-glamour. LaBelle's Afro-futurism was a strategic move to make the group look freakish and alien, to make blackness something otherworldly and uncanny.

Aviance, like LaBelle, reconstructs blackness as a mysterious Lost-in-Space aesthetic. Other comparisons can be drawn between the punk performance style of Klaus Nomi, the deranged disco divinity of Grace Jones, the insane and beautiful drag of Leigh Bowery, and the spaced-out elegance of the hip-hop artist Missy Misdemeanor Elliot. But Aviance's look is definitely his own. I have seen him in many outfits, including fantastic gold lamé jumpsuits, sheer polka-dot minidresses, and leopard-skin body stockings. Although he does not wear wigs, he sometimes adorns his bald head with a hat.

Both his appearance and his performances are in no way attempting to imitate a woman. He is instead interested in approximating a notion of femininity. Queer theory has made one lesson explicitly clear: the set of behaviors and codes of conduct that we refer to as feminine or masculine are not slaves to the biological.[13] Women, straight and gay, perform and live masculinity in the same way as many a biological man inhabits femininity. Sometimes technology aligns people's gender identity and their biological self. Others relish the antinormative disjuncture between their biological gender and their performed or lived gender. Aviance's masculinity, partially informed by his biological maleness, is never hidden—he wears no wig, and he does not tuck (conceal or hide the male genital bulge while in drag). Indeed, in his performance we see a unique cohabitation of traditional female and male traits.

To perform such a hybrid gender is not only to be queer but to defy troubling gender logics within gay spaces. Bollen's chapter on queer performativity and the dance floor catalogs different dancing styles—such as girly poofter (Australian slang for campy and feminine male dancing) and the standard macho style of dancing that dominates many gay dance venues. Bollen notes but does not delve into the femmephobia apparent on many queer dance floors, where those who break the gay-clone edict to act like a man are de-eroticized and demoted to second-class citizenship.

I observe that tension when I find myself at the Roxy, the sceniest place to be for a certain stratum of New York gay men. I am overwhelmed by the throngs of shirtless dancers with gym-crafted bodies. Their dance style is aggressive yet rigid; the moves they make are meant to show off the rewards of hours of gym workouts. They do not spread out but instead dance closely together, almost in packs. They are often awash in the effects of club drugs, such as Ecstasy and Special K, and huddle together as they dance. For the most part, they do not let themselves flow and keep close to one another, enjoying the ways in which their gym-sculpted muscles rub up against those of the next clonish dance-floor compatriot.

Through the mist of the smoke machine I watch Aviance elevate himself above the crowd. He is dancing on a small platform that is about five feet high, the kind of ministage usually occupied by a gym-built go-go boy. Go-go boys mostly just bump and grind. There is not much room for steps, and Aviance does not need them. This particular dance is about his hands. His hands move in jerky, mechanical spasms. They frame his face and his outfit. He dances to the house music that the DJ is playing especially for him. He is elevated from the dance floor but also surrounded by dancers who are now dancing with him. He is both onstage and one of the throng, one with the music. It makes sense that he is elevated. He is there not because he is simply a better dancer than the other clubgoers around him (he is) but because he is the bridge between quotidian nightlife dancing and theatrical performance.[14] He defies the codes of masculinity that saturate the dance floor. His gestures are unapologetically femme. His fingers swiftly minister to his face, as though applying invisible makeup. His movements are coded as masculine (strong abrupt motions), feminine (smooth flowing moves), and, above all, robotic (precise mechanical movements).

What does it mean that in this space, where codes of masculinity dominate, Aviance is a local deity? What work does his performance do in this venue? Furthermore, what about his blackness in this space that is overrun by sweaty and shirtless white torsos? One response would be that he is a fetish in this space, a magic juju that lets white and effeminate gay men be fabulous while not being progressive around gender, race, and sexuality. Such a reading would miss the point. Aviance is extremely aware of the audience, and when the time comes to play the race man/woman, he will certainly do so. I have seen it occur onstage on many occasions. At La Nueva Esculeita, a Latino queer space in midtown, I have seen him convert the dance club's stage to a pulpit between musical numbers and have witnessed him denouncing the fascist regime of the city's mayor and his racist police force. Aviance speaks out regularly at venues both white and racialized. He has also read the racism of New York's privileged gay community. Aviance is conscious about the ways in which he can be made into a fetish, but he disidentifies with such a role in very particular ways.

Marxism tells us the story of the commodity fetish, the object that alienates us from the conditions of possibility that brought whatever commodity into being.[15] The fetish, in its Marxian dimensions, is about occlusion, displacement, concealment, and illusion. Some drag artists prefer the gender title of illusionist. Aviance does not work in illusion; he becomes many things at once. His performance labors to index a fantastic female glamour, but his masculinity is never eclipsed. If the fetish is about illusion, Aviance disidentifies with the standard notion of the fetish and makes it about a certain demystification.

When he is on that stage, he performs gestures that few others can perform. His gestures are not allowed in the strict codes of masculinity followed by the habitués of most commercial queer dance spaces. Paul Franklin's chapter on Charlie Chaplin's gestures speaks to the fear of effeminacy that has haunted the history of the male dancer in the West. The same arguments are lucidly conveyed in Ramsay Burt's writing on the Male Dancer.[16] This antieffeminate bias has, ironically, resurfaced in many gay male dance spaces. As an icon, a beacon above the dance floor, Aviance uses gestures that permit the dancers to see and experience the feelings they do not permit themselves to let in. He and the gestures he performs are beacons for all the emotions that the throng is not allowed to feel.

These pumped-up gym queens started out, in most cases, as pudgy or skinny sissy boys who attempted to hide their gestures. Many of them, like the I from my earlier autobiographical account, attempted to walk like men and hide the telltale queer gesture. This culture needs to be critiqued for the normative gender paradigms to which it subscribes as well as for the exclusionary logics it applies to people who do not make its normative (often white and decidedly masculine) cut. Nonetheless, though this symbolic violence is not justifiable, one can certainly understand this desire to be masculine. These men did not stop at straightening out the swish of their walk; they worked on their bodies and approximated a hypermasculine ideal.

I do not want to extend energy in moralizing against this route to survival in a heteronormative world. It makes sense, especially when we consider that these men came into masculinity as they were surrounded by the specter of the AIDS pandemic. The AIDS catastrophe provides a lot of reasons to build up the body. But imagine how hard it must be to try to look and act so butch all the time. Indeed, these men become their own fetish of masculinity in that they hide the conditions of possibility that lead to their becoming butch. Aviance reveals these conditions. That is the function of the counterfetish. He performs the powerful interface between femininity and masculinity that is active in any gender, especially queer ones. In this fashion he is once again a counterfetish, elucidating the real material conditions of our gender and desire.

Imagine the relief these gym queens feel as Aviance lets himself be both masculine and feminine, as his fabulous and strange gestures connote the worlds of queer suffering that these huddled men attempt to block out but cannot escape, and the pleasures of being swish and queeny that they cannot admit to in their quotidian lives. Furthermore, imagine that his performance is something that is instructive, that recodifies signs of abjection in mainstream queer spaces—blackness, femininity/effeminacy—and makes them not only desirable but something to be desired. Imagine how some of those men on the dance floor might come around to accepting and embracing the queer gesture through Aviance's exemplary performance. More important, imagine what his performance means to those on the margins of the crowd, those who have not devoted their lives to daily gym visits and this hypermasculine ideal, those whose race or appearance does not conform to rigid schematics of what might be hot. Those on the margins can get extreme pleasure in seeing Aviance rise from the muscled masses, elevated and luminous.

For the racialized cognoscenti, his gestures function like the sorrow songs of W. E. B. Du Bois's *The Souls of Black Folk*. In that paradigm-shifting text Du Bois meditates on the power of Negro music and the embedded and syncretic meaning found in these testaments to the culture of slavery.

What are these songs, and what do they mean? I know little of music and can say nothing in technical phrases, but I know something of
men. Knowing them, I know that these songs are the articulate message of the slave to the world. They tell us that life was joyous to the
black slave, careless and happy. I can easily believe this of some, of
many. The Old South cannot deny the heart-touching witness of these
songs. They are the music of an unhappy people, of the children of
disappointment; they tell of death and suffering and unvoiced longing
toward a truer world, of misty wanderings and hidden ways.[17]

I risk sounding a bit overdramatic by using this analogy. I nonetheless invoke this classic text in African American letters for the express purpose
of calling attention to the pathos that underlies some of these gestures.
Vogueing, for instance, is too often considered a simplistic celebration
of black queer culture. It is seen as a simple appropriation of high fashion or other aspects of commodity culture. I am proposing that we might
see something other than a celebration in these moves—the strong trace
of black and queer racialized survival, the way in which children need to
imagine becoming Other in the face of conspiring cultural logics of white
supremacy and heteronormativity. The gesture contains an articulate message for all to read, in this case a message of fabulousness and fantastical
becoming. It also contains another message, one less articulated and more
ephemeral but equally relevant to any understanding of queer gestures,
gestures that, as I have argued, are often double- or multivalenced. So
while the short-sighted viewer of Aviance's vogueing might see only the
approximation of high-fashion glamour as he moves and gestures on the
stage, others see/hear another tune, one of racialized self-enactment in
the face of overarching opposition.

Conclusion: The Not-Vanishing Point

Even New York clubs eventually close for the night; most close the next
afternoon, but they do close. The performances come to an end. Club kids
stumble into taxis in broad daylight, and Aviance and other performers
pack up their outfits and makeup and go home for a restorative nap. Is this
performance's end? That moment when the venue closes? Has the vanishing point been reached? In Marcia Siegel's influential book of dance criticism, *At the Vanishing Point: A Critic Looks at Dance*, Siegel provocatively

links dance to the notion of a vanishing point: dance exists as a perpetual vanishing point.[18] At the moment of its creation it is gone. All the years of training in the studio, all the choreographer's planning, the rehearsals, the coordination of designers, composers, and technicians, the raising of money and the gathering together of an audience—all these are only a preparation for an event that disappears in the very act of materializing. No other art is so hard to catch, so impossible.

Siegel certainly knows that every vanishing point signals a return, the promise of the next performance, of continuation. She argues that dancers and audiences must have been aware of this ephemerality and are used it. I agree with the revered critic. Queer dance is hard to catch, and it is meant to be hard to catch—it is supposed to slip through the fingers and comprehension of those who would use knowledge against us. But it matters and takes on a vast material weight for those of us who perform or draw important sustenance from performance. Rather than dematerialize, dance rematerializes. Dance, like energy, never disappears; it is simply transformed. Queer dance, after the live act, does not just expire. The ephemeral does not equal unmateriality. It is more nearly about another understanding of what matters. It matters to get lost in dance or to use dance to get lost: lost from the evidentiary logic of heterosexuality.

For queers, the gesture and its aftermath, the ephemeral trace, matter more than many traditional modes of evidencing lives and politics. The hermeneutics of residue on which I have called are calibrated to read Aviance's gestures and know these moves as vast storehouses of queer history and futurity. We also must understand that after the gesture expires, its materiality has transformed into ephemera that are utterly necessary.

5

Cruising the Toilet

LeRoi Jones/Amiri Baraka, Radical
Black Traditions, and Queer Futurity

AMIRI BARAKA DENOUNCED much of the life of LeRoi Jones, a writer, editor, and bon vivant in the bohemia of New York City's Greenwich Village during the late 1950s and early 1960s. A difficult play by LeRoi Jones (Baraka), *The Toilet*, is emblematic of the life that Baraka eschews with hardly a backward glance.[1] *The Toilet* was produced in 1964, on a double bill with a play by Frank O'Hara, one of the members of the demimonde that Jones inhabited. Though I read the play as a narrative of violence and negation, it does nonetheless generate the possibility of a critical and utopian practice of hope in the face of loss. *The Toilet* signals a queer past with which Baraka, through tragedy in his own life, must reconcile. Following Ernst Bloch's *Principle of Hope*, I am interested in the socially symbolic performative dimension of certain aesthetic processes that promote a modality of political idealism.[2] I see myself participating in a counternarrative to political nihilism, a form of inquiry that promotes what I am calling queer futurity. Previous aesthetic and cultural production—such as this somewhat minor play that was performed within a now-expired artistic enclave—offers a powerful critique via counterexample of the political impasse of the present. This temporal operation is enabled by a Blochian investment in both the not-yet-here (the future) and the no-longer-conscious (the past). *The Toilet* represents a violent and tragic queer past that, when seen through the optic of queer utopia, becomes a source for a critique of a limited and problematic straight time. I suggest that the performative force of the gesture interrupts straight time and the temporal strictures it enacts.

This chapter takes its lead from Fred Moten's brilliant *In the Break: The Aesthetics of the Black Radical Tradition*.[3] Moten describes the conterminous relationship between black radical politics and improvisational aesthetic practices associated with blackness. Looking at the racial blind spots in Sally Banes's historiography of New York's historical downtown bohemia, *Greenwich Village 1963: Avant-Garde Performance and the Effervescent Body*,[4] Moten counters Banes's now almost canonical rendering of a downtown art scene that excludes black artists such as LeRoi Jones, Cecil Taylor, and Samuel Delany. Here I am interested in casting light on not only those important historical figures but also others such as Mario Montez (the Warhol screen superstar who played Juanita Castro) or Dorothy Dean (the black woman who was the acknowledged ultimate fag hag of the day and worked as the sharp-tongued bouncer at Max's Kansas City). These characters inhabit what Moten calls the B-side of this avant-garde's history, in which Banes is uninterested.[5] Although I am not proposing an alternative canon of what is an already existing, and in some ways already "alternative," canon of the American avant-garde, I do want to look at these minoritized historical players because they disrupt dominant historiographies of queer avant-gardism and radical aesthetics and politics.[6] Gloria Anzaldúa famously indicated that *jotería* (queers) could be found at the base of every liberationist social movement.[7] And while tales of social movements in the United States continue to ignore *jotería*, to an even larger degree disciplinary accounts of avant-garde aesthetics underplay both explicitly queer presences and (perhaps especially) racialized participation, labor, and influence. Anzaldúa's injunction to look for *jotería* is a call to deploy a narrative of the past to enable better understanding and critiquing of a faltering present. In this sense her call for mestiza consciousness is a looking back to a fecund no-longer-conscious in the service of a futurity that resists the various violent asymmetries that dominate the present.

The Toilet holds a pivotal place in Jones/Baraka's history of artistic production. It has been called the most homoerotic play in a spate of other homoerotic or queerly valenced works by Jones/Baraka, such as *The Baptism*, mostly produced during the early 1960s. My project here, however, is not to "bring out" Jones or Baraka. Any such gesture would be reductive. Instead, I want to discuss the negotiation of animating queer energies in *The Toilet* to consider what queerness might tell us about the temporal particularity of the Greenwich Village lifeworld of the 1960s and what its resonances might mean today. When I refer to the animating force of queerness I specifically want to discuss a mode of queer performativity—that is, not the fact of a queer identity but the force of a kind of queer doing. My methodological concern at this point is an attentiveness to the

Tony Just, "London," 2004. Copyright Tony Just, Courtesy of the Gavin Brown Enterprise/Gallery.

Tony Just, "Celebrate Trees." Copyright Tony Just, Courtesy of the Gavin Brown Enterprise/Gallery.

"Catch One." Copyright Kevin McCarty.

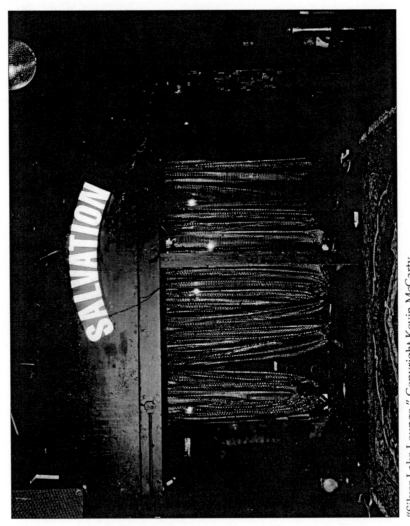

"Silver Lake Lounge." Copyright Kevin McCarty.

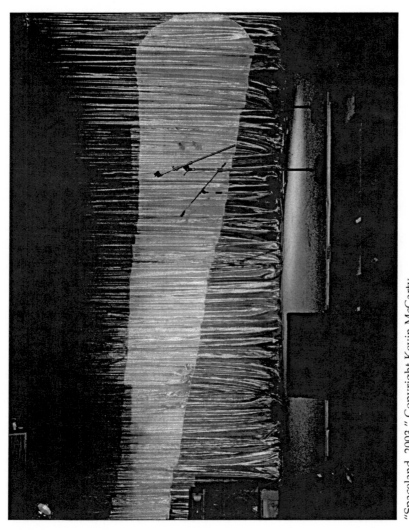

"Spaceland, 2003." Copyright Kevin McCarty.

"The Parlour." Copyright Kevin McCarty.

Installation, Reprint 1994. *Silver Clouds* (Warhol Museum Series), 1994, refabricated for The Andy Warhol Museum in cooperation with The Andy Warhol Foundation for the Visual Arts, Inc.; and Billy Klüver, 1994, helium-filled metalized plastic film (Scotchpak), 36 × 51 in. (91.4 × 129.5 cm), Andy Warhol (artist), Billy Klüver (contributor), Manufactured by CTI Industries Corp., Barrington, IL, The Andy Warhol Museum, Pittsburgh, © 2008 The Andy Warhol Foundation for the Visual Arts/ARS, New York.

Paintings, 1986, *Self-Portrait*, acrylic and silkscreen ink on linen, 40 × 40 in.
(101.6 × 101.6 cm), Andy Warhol (artist), The Andy Warhol Museum, Pittsburgh; Founding Collection, Contribution, The Andy Warhol Foundation for
the Visual Arts, Inc., © 2008 The Andy Warhol Foundation for the Visual
Arts/ARS, New York.

productive and counterproductive deployments of the past. Jones himself has been outed at different intervals by former acquaintances. His former lover and the mother of two of his children, the poet Diane di Prima, in her memoir *My Life as a Woman* has more than intimated that whereas she was not overly threatened by the other women with whom Jones spent time, she was afraid that she would ultimately lose her lover to a man.[8] She also characterized the federal government's crackdown of their important literary journal of the scene, *The Floating Bear*, as having to do with an essay by William Burroughs and a "homosexual play" by Jones. An outing that seems especially bitter and vindictive is by Joe LeSueur, Frank O'Hara's roommate. In his autobiographical text *Digressions on Some Poems by Frank O'Hara*, LeSueur indulges in some especially spiteful prose that I cite at some length because I feel it is especially illuminating when one considers Jones's place in this downtown milieu:

> Neat, compact, physically appealing, conservatively dressed, clearly intelligent, obviously gifted, son of a New Jersey postman—here was a young black man who seemed to harbor no anger or resentment, so that his easy smile, sparkling eyes, and courtly manners quickly won over everyone he met in the downtown art and poetry community of the late fifties, which was when Frank became friends with him and he would drop by, first when we were living at 90 University Place, later at East 9th street, sometimes staying over and sharing Frank's bed, while I, the very soul of discretion, was in my own bed, minding my own business, never asking questions, never saying a word to anyone later about what I thought might be going on Roi being a married man, father, a stud, a heterosexual! And how am I repaid for that discretion, keeping to myself what I could dine out on? Almost twenty years after Frank's death, I picked up a copy of *The Autobiography of LeRoi Jones/Amiri Baraka* and found my answer when I came upon a passage [referring] to me as Frank O'Hara's boyfriend with a compliment thrown in about my movie star good looks, which by no means assuaged my pique. The passage, which I'm unable to quote, smacked of a veiled homophobia and was utterly disingenuous, inasmuch as he knew that Frank and I weren't lovers.[9]

LeSueur's invocation of Jones is explicitly racist, as evidenced by his descriptive language, which includes his condescending reference to the "clearly intelligent, obviously gifted" artist; his reliance on clichés used to describe black people, including the phrases "easy smile" and "sparkling eyes"; and the fetishistic deployment of the word "stud." LeSueur felt rage toward what he experienced as a personal betrayal. This quotation is more than a minor poet's sense of interpersonal slight and general bitterness. Many members of that scene registered Jones's passage from token insider to angry militant outsider in memoirs and diaries. In LeSueur's chronicle we see another fairly standard move: the response to Jones's "veiled homophobia" feels like full-fledged homophobia, conveyed via a language of racism, articulating a feeble complaint of hypocrisy. The charge of homosexuality and its entwinement with homophobia has not only been a tactic deployed by white writers. In Jerry Gafio Watts's biography, *Amiri Baraka: The Politics and Art of a Black Intellectual*, the author comments on Baraka's performances of hypermasculinity.[10] According to Watts's racial stereotypes of black hypermasculinity, that included justifications for the rape of white women and violent bursts of homophobic rhetoric that "masked Jones's homosexual past."[11] The performance of calling out Jones's queer past is a temporal move to which I would like to return in this chapter. But I wish to do so while resisting the moralizing impulse that drives LeSueur and Watts. Moten's characterization of Jones's hazy queerness is the most useful description I have encountered. His take on the Baraka of the early 1960s describes the narration of a "homosexual, interracial seizure" and its concomitant disavowal. *Seizure* means both arrogation and fit in this instance. I am also interested in another aspect of this queerness, which does not line up with most contemporary understandings of the term. I mean to describe this moment, the time and place of this relational field, where Jones, along with di Prima, the Judson dancer Fred Herko, and the jazz musician Cecil Taylor, sat together in di Prima's apartment and stapled together *The Floating Bear*. That pivotal journal included poems by Frank O'Hara, collages by the enigmatic Ray Johnson, and an essay by William S. Burroughs. Much of the work published there signals a kind of queer potentiality that existed before the stultifying effects of some identitarian narratives installed after the modern gay movement took hold.[12] A Blochian understanding of temporality, especially its emphasis on the power of futurity, is key to understanding Baraka and his place. As Bloch makes clear, the past, even a willfully idealized one such as the one I rehearse in this chapter, tells us something about the present. It tells us that something is missing, or something is not yet here. Bloch's unorthodox and messianic Marxism resonates alongside the black radical tradition that Moten invokes after Cedric Robinson. Robinson's temporal mapping of black resistance and endurance to capitalism predates Karl Marx and is reminiscent of the temporal work that Bloch advocates. If the condition of possibility for blackness is a certain radicalness in relation to capitalism's naturalizing temporal logic, the black radical tradition is engaged in a maneuver that helps elucidate queer futurity. I wish to look at one particular moment of that tradition, exemplified in *The Toilet*, that intimated another way of being within both blackness and homosexualness—precisely at the point of what Moten describes as the homosexual-interracial seizure.

For Bloch, aesthetic production does more than socially symbolic work. Indeed, there is a performance of futurity embedded in the aesthetic. Bloch's protocols of aesthetic analysis directed an eye toward what he called the anticipatory illumination of art. Queerness in my formulation is also not quite here and no longer conscious. Queerness, if it is to have any political resonance, needs to be more than an identitarian marker and to articulate a forward-dawning futurity. The dialectical movement that I am attempting to explicate is the interface between an engagement with the no-longer-conscious and the not-yet-here. This Blochian hermeneutic is especially felicitous when considering the queer residue and simultaneous potentiality that lay at the center of the example that Jones/Baraka and *The Toilet* generate.

The Toilet is a one-act play set in a high school restroom. At the end of the school day a group of black students enters the lavatory. They are expecting some event, which is revealed to be a fight between two young men, one black and one white. The would-be combatants—Ray, known by his schoolmates as Foots, and Jerry Karolis, who is described as a "paddy"—do not appear until about the middle of the play. The action that dominates the first half of the drama is the playful badgering and verbal taunting of Foots's assembled friends. It is clear from the dialogue that Foots, who is described as small and compact, is nonetheless the unofficial leader of this cohort. He is also the only member who is described as a good student. Another dominant member is Ora, a violent bully who threatens the other young men in an extremely menacing fashion. His name connotes the oral of sexuality but also the question of aural that, for Moten, plays an indexical role in a black radical tradition. Moreover, there is the oral threat of the secret, either open or not, that is always relational to the question of sex, secrets, and disclosure.

While the boys verbally joust, there is a manhunt for Karolis under way in the halls. When two other boys, one black and one white, enter the restroom, the white one, Donald Farrell, soon discovers that the point of this gathering is a gang assault on Karolis. Ora does not permit Farrell to defend Karolis verbally by revealing what might be a floating truth, the open secret of Karolis and Ray's relationship.

Ora punches Farrell in the stomach, and Farrell falls, doubled over in pain, his lips temporarily sealed. Then Karolis is dragged into the restroom by Knowles and Skippy, the two young men sent to fetch him. His face is bloody. He has already been severely beaten. Ora taunts Karolis, telling him that he has a nice sausage for him. The verbal play hums somewhere between a taunt and the threat of sexual violation. At this point Foots makes his appearance. Once Foots enters, there is a shift in the play's text, and scene direction becomes as important as dialogue. Here is the moment in the text when Foots first notices his intended opponent.

> foots: Yeah somebody told him Knowles said he was gonna kick Karolis' ass. (Seeing karolis in the corner for the first time. His reaction is horror and disgust . . . but he keeps it controlled as is his style, and merely half whistles.) Goddamn! What the fuck happened to him? (He goes over to Karolis and kneels near him, threatening to stay too long. He controls the impulse and gets up and walks back to where he was. He is talking throughout his action.) Damn, what you guys do? Kill the cat? (T, 52)

Scene direction is the play's choreography of the gestural that is especially attuned to the temporality of reading the play along the provisionally parallel lines of the black radical tradition and the project of queer futurity. Moten's analysis has also pointed to the emphasis on movement in the play. He is especially astute about Foots's relation to movement, how his feet are indeed always moving and running, like his mouth. Of course he is also running from the force field of queer desire, the threat that animates the open secret, a secret that threatens to keep him hovering above Karolis for too long, a force he needs to resist, an impulse that needs to be controlled. (This is the secret that LeSueur supposedly kept to himself, that the jilted lover di Prima puts forth in her memoir, and that Watts blurts out in his three-hundred-plus-page condemnation of Baraka.) What happens at this moment in the play can be seen as a choreography, a dance macabre, scored by the death drive, a tune that is, as Lee Edelman argues, endemic to queerness.[13] The dance is also the choreography of childhood violence and brutality, another queer past that haunts queers in the present, much in the same way that the past of The Toilet haunted the black nationalist Baraka.

Foots wants to put an end to this dance, not wanting to perform it for an audience. He tells his friends that Karolis was supposed to be beaten by him and that the after-school rumble has been ruined for him. Ora tells Foots to drag Karolis on his feet so that he can knock Karolis down again. Ora insists that the fight go on as promised, despite Karolis's pathetic state. Farrell then gets up. Foots suggests that he get out, that he has no business there. Farrell asks to take Karolis with him and asks why he is about to be beaten. Ora reveals that Karolis sent a letter to Foots in which he exclaimed that Ray/Foots was beautiful and that he wanted to give him a blowjob. Farrell protests this impending attack and is about to suggest, it would seem, that there is more to the relationship between the two than the story of Karolis's writing a mash note out of the blue would indicate. It would seem that this relationship has the status of what can be called semipublic knowledge. There is, of course, another reading to be made about letters, purloined and otherwise. But this is not the moment to make an argument for what "remains of the signifier when it has no more signification," as Barbara Johnson argued in the case of Poe's purloined letter.[14] Instead, signification abounds, potentiality cloaked as innuendo. Before Farrell is finally ejected by Ora, Karolis stares at Foots and addresses him by his other name: "Oh Ray, come on. Why don't you come off it?" (*T*, 56).

The not-so-unspeakable is almost spoken at this moment. And, on that cue, just when it seems as if further carnage has been averted, Karolis, Lazarus-like, rises from the corner where he has been slumped. He exclaims, "Nobody has to leave. I *want* to fight you Ray. (He begins to pull himself up. He is unsteady on his feet, but determined to get up . . . and to fight.) I *want* to fight you." "Want" is the word emphasized through italics in the text, and thus desire is transposed. Karolis pushes "himself off the wall slightly and [wipes] his face with his sleeve" (*T*, 57). He calls out to Foots but modifies the structure of address, in the same way Farrell did a beat earlier: "No, Ray. Don't have them leave. I want to fight you." One onlooker calls out, "Get it on fellas." The scene's narration speeds up:

> karolis: Yeh! That's why we're here, huh? I'll fight you, Foots! (Spits the name.) I'll fight you. Right here in this same place where you said your name was Ray. (Screaming he lunges at Foots and manages to grab him in a choke hold.) Ray, you said your name was. You said Ray. Right here in this filthy toilet. You said Ray. (He is choking Foots and screaming. Foots struggles and is punching Karolis in the back and

stomach, but he cannot get out of the hold.) You put your hand on me said Ray! (*T*, 58)

Karolis has the upper hand in the fight, but the gang joins in and saves Foots. Karolis is beaten down and lies in the center of the room, limp. Ora drapes him in wet toilet paper, and the rest of the group keeps him from sticking the beaten boy's head in the toilet. Foots is mocked by his friends, a leader deposed. Before exiting, Ora takes a paper cup, dips it in the commode, and throws it in Foots's face. He leaves the room as well. Karolis struggles to get up but collapses on the dirty floor. Turning from paraphrase to Jones's actual stage notes, we see that the play's last moment is completely gestural:

> After a minute or so Karolis moves his hand. Then his head moves and he tries to look up. He draws his legs up under him and pushes his head off the floor. Finally he manages to get to his hands and knees. He crawls over to one of the commodes, pulls himself up, then falls backward awkwardly and heavily. At this point, the door is pushed open slightly, then it opens completely and Foots comes in. He stares at Karolis' body for a second, looks quickly over his shoulder, then runs and kneels before the body, weeping and cradling the head in his arms. (*T*, 58–59)

The play's final moment is worth dwelling on, although I do not want to cast the gesture of tenderness as redemptive. I am not interested in cleansing the violence that saturates almost every utterance and move in the play. But I nonetheless want to consider how we might read this ending within the nexus of the historical moment, relational to an author's status as outsider among outsiders in a lost bohemia, an expired avant-garde. Baraka renounces queerness a few years later. He even shouts down the play's set designer, Larry Rivers, the straight painter who was also Frank O'Hara's art-boy, semi-rough-trade lover, in a public forum.[15] This moment nonetheless tells a story that suggests some kind of futurity, a relational potentiality worth holding on to. Battered and bruised, shattered by internal and external frenzies of homophobic violence, the combatant lovers nonetheless have this moment of wounded recognition that tells us that this moment in time and in this place, the moment of a pain-riddled youth, is not all there is, that indeed something is missing. The gestural speaks to that which is, to use Bloch's phrase, the not-yet-here. The gesture is not the coherence or totality of movement. Gesture for Giorgio Agamben is exemplary of the politics of a "means without ends." The gestural exists as an idealist manifestation and not as a monolithic act directed toward an "end": "What characterizes gesture is that in it nothing is being produced or acted, but something is being endured and supported."[16] The gesture interrupts the normative flow of time and movement. The image of the lover holding/enduring/supporting the other's battered body is poignant when we recall that Foots, who is always doing/running his mouth or his feet, is finally still, living within the queer temporality of the gestural, a temporality that sidesteps straight time's heteronormative bent. The politics of queer utopia are similarly not based on prescriptive ends but, instead, on the significance of a critical function that resonates like the temporal interruption of the gesture. Bloch rejected what he called "abstract utopias" that, within the frame of Agamben's writing, would indeed be a prescriptive "end."[17] The queer futurity that I am describing is not an end but an opening or horizon. Queer utopia is a modality of critique that speaks to quotidian gestures as laden with potentiality. The queerness of queer futurity, like the blackness of a black radical tradition, is a relational and collective modality of endurance and support. The gesture of cradling the head of one's lover, a lover one has betrayed, is therefore not an act of redemption that mitigates violence; it is instead a future being within the present that is both a utopian kernel and an anticipatory illumination. It is a being in, toward, and for futurity.

Lee Edelman, in his powerful polemic *No Future: Queer Theory and the Death Drive*, wishes to alert his readers to the fact that "the structuring optimism of politics of which the order of meaning commits us, installing as it does the perpetual hope of reaching meaning through signification, is always, I would argue, a negation of this primal, constitutive and negative act."[18] Political hope fails queers because, like signification, it was not originally made for us. It resonates only on the level of reproductive futurity. Instead, Edelman recommends that queers give up hope and embrace a certain negation endemic to our abjection within the symbolic. What we get, in exchange for giving up on futurity, abandoning politics and hope, is a certain jouissance that at once defines and negates us. Edelman's psychoanalytic optic reveals that the social is inoperable for the always already shattered queer subject.[19]

I have attempted to outline this polemic in a fashion that displays some of my admiration for it. I agree with and feel hailed by much of *No Future*. Indeed, when I negotiate the ever-increasing sidewalk obstacles produced by oversized baby strollers on parade in the city in which I live, the sheer magnitude of the vehicles that flaunt the incredible mandate of reproduction as world-historical virtue, I could not be more hailed with a statement such as, "Queerness names the side of 'not fighting for the children,' the side of outside the consensus by which all politics confirms the value of reproductive futurism."[20] But as strongly as I reject reproductive futurity, I nonetheless refuse to give up on concepts such as politics, hope, and a future that is not kid stuff. Maybe there are moments after the frenzy of negation that is symbolized as extreme violence in *The Toilet*, such as Karolis cradling Foots's head, that might display an ethics of embracing one's constituting negation. Perhaps that gesture is a manifestation of queerness's jouissance. It certainly reads like a smoldering moment in a Jean Genet text. Edelman's emphasis on queer jouissance, his charge that we take up our abjection within the social, is calibrated on embracing the necessary failure within the symbolic and within the protocols of reason. A reading aligned with this polemic would reject an understanding of this bloodied embrace between men as indicating any notion of a principle of hope. Thus, Jones's only justification for the play's ending would be rebuffed by an Edelman-inspired reading. In a 1978 interview, well after the heyday of his nationalist separatism and his immersion in a particular Marxist-Stalinist configuration, Baraka described the end of the play as tacked on, explaining that it was meant to end with the fight.

> I sat there for a while thinking, was this really the way it had to end? The whole thing needed some kind of rapprochement—there was a question of wanting to offer that kind of friendship that existed across traditional social lines. At the time I was married to a white woman, and most of the friends I had were white, on the Lower East Side. I didn't go around thinking in my mind this is the case, but I think that is why that kind of ending seemed more appropriate to me at the time.[21]

We know that many of these white friends on the Lower East Side, such as O'Hara and Allen Ginsberg, were also a little lavender. The interview works as a mild disavowal of the play's ending, a display of ambivalence that ignores its queer affect and tenor. The author's need to justify his end as the appeasement of his immediate social world needs further scrutiny. A turn to Hegel via Judith Butler's recent meditation on the longing for recognition can further explicate the stakes in this moment of contact and interracial intimacy.[22] Butler tells a tale of recognition, made famous by G. W. F. Hegel in *The Phenomenology of Spirit*.[23] It is a representative moment that signals the spirit of German philosophical idealism in which Bloch and other utopian thinkers participate, and it further illuminates the play's ending. Reflecting on the paradigm of the master and the bondsman, Butler outlines the relation to self and other:

> The moment in "Lordship and Bondage" when the two self-consciousnesses come to recognize one another is, accordingly, in the "life and death struggle," the moment in which they each see the shared power they have to annihilate the Other and, thereby, destroy the condition of their own self-reflection. Thus, it is as a moment of fundamental vulnerability that recognition becomes possible, and need becomes self-conscious. What recognition does at such a moment is, to be sure, to hold destruction in check.[24]

The Hegelian narrative is enriched when we insert Frantz Fanon's contribution to the very central philosophical thematic of self/other and the drama of recognition. If we consider the vicissitudes of the fact of blackness, the radical contingency that is epidermalization, the narrative fills out further and the tale of vulnerability is fleshed out. Recognition, across antagonisms within the social such as sex, race, and still other modalities of difference, is often more than simply a tacit admission of vulnerability. Indeed, it is often a moment of being wounded.[25] In this sense I offer *The Toilet* as a tale of wounded recognition. It marks and narrativizes the frenzy of violence that characterizes our cross-identificatory recognition. *The Toilet* teaches us that the practice of recognition is a brutal choreography, scored to the discordant sounds of desire and hate. With that stated, its semidisowned ending speaks to the sticky interface between the interracial and the queer. The interracial and the queer coanimate each other, and that coanimation, which is not only about homosexuality but about blackness and how the two touch across space and time, takes the form of not only the amalgamation of movements that rate a seizure but also the fragmented gesture that signals an endurance/support, queerness's being in, toward, and for futurity. Utopian hermeneutics like those invoked in the project of queer futurity consider the forward-dawning significance of the gesture.

Thus, the play's dramatic conclusion is not an end but, more nearly, an Agambenian means without an end. Recognition of this order challenges theories of antirelationality that dominate queer criticism, such as Edelman's and the Leo Bersani of "Is the Rectum a Grave?" and, to a lesser degree, *Homos*.[26] The act of accepting no future is dependent on renouncing politics and various principles of hope that are, by their very nature, relational. By finishing on a note not of reconciliation but of the refusal of total repudiation—a gestural enduring/supporting—*The Toilet* shows us that relationality is not pretty, but the option of simply opting out of it, or describing it as something that has never been available to us, is imaginable only if one can frame queerness as a singular abstraction that can be subtracted and isolated from a larger social matrix.

In *No Future* Edelman takes on Cornel West's referencing of futurity in an op-ed for the *Boston Globe* that he wrote with Sylvia Ann Hewitt titled "A Parent's Bill of Rights."[27] The title is disturbingly smug (as if biological parents of the middle class did not already have uncontested rights to their children!), and the editorial is a neoliberal screed on behalf of the culture of the child. But Edelman's critique never considers the topic of race that is central to the actual editorial. West's pro-children agenda aligns with his other concerns about the crises of African American youth.

Edelman's critique of the editorial, with which for the most part I am deeply sympathetic, is flawed insofar as it decontextualizes West's work from the topic that has been so central to his critical interventions: blackness. In the same way all queers are not the stealth-universal-white-gay-man invoked in queer antirelational formulations, all children are not the privileged white babies to whom contemporary society caters. Again, there is for me a lot to like in this critique of antireproductive futurism, but in Edelman's theory it is enacted by the active disavowal of a crisis in afrofuturism.[28] Theories of queer temporality that fail to factor in the relational relevance of race or class merely reproduce a crypto-universal white gay subject that is weirdly atemporal—which is to say a subject whose time is a restricted and restricting hollowed-out present free of the need for the challenge of imagining a futurity that exists beyond the self or the here and now.

The question of children hangs heavily when one considers Baraka's present. On August 12, 2003, one of his daughters, Shani Baraka, and her female lover, Rayshon Holmes, were killed by the estranged husband of Wanda Pasha, who is also one of Baraka's daughters. The thirty-one- and thirty-year-old women's murders were preceded a few months earlier by another hate crime in Newark, the killing of fifteen-year-old Sakia Gunn. Gunn was a black transgendered youth who traveled from Hoboken to

Greenwich Village and the Christopher Street piers to hang out with other young queers of color. Baraka and his wife, Amina, have in part dealt with the tragic loss of their daughter by turning to activism. The violent fate of their child has alerted them to the systemic violence that faces queer people (and especially young people) of color. The Barakas have both become ardent antiviolence activists speaking out directly on LGBT issues. Real violence has ironically brought Baraka back to a queer world that he had renounced so many years ago. Through his tremendous loss he has decided to further diversify his consistent commitment to activism and social justice to include what can only be understood as queer politics. In the world of *The Toilet* there are no hate crimes, no lexicon that identifies homophobia per se, but there is the fact of an aggression constantly on the verge of brutal actualization. The mimetic violence resonates across time and to the scene of the loss that the author will endure decades later. This story from real life is not meant to serve as the proof for my argument. Indeed, the play's highly homoerotic violence is in crucial ways nothing like the misogynist violence against women that befell the dramatist's family or the transgenderphobic violence that ended Gunn's young life. I mention these tragedies because it makes one simple point. The future is only the stuff of some kids. Racialized kids, queer kids, are not the sovereign princes of futurity. Although Edelman does indicate that the future of the child as futurity is different from the future of actual children, his framing nonetheless accepts and reproduces this monolithic figure of the child that is indeed always already white. He all but ignores the point that other modes of particularity within the social are constitutive of subjecthood beyond the kind of jouissance that refuses both narratological meaning and what he understands as the fantasy of futurity. He anticipates and bristles against his future critics with a precognitive paranoia in footnote 19 of his first chapter. He rightly predicts that some identitarian critics (I suppose that would be me in this instance, despite my ambivalent relation to the concept of identity) would dismiss his polemic by saying it is determined by his middle-class white gay male positionality. This attempt to inoculate himself from those who engage his polemic does not do the job. In the final analysis, white gay male crypto-identity politics (the restaging of whiteness as universal norm via the imaginary negation of all other identities that position themselves as not white) is beside the point. The deeper point is indeed "political," as, but certainly not more, political than Edelman's argument. It is important not to hand over futurity to normative white reproductive futurity. That dominant mode of futurity is indeed "winning," but that is all the more reason to call on a utopian po-litical imagination that will enable us to glimpse another time and place: a "not-yet" where queer youths of color actually get to grow up. Utopian and willfully idealistic practices of thought are in order if we are to re-sist the perils of heteronormative pragmatism and Anglo-normative pes-simism. Imagining a queer subject who is abstracted from the sensuous intersectionalities that mark our experience is an ineffectual way out. Such an escape via singularity is a ticket whose price most cannot afford. The way to deal with the asymmetries and violent frenzies that mark the pres-ent is not to forget the future. The here and now is simply not enough. Queerness should and could be about a desire for another way of being in both the world and time, a desire that resists mandates to accept that which is not enough.

6

Stages

Queers, Punks, and the Utopian Performative

You can't tell who was and who wasn't in a band. We did not like poseurs but we liked to pose for pictures. Because we knew there was something about the night that would be remembered even if we couldn't remember it. We were young and naive in a way that seems to be a lost art. We were snotty and compassionate and deliberate and reckless but we knew exactly what we were doing. We were ghosts then and we are ghosts now. We will haunt your malls and catwalks forever. Ha Ha.

—Exene Cervenka[1]

Utopian Performatives

How does one stage utopia? Which is to say, how do we enact utopia? In the various chapters of this book, some form of that question is almost always articulated. It is one of those good questions that help writers clarify their arguments, to propel their thinking forward. One thing I have learned from this question is that utopia is an ideal, something that should mobilize us, push us forward. Utopia is not prescriptive; it renders potential blueprints of a world not quite here, a horizon of possibility, not a fixed schema. It is productive to think about utopia as flux, a temporal disorganization, as a moment when the here and the now is transcended by a *then* and a *there* that could be and indeed should be.

But on some level utopia is about a politics of emotion; it is central to what Ernst Bloch called a "principle of hope."[2] It is my belief that minoritarian subjects are cast as hopeless in a world without utopia. This is not to say that hope is the only modality of emotional recognition that structures belonging; sometimes shame, disgust, hate, and other "negative" emotions bind people together—certainly punk rock's rejection of normative feelings stands as the most significant example of the emotional work of negative affect. But in this instance, I dwell on hope because I wish to think about futurity; and hope, I argue, is the emotional modality that permits us to access futurity, par excellence.

Queers, for example, especially those who do not choose to be biologically reproductive, a people without children, are, within the dominant culture, people without a future. They are cast as people who are developmentally stalled, forsaken, who do not have the complete life promised by heterosexual temporality.[3] This reminds one of the way in which worried parents deal with wild queer children, how they sometimes protect themselves from the fact of queerness by making it a "stage," a developmental hiccup, a moment of misalignment that will, hopefully, correct itself or be corrected by savage pseudoscience and coercive religion, sometimes masquerading as psychology. In this chapter, I consider the idea of queerness as a "stage" in a way that rescues that term from delusional parents and others who attempt to manage and contain the potentiality that is queer youth. In this chapter I enact a utopian performative change in the signification of the phrase "it is only a 'stage,'" deployed in the name of the queer child—in this case, the queer wild child of punk subculture. I enact this change through a reading of visual artist Kevin McCarty's representations of illuminated stages at gay bars and independent rock clubs and through a more general reading of punk rock's ethos as conjured and connoted by McCarty's images and my readings of them. I argue that the artist's work indexes a punk/queer utopian scene that I read for its utopian potentiality and also, furthermore, that the work itself is a photographic instance of the utopian performative.[4]

This argument is not aligned with any of the dominant performance theories that held sway during the early nineties, such as Peggy Phelan's axiom that the ontology of performance was disappearance and that performance itself represented a unique mode of representation without reproduction.[5] Instead, a materialist current influences this analysis. For example, I see this project working in tandem with a book such as Miranda Joseph's *Against the Romance of Community*. In that book, Joseph offers an important critique of Phelan's version of the performance's power: "in order to claim that performance resists exchange value, or equivalence, and thereby approaches the unrepresentable real itself, Phelan discounts the work of the audience; their productive consumption of the work, their act of witness is for her the memory of something presented by somebody else."[6]

Joseph, then, suggests that performance's temporality is not one of simple presence but instead of futurity. In Joseph's lucid critique we see that performance is the kernel of a potentiality that is transmitted to audiences and witnesses and that the real force of performance is its ability to generate a modality of knowing and recognition among audiences and groups that facilitates modes of belonging, especially minoritarian belonging. If we consider performance under such a lens, we can see the temporality of what I describe as a utopian performativity, which is to say a manifestation of a "doing" that is in the horizon, a mode of possibility. Performance, seen as utopian performativity, is imbued with a sense of potentiality. Giorgio Agamben has outlined the temporality of the philosophical concept of potentiality by following a line of thought that begins with Aristotle. Agamben underscores a distinction made by Aristotle between potentiality and possibility.[7] Possibilities exist, or more nearly, they exist within a logical real, the possible, which is within the present and is linked to presence. Potentialities are different in that although they are present, they do not exist in present things. Thus, potentialities have a temporality that is not in the present but, more nearly, in the horizon, which we can understand as futurity. Potentiality is and is not presence, and its ontology cannot be reduced to presentness. Agamben reads this notion of potentiality alongside Jacques Derrida's notion of the trace. It is something like a trace or potential that exists or lingers after a performance. At performance's end, if it is situated historically and materially, it is never just the duration of the event. Reading for potentiality is scouting for a "not here" or "not now" in the performance that suggests a futurity.

I continue this writing, then, by readjusting my opening question— "How do we stage utopia?"—by suggesting that utopia is a stage, not merely a temporal stage, like a phase, but also a spatial one. Sir Thomas More initially positioned Utopia as a place, an island, and later that formulation was amended to become a temporal coordinate. Utopia became a time that is not here yet, a certain futurity, a could be, a should be. Utopia, according to Bloch, is a time and a place that is not yet here. Bloch, along with other Frankfurt School thinkers such as Theodor Adorno and Herbert Marcuse, contended that utopia is primarily a critique of the here and now; it is an insistence that there is, as they put it, "something missing in the here and the now."[8] Capitalism, for instance, would have us think that it is a natural order, an inevitability, the way things would be. The "should be" of utopia, its indeterminacy and its deployment of hope, stand against capitalism's ever expanding and exhausting force field of how things "are and will be." Utopian performativity suggests another modality of doing and being that is in process, unfinished. It is to be deciphered by noting what Bloch has called the anticipatory illumination that radiates from certain works of art.

Also pivotal to my formulation is the work of the previously discussed Italian philosopher Agamben. I have outlined his emphasis on potentiality and his privileging of this concept over that of possibility. Furthermore, the notion of the utopian performative that I am attempting to outline in this chapter is a notion that is inspired by Agamben's notion of a "means without an end."[9] For Agamben, politics is disabled by a certain emphasis on "ends," which is to say politics depends on a performative doing, a perpetual becoming. Performances that display and illuminate their "means" are, like punk, a modality of performance that is aesthetically and politically linked to populism and amateurism. The performative work of "means," in the sense I am using it, is to interrupt aesthetics and politics that aspire toward totality. This too is one of the ways in which I want to resist the Hegelian shell game of absence and presence (appearance and disappearance) that dominates previous performance theories. An emphasis on means as opposed to ends is innately utopian insofar as utopia can never be prescriptive of futurity. Utopia is an idealist mode of critique that reminds us that there is something missing, that the present and presence (and its opposite number, absence) is not enough.

Two years ago, I spent a sabbatical in Los Angeles. I grew up listening to X, the Germs, Gun Club, and other bands that made up the LA punk scene of the eighties. I lived in the LA punk scene via my semisubcultural existence in suburban Miami; this was possible through a grungy alternative record store located in a strip mall, called Yesterday and Today Records; a few punk and new wave clubs such as Flynn's on the Beach and Club Fire and Ice; and issues of *Creem*, a magazine that covered the edgier rock scene but could still be purchased in a Miami supermarket. Through my deep friendships with other disaffected Cuban queer teens who rejected both Cuban exile culture and local mainstream gringo popular culture, and through what I call the utopian critique function of punk rock, I was able to imagine a time and a place that was not yet there, a place where I tried to live. LA and its scene helped my proto-queer self, the queer child in me, imagine a stage, both temporal and physical, where I could be myself or, more nearly, imagine a self that was in process, a self that has always been in the process of becoming.

Years later, while in Los Angeles, I started hanging out with an artist, Kevin McCarty, with whom I shared an interest in punk and postpunk music, subculture, and utopia. Our friendship has endured various mutations, moments of volatility and great fun, and our mutual neuroses have fueled our queer intimacy. Our friendship is ultimately based on convergent worldviews in relation to politics and aesthetics. On a recent studio visit I saw a series of works that helped me organize and substantiate my thinking about the time, space, and utopian function of punk in relation to queer subcultural becomings. Writing about living artists helps one further debunk the false principle of the critic's objectivity. Queer intimacies underwrite much of the critical work I do. Yet I reject the phrase "advocacy criticism" and instead embrace the idea of the performative collaboration between artist and writer.

With that stated, I must add that from my side this connection between theory and art feels incredibly one-sided, and not only in the case of McCarty but also in my work on Carmelita Tropicana, Vaginal Davis, Isaac Julien, and others, because their work and the queer friendships and the intimacies I share with them enable my critical project. Attempting to imagine a convergence between artistic production and critical praxis is, in and of itself, a utopian act in relation to the alienation that often separates theory from practice, a sort of cultural division of labor.

McCarty's series of photographs titled *The Chameleon Club* is named after a space from the artist's biography, about which I have more to say later. The series lines up portraits of stages from different club spaces in Los Angeles such as Spaceland and Catch One. Spaceland is a bar and music venue in the now hipster Los Angeles neighborhood Silverlake. Spaceland is where the indie music kids and "not-so-kids" (I position myself within this bracket) go to hear the cutting-edge music of the day. Catch One is a predominantly black gay space where lesbian and transgendered people also go. It is a space that is not on the West Hollywood–centered gay map of Los Angeles. McCarty's extraordinary pictures exercise a great deal of formalist mastery that renders the stage as monumental. When the space is empty of people, the dark and dramatic lighting is set to make the performance sites look as though they were shot while the club was open and running. McCarty's pictures share some formal and contextual qualities with the beautiful work of Hiroshi Sugimoto, who famously photographs empty spaces. One of the crucial differences is the nature of the empty stages photographed. McCarty's work is perhaps a little less universal than Sugimoto's images insofar as the Los Angeles–based photographer images spaces that are vibrantly resonant with the space of subculture.

After I left LA, Kevin gave me a large print of the Catch One picture. The stage is small but appears large and luminous. The stage itself is black, and it rises from a black-and-white checkerboard floor. The black curtains that flank the stage are layered with gleaming silver hubcaps. The hubcaps sparkle through the photographer's gaze and its photographic representation. The back of the stage is illuminated by rows of simple white light strings. They are separated by a world of difference, but they nonetheless remind me of the light strings utilized by Félix González-Torres in his art installations. González-Torres's light strings symbolized the flickering status of queer lives in an epidemic, but they did not hang in the uniform fashion of the lights in McCarty's imaging of Catch One. I nonetheless look at these lights, lighting up the photograph from its deepest point and offering a warm secondary illumination from their reflection on the actual stage's shiny black floor, and I think of that city, Los Angeles, a place I grew to love, and this one queer, predominantly black space that I had access to.

The only negative critique I have heard of this picture that rests on my wall is from people who have seen it in my apartment and think that it is perhaps too beautiful. The suggestion is that it is too pretty in the face of the adversity that queers of color face on a daily basis. I have presented on this series at different professional conferences, and on more than one

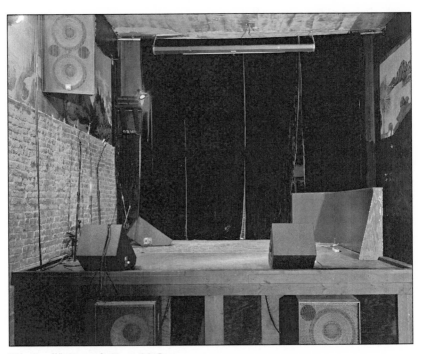

"The Smell." Copyright Kevin McCarty.

"Catch One." Copyright Kevin McCarty.

occasion a gay black man in the audience has recognized the space and approached me afterward. What I have learned from those encounters is that seeing this space of black queer belonging framed by McCarty's meticulous attention helps us see our connectedness outside of the actual temporality of club life. The utopian performative charge of this image allows one to see the past, the moment before an actual performance, the moment of potentiality; and the viewer gains access to the affective particularity of that moment of hope and potential transformation that is also the temporality of performance.

The stage at Catch One juts out into the audience; it looks like a catwalk, and its edges are lined with small shimmering light bulbs. The catwalk feature makes one think about a queer appropriation of high fashion, to which Exene Cervenka's quotation in the epigraph to this chapter refers. Cervenka's commentary, like McCarty's image of the stage from queer Catch One, calls attention to the way queer and punk subcultures have been informing and haunting the world of mainstream fashion for quite a while. The bluish lighting of Catch One reminds one of the moment I cited in chapter 3 of this book, that key moment in Delany's memoir *The Motion of Light in Water* in which Delany describes seeing a mass of gay men having sex under a blue light at the now closed St. Mark's Bath in the East Village. It was during this moment of utopian rapture when he first realized he was not a solitary pervert but part of a vast world of gay men who fucked, connected, and had actual lives.[10]

The theatricality of McCarty's images has much to do with the lighting, which seems to be generated from the stage itself, bottom-up instead of top-down light, giving the effect that the space is glowing with possibility. That effect recalls Bloch's formulation in regard to certain aesthetic modes, such as, for example, what he called the ornamental. Bloch privileges the ornamental over the functional, which does not let us see anything in it except the use that capitalism has mapped out for it in advance. The ornamental, on the other hand, has an indeterminate use value that challenges the protocols of capitalism, and in it one can view Bloch's anticipatory illumination of art. The glow that McCarty's photos generate is that anticipatory illumination, that moment of possibility right before an amazing band or performance manifests itself on stage and transforms the world for the performance's duration and, for many of those in attendance, beyond. The best performances do not disappear but instead linger in our memory, haunt our present, and illuminate our future.

When McCarty displays the images of Catch One and Spaceland he wants them to be one piece, the two images side by side, adjacent, giving a sense that there is a door between them, joining the space of punk and queer subcultures. Popular culture is the stage where we rehearse our identities. McCarty's work stands as a powerful amendment to this formulation by displaying the actual and metaphorical stages where queers and punks rehearse self. The artist explains his rationale for his objects of study in an autobiographical artist statement:

Located somewhere in the middle of nowhere, surrounded by cow fields, and suburban home developments, situated in between the ruins of downtown Dayton, Ohio, a post industrial wasteland, and Wright Pat Air Force base, sat the Hills and Dales shopping center. In a retail space, in the rear of a strip mall the Chameleon Club opened. One entered what would be the sales floor and made their way back, though a single doorway to the storeroom, which had been converted, into a punk rock club. The only furnishings were a plywood stage at the far end flanked by a PA. The dry walling was incomplete exposing cinder blocks. To the right of the stage was a doorway that led to 1470's, the largest gay bar in Dayton. When you paid admission to the Chameleon Club you could buy drinks at 1470's. The punks would pass back and forth, but no one from 1470's came to the Chameleon Club. With their costumes and their lyrics the kids on the music scene performed their identities at the temporary venue. For the punks geographic location was not relevant as long as there was a stage, a soundman and an audience. Behind the bare cinder blocks of the Chameleon Club one could hear the beats of dance music. The sweating bodies of intoxicated gay men crowded the dance floor only to be revealed through the artificial fog by streaks of red, blue, and green lights circling above their heads. Here men forgot about the bluecollar oppressive city they called home and imagined a world where they could be free from shame and embarrassment. Neither place was mine. I observed both from the outside. My utopia existed at the doorway on the threshold—neither space at one time and in both simultaneously.[11]

This statement resonates alongside my own autobiography. I was certainly crossing what was for me a metaphorical threshold between the punk world and gay life. Punk made my own suburban quotidian existence radical and experimental—so experimental that I could imagine and eventually act on queer desires. Punk rock style may look apocalyptic, yet its temporality is nonetheless futuristic, letting young punks imagine a time and a place where their desires are not toxic. McCarty talks about a space between these two zones, between the queer 1470 and the punk Chameleon Club. In part, he is narrating a stage of in-between-ness, a spatiality that is aligned with a temporality that is on the threshold between identifications, lifeworlds, and potentialities. The work and the artist's statement resonate beyond my own biography.

In an early gay and lesbian studies anthology edited by Karla Jay and Allen Young, *Lavender Culture*, there is another report about queer bars in Ohio. In a short piece by John Kelsey titled "The Cleveland Bar Scene in the Forties," the author reports the fundamental importance of these spaces: "There was, of course, nothing spectacular about Cleveland's gay male bars in the forties, but the point is simply this: they existed. Gay men had places to meet, not only in San Francisco or New York, but in a city easily scoffed at or ignored by sophisticates on either coast."[12] Kelsey's narration of the forties resonates powerfully next to McCarty's artist statement. McCarty's impressions from the nineties, fifty years after Kelsey's

moment, would probably still agree with a point Kelsey makes: "The curi-
ous combination of exploitation and liberation helped define the mood
in gay bars then as it is now, though perhaps both elements were more
extreme in those days."[13] The calculus of exploitation and liberation dogs
queer culture. Kelsey talks about seeing a few good female impersonators
and also states, "If the professional entertainment was bad, the amateurs
were unbelievably awful."[14] He characterizes a typical afternoon at the
Hide-Out Club's Sunday afternoon of amateur performances as a scene
where

> male typists in Grandma's cast-off finery would take the stage, forget
> lyrics, and flee in tears. And stockroom boys would take absolutely
> dreadful spills during their ballet-tap routines. One I much enjoyed
> was a short, middle-aged man who would sing part of it in the voice of
> Nelson Eddy, and part in the voice of Jeanette MacDonald.[15]

The celebration of an aesthetics of amateurism are reminiscent of punk
rock's aesthetics. The performances of amateurism, in both punk and
Kelsey's example of queer performance, signal a refusal of mastery and an
insistence on process and becoming. Again, such performances do not disappear but instead remain and, like performatives in J. L. Austin, do things
in the future.[16] In Kelsey's example, the short, squat singer of "Indian
Summer" is loved decades after his performance, and that one audience
member's testimonial stands as one of the things that remains after the
performance. The performance, in its incompleteness, lingers and persists,
drawing together the community of interlocutors. Utopian performativity
is often fueled by the past. The past, or at least narratives of the past, enable utopian imaginings of another time and place that is not yet here but
nonetheless functions as a doing for futurity, a conjuring of both future
and past to critique presentness.

McCarty's work is fueled by a past recollection from his biography that
he takes to another time and place and uses to capture this ideality that
is the potentiality of utopian performativity. His stages are lit as though a
performance is about to emerge from the realm of potential to actuality.
The lure of the work is its performative dimension, which I would describe
as a doing as dwelling, which is to say that I am particularly interested in
the way in which the images dwell in potentiality, aestheticizing that moment, transmitting the power of its ideality. Thus, the aesthetic fuels the
political imagination.

"La Plaza." Copyright Kevin McCarty.

I am especially partial to the image of La Plaza. The club itself is one of the oldest Latino gay clubs in LA. The place has a sort of ranchera or country-western feel to it. Often many of the patrons dress to go with the decor. It is not the sanitized, glamorous country-western feel that has become a fashionable commodity within middle-class, and mostly white, gay circles. Instead it is, more nearly, a sort of gay Mexican cowhands feel. But that is not true of the stage at this humble little bar. The curtains shine with an extravagance that seems out of place with the rest of the locale. As soon as showtime starts, the heavy theatrical lights burst on and illuminate the seemingly beaded curtains. Once the show begins, old-school glamorous transvestites take the stage. The entire spectacle is in Spanish. The hostess glimmers with the same intensity as the curtains. All the performances are standard exercises in lip-syncing. About two-thirds of the songs are Spanish anthems, and the rest are English pop songs. Then contestants come onstage, and they are introduced in relation to the province or village they are from in Mexico. The codes that organize time and space

"Silver Lake Lounge." Copyright Kevin McCarty.

are disrupted in this performance space. The first time I visited the club I felt as though I was in Guadalajara in the 1950s. This spatial and temporal displacement mimetically resonates with the lush photograph of the stage. Again we see potentiality, another vista is offered, and in Los Angeles the site, La Plaza, conjures stories of migratory crossing, legal and illegal, and one sees these bodies, whose lifeworld is always in flux, about to belong, on the cusp of materialization.

A white neon sign that reads "Salvation" hangs over the stage at the Silver Lake Lounge, another predominantly Latino gay club where I have seen rough strippers and messy drag queens perform their crafts. Queer culture, in its music and iconography, often references salvation. One hears the refrain of a famous club anthem, "Last Night a DJ Saved My Life." There is indeed something about the transformative powers of nightlife that queers and people of color have always clung to. The contrast in the Silver Lake Lounge composition is a strong one, a contrast between the idea of salvation and the clear seediness of the actual space. The bright shining ideality of salvation hangs over a space that is dark and not very promising except that the concept literally is writ large on top of the picture—in this visual study is embedded the nature of a utopian performativity within subaltern spaces. Sometimes the utopian spectator needs to squint to see the anticipatory illumination promised by utopia, yet at other times, its visuality and (non)presence cannot be denied.

The stage from Spaceland is lit a certain deep pink that makes it feel like a band of screaming angry teens will hop onstage and tear it up with their savage guitars. The photograph returns me to my early punk shows. I remember the potentiality that those scenes of spectatorship promised even before performers showed up onstage. The hum of other men's bodies, bodies that for whatever reason, for that moment, rejected a trajectory that was attuned to the normal. Being at Spaceland makes me feel old. I remember the Cat's Cradle in Chapel Hill, North Carolina, and seeing my favorite bands there during the relentless social tedium of graduate school. That is where I started to feel too old to go to shows yet nevertheless felt the show and stage, the transformation of time and space offered by the performance, as forgiving and still permitting me access to this network of queer belongings.

"Spaceland, 2003." Copyright Kevin McCarty.

"The Parlour." Copyright Kevin McCarty.

I feel the sense of belonging with even greater intensity when I look at the opulent image of the now defunct Parlor Club on Santa Monica Avenue. The tiny stage is clearly overdecorated, with its elaborate chandelier and its rich red drapes with golden tassels. I visited the club during my regular trips to Los Angeles, when my dear friend and frequent object of study Vaginal Davis hosted her Friday-night party Bricktop there. The Parlor Club's tiny stage often looks like it is about to buckle under Davis's massive frame as she inhabits the stage, perhaps performing some surprisingly delicate flapper dance.[17]

Of all the spaces McCarty has chosen to depict, this one is most clearly and concretely the space where punk and queerness meet. Indeed, in the pagan church of punk queerness, Davis is both high priestess and black pope. Davis is one of my favorite people in Los Angeles and something of a heroine from my queer coming of age. In her zines such as *Fertile LaToya Jackson* and *Shrimp* (a journal dedicated to the sucking of toes), I found an incredible resource for imaging a futurity where my, for lack of a better word, "antinormativity" could flourish. Through our friendship and queer intimacy we have performed, through a certain sick reappropriation, a rei-magined modality of the patronage system. She does her work, and I tes-tify to the *New York Times* and the *Los Angeles Times*—with my academic credentials and letterhead well in place—that she is a certified art star in the tradition of Dada and Surrealism. I then get to see her work, which inspires me to no end. Her Friday-night emporium of queer punk vintage retro sleaze was like no other venue I know of. McCarty's picture of the Parlor Room and its stage, with its dense Victorian luster, beautifully cap-tures the ethos of the party. I would summarize that ethos as a use of past decadence to critique the banality of our presentness for the purpose of imaging and enacting an enabling of queer futurity.

Installed at a gallery, the images of punk clubs are hung next to images of a gay bar's stage. The placement of these images next to one another speaks to subjectivities that travel through the swinging door between both temporal and spatial coordinates. For those of us whose relationship to popular culture is always marked by aesthetic and sexual antagonism, these stages are our actual utopian rehearsal rooms, where we work on a self that does not conform to the mandates of cultural logics such as late capitalism, heteronormativity, and, in some cases, white supremacy.

The empty stage was used in pieces by the generation of queer artists before McCarty. Félix González-Torres brought into the gallery a blue platform that was also outlined with light bulbs. Paid go-go dancers, who would appear at odd moments, often wearing Walkmen, would dance sug-gestively on the stage. That stage was always one of potentiality, empty one moment and overflowing with sex and movement the next. Whereas that work shares a utopian impulse with McCarty's, the empty stages of Jack Pierson's photographs look melancholic and emptied out of possibility. Pierson's images are snapshots of the disappointment that is part of uto-pia—the hangover that follows hope. At this moment it seems that queer visual culture needs to nourish our sense of potentiality and not reinforce our feeling of disappointment. If we are to go on, we need a critical mo-dality of hope and not simply dramatization of loss and despair.

The source material for McCarty's images is the past—not a nostalgic past but a past that helps us feel a certain structure of feelings, a circuit of queer belonging. When I look at his images, I remember the sexually am-biguous punk clubs of my youth where horny drunk punk boys rehearsed their identities, aggressively dancing with one another and later lurching out, intoxicated, to the parking lot together. For many of them, the mosh pit was not simply a closet; it was a utopian subcultural rehearsal space. In an earlier image of McCarty's, a makeshift subculture is shown in a collection of concert tickets pinned to a white wall with pins that resemble those used to mark places on maps. This reminds one of Oscar Wilde's *The Soul of Man under Socialism*, quoted in the epigraph to this book's introduction: "A map of the world that does not include utopia is not worth glancing at."[18] That earlier piece of McCarty's helps us understand the temporality of utopia, the way in which the past is used in the service of mapping a future, a place of possibility and transformation. Heteronormative culture makes queers think that both the past and the future do not belong to them. All we are allowed to imagine is barely surviving the present. This mapping of hope and affect on a white wall brings me back to the various shows where I rehearsed and planned a future self, one that is not quite here but always in process, always becoming, emerging in difference.

This chapter opened with Exene Cervenka's recent writing from the catalog called *We're Desperate: The Punk Rock Photography of Jim Jocoy*. In that book, there is a performance shot of Darby Crash, one of punk history's most fucked-up and damaged queer teens. In the punk biography *Lexicon Devil: The Fast Times and Short Life of Darby Crash and the Germs*, the late Tomata Du Plenty, lead singer for rival band the Weirdos, describes Darby offstage in relation to his staged self:

> Darby was fascinating in a parking lot. I think that's where he was really a star. Watching his behavior in a parking lot, that's what made Darby Crash, that's what made him a legend, certainly not his onstage performances! Oh, they were so boring! I couldn't sit through a Germs set, please. Torture! But I could certainly sit on the curb with a 40-ounce and listen to him for hours. He was an interesting, interesting boy.[19]

The stage and the parking lot are adjacent in much the same way that there is a phantom door between Catch One and Spaceland in McCarty's work. On one asphalt stage in Los Angeles, one queer punk watches another hold forth, and across the country, under a different shape of palm tree, but still in a parking lot, my best friend Tony and I sit in his beige Nissan Sentra and we speculate about this band the Germs and the provocative lyrics to such songs as "Sex Boy" and "Richie Dagger's Crimes." What can they possibly mean? we asked ourselves, almost already knowing. While we sat in that car, my parents worried about where I was and what I was doing with whom, and I know they must have been trying to comfort themselves by letting themselves think that I was merely at a stage. What we were learning in that parking lot as the Germs song "Forming" played was that there was another stage out there for us, both temporal and spatial, one in which potentiality, hope, and the future could be, should be, and would be enacted. Today I write back from that stage that my mother and father hoped I would quickly vacate. Instead, I dwell on and in this stage because I understand it as one brimming with a utopian performativity that is linked to the ideality that is potentiality. This potentiality is always in the horizon and, like performance, never completely disappears but, instead, lingers and serves as a conduit for knowing and feeling other people.

7

Utopia's Seating Chart

Ray Johnson, Jill Johnston, and
Queer Intermedia as System

for Luke

The solution to the problem of identity is, get lost.

—Jill Johnston

THE STONEWALL RIOT was a manifestation of pent-up energies that erupted on the streets of Greenwich Village in 1969. Today I live and work in the Village, and it is hard to find any residue of those energies. Yet the task of finding traces of those transformative political potentialities is nonetheless important, and in my research I often return to that moment of countercultural fecundity. Stonewall is of course the birth of the modern gay and lesbian movement and the initial eruption that led to a formalizing and formatting of gay and lesbian identities. Although this turn to the identitarian was important and even historically necessary, it is equally important to reflect on what was lost by this particular process of formalization. Before this bold rebellion there was another moment in which the countercultural map was perhaps a bit queerer, which is to say more expansive and including of various structures of feeling and habits of being that the relatively restrictive categories of gay and lesbian identities are incapable of catching.

When I turn to the ephemeral archives of queer New York I am interested in locating the anti-identitarian germ of this rebellion. Avant-garde cultural work from this period can be viewed from a certain vantage point from which the complexity of these then inchoate identities can be seen clearly. This approach looks at the work of certain cultural producers as ephemeral archives of these previous understandings and cartographies of the world. I am most interested in identifying a certain utopian component in these archives. This archival turn is intended to do more than simply unpack the past, to move from then to now. It is instead to calibrate a critical optic that can potentially perceive the residue of the utopian impulse that animated preidentitarian queer politics, and move from *then* to *here*. This move *from then to here* is a move to think about the coterminous nature of the temporal and spatial in the queer utopian methodology that I am suggesting. The time of the past helps mount a critique of the space of the present. This is not revisionary history or metahistory; it is a critical deployment of the past for the purpose of engaging the present and imagining the future. The purpose of calibrating such an optic is then to deploy the knowledge gleaned from queer ephemeral archives for the purposes of reanimating and reviving this utopian impulse.

To that end, I turn to two figures from that period: cultural critic Jill Johnston and conceptual artist Ray Johnson. With the homophonic surnames acknowledged, the pairing has to do with similar antidisciplinary protocols in their artistic work, what I call the "intermedia" approach of their cultural production. This intermedia process leads to a perpetual unfinished system that is by its very nature antisystemological, and thus analogical to the preidentitarian moment in which I am so interested. Intermedia is a radical understanding of interdisciplinarity. The usage of intermedia that I am suggesting is interdisciplinary in relation to both art-making protocols and taxonomies of race, gender, and sex.[1] I transport Johnston and Johnson from their historical perch and attempt to understand them alongside each other, as well as in the historical moment that enabled their projects. The project here is to understand how this work represents a much larger communal vibe, not to cast the two cultural producers as some kind of individualistic heroes. The work of Ernst Bloch, especially his interest in discerning the utopian aura of art, is crucial to my endeavor. Once again, I follow a flight plan that by now has hopefully become familiar in this book: I turn to the past in an effort to imagine a future. But before I engage that project, I sketch a map of how I got from then to here.

No one knows how many members belonged to the New York Correspondence School. I would like to think that the membership was vast and far-reaching, a virtual army of lovers who mailed obtuse yet beautiful objects to one another, objects that remade the world in significant and startling ways. The New York Correspondence School (NYCS) debuted in 1970 at the Whitney Museum of Modern Art with the show "Ray Johnson: New York Correspondence School" (September–October 1970). This, of course, was the school's public debut, and in that way a very limited aspect of the story. To understand the NYCS we should begin with a sketch of its founder, architect, and author: Ray Johnson. Johnson was not only a member of this club but also its president.[2]

Johnson alternated between the spelling "correspondence" and "correspondance," the latter spelling connoting the strange choreography of his mail art. Considering Johnson's close association with the Judson Memorial Dance Theater and his attendance at Robert Dunn's famous dance classes, the visual artist's indexing of dance as a process, as it was being conceived in the postmodern dance circles in which he traveled, is worth paying attention to.[3] The dancers Johnson would send out onto the stage were his mailings. The stage was the world via the postal system. The art of the NYCS had much to do with Johnson's sending of ephemera, information, collages, and all manner of unconventional mailings. These mailings were correspondences in that they sometimes called people to respond. His recipients, all of whom formed the membership of the NYCS, were invited to write back and present their own work or alter his previous mailing. He often sent his collages, which he called "Moticos," through the mail. The recipients of Moticos found in them a pastiche of Lucky Strike packaging, movie-star publicity photos, and fashion-magazine layouts. Moticos were an art that moved, performing objects insofar as they danced along the runways and stages provided by the world postal system. They were performative art objects that flowed like queer mercury throughout the channels of majoritarian communication and information.

I will continue this sketch of who Ray Johnson was and what he did by describing my first encounter with him. In this next phase of my description, which veers from anything resembling a traditional art-historical methodology, I want to show my associative belonging to this work. This turn to the associative is not random; instead it is meant to echo performatively the associative style of both Johnson and Johnston. At times my prose also echoes this work. I never met Johnson, but I know him through my dear friend Luke Dowd, who first told me about him. Johnson's friend and most famous collector, William Wilson, had bought a piece of Luke's work in a gallery. When Wilson had purchased the work he did not know that the young artist whose work he had found compelling enough to add to his collection was the son of another artist, John Dowd, a queer artist who was a friend of Wilson's and Johnson's. Before John Dowd had died of an AIDS-related illness in San Francisco he was involved with General Idea, a group of Toronto-based conceptual artists who were, to some degree, inspired by the NYCS. Luke told me about this chance meeting with Wilson and his familial connections. That happened before the large retrospective of Johnson's work was exhibited at the Whitney Museum of American Art (January 14, 1999–March 21, 1999). I was intrigued by Luke's description of Johnson's work, and this interest was further fed by a conversation I had with the artist Nayland Blake, who was, at the time, considering teaching a course on Johnson, Jack Smith, and Joseph Cornell—the latter two whose work I had (and continue to have) a great interest in.

At that point I became somewhat obsessed with Johnson. Through the machinations of New York City's vast interlibrary loan system I acquired two slim catalogs of Johnson's work from the early eighties. The work did not disappoint my hyped expectations. The art I encountered was ingenious and funny. The work abounded with verbal and visual puns. The collages included tributes to Gertrude Stein and Marianne Moore, two of my sapphic modernist heroes. My only frustration was that there was hardly any mention of the NYCS in the two artist's catalogs. I would need to wait until the 1999 Whitney retrospective on the artist's work for the opportunity to immerse myself in the NYCS.

I also learned about Johnson's brilliant response to Allan Kaprow and the Happenings movement in contemporary art: his "Nothings."[4] One particularly interesting nothing is recorded in a recent documentary on the artist, *How to Draw a Bunny*,[5] in which Johnson walks into a room where there is only a cardboard box then removes his belt and proceeds to whip the box. As he does so, he slowly attempts to articulate the word "Kafka" and is unable to say the writer's proper name. There is a conceptual minimalism to the piece that calls attention to the overabundance that was associated with Happenings. This performative insistence on "the nothing" (the not there) over the presentness of the happening (what is there) is both queer and utopian. Utopia is always about the not-quite-here or the notion that something is missing. Queer cultural production is both an acknowledgment of the lack that is endemic to any heteronormative rendering of the world and a building, a "world making," in the face of that lack. A nothing is a utopian act insofar as it acknowledges a lack that is normalized as reality and attempts to work with and through nothingness and ephemerality: it is both a critique and an additive or reparative gesture.[6] Queer utopian practice is about "building" and "doing" in response to that status of nothing assigned to us by the heteronormative world.

Walking through the exhibit with another good friend, the playwright Jorge Cortiñas, I found myself awash in Ray Johnson's conceptual madness. I learned about Johnson's biography—his training at Black Mountain and the profound influence of his teachers, Joseph Albers and John Cage, on his work. I took pleasure in looking at Johnson's punning bitchy swipes at macho abstract expressionists such as Jackson Pollock. He poked fun at his queer contemporaries, especially Andy Warhol. I found out about his charming and somewhat demented relationship with the artist May Wilson, collector and critic William Wilson's mother. But I was most impressed by the correspondences. I marveled at their freakishness. The work was small and subtle, and it was clear that critics whose imaginations were limited would simply dismiss it. When I looked at the collages I could see the clear-cut influence of artists such as Yvonne Rainer and Merce Cunningham, artists committed to antiformalism and spontaneity, and I could see the resonance with the conceptual work of Fluxus. I looked at the letters and remembered Samuel Delany's autobiographical narrative about the bathhouses of New York, his first visit to the St. Mark's Baths. Once again, the strange blue light of the public sex facility that permitted the author to see a comforting mass of perverts comes into focus, developing into something of a visual throughline for this text. These letters function something like the representation of those writhing pre-Stonewall bodies. Viewing Johnson's postings, his mail art, was like entering a secret world I had somehow half known. It was edifying. The letters represented a vast system of associations and correspondences that made a world that was not quite here yet nonetheless on the horizon. It was a queer world of potentiality.

I have taken the time to narrate my encounter with Johnson in an effort to convey the sensation of stumbling upon the queer world of Johnson and the NYCS. How did I chance upon Johnson's world? Mostly through coincidence: such as the fact that Johnson's collector, William Wilson, bought the work of a friend, which occasioned the discovery that this friend's late father was a friend of Johnson's. But I also encountered Johnson's world through a more impersonal, commonly navigated route, such as the Whitney retrospective. Yet through these decidedly different ports of entry I found myself in the midst of the world of the NYCS. I am not just an archivist or a scholar. I am also part of a queer relational orbit, a force field of belonging. Through associations both common and unique I acquired information about Ray Johnson and his work. Johnson's work allows one to see worlds that are both real and imagined, existing in a spatiotemporal coordinate between the real and the virtual. Johnson's correspondence school works as a map, or schematic, of a world that can only potentially exist. This potential, born out of spatiotemporal conditions of (im)possibility, can be deciphered as utopian. These conditions of (im)possibility reflect Johnson's rejection of "objective" reality. This rejection challenges objective reality's tenets, which include conventional understandings of not only the temporal and the spatial but also the ontological itself. For example, one did not actually need to be present at a meeting of the NYCS to be there.

Now I turn to a maverick critic who was a contemporary of Ray Johnson, the lesbian dance and art critic Jill Johnston, and her collection of writings culled from her *Village Voice* column, *Marmalade Me*.[7] Johnston's perspective on critical practice interests me and inspires my approach to this chapter and the larger project with which it is associated. Johnston was a student of literature who moved to New York from her native London (perhaps her Englishness, as well as her sexuality, contributed to her status as cultural outsider). The avant-garde art world of New York was the place where Johnston could join other outsiders and find a critical sense of belonging. Johnston was not only a commentator on the scene she covered; she was also often, to varying degrees, a participant. For instance, like Ray Johnson, she audited Dunn's famous dance workshops and other cultural happenings that led to the formation of the Judson Memorial Theater. Johnston, through the performance of her wildly associative writing style, would narrate her experiences on and off the stage, including her use of drugs and her acting out at parties.

Deborah Jowitt, in an introduction to a recent edition of *Marmalade Me*, wrote, regarding Johnston's style, "I'm also tempted to see in the rambling meditations structural analogies to Yvonne Rainer's epochal *Trio A*—a long chain of movements performed in such a way as to render no movement more important than any other one."[8] Rainer's piece, one of the most important pieces of choreography in the history of postmodern dance, challenges codes of difference and value within dance practice. Rainer's work is a challenge to dance's hierarchy of value because it brackets, yet does not abandon, technique in an effort to relativize the difference between movement that was not traditionally considered "dancelike" with moves that were established as such in dance's canon. This idea is reflected in Johnston's dance criticism, which began in the *Voice* as a column specifically addressing dance and progressed into a column about almost everything. Through this analogy one is reminded of Johnson's punning of *correspondence* and *correspondance*. Johnson's collage work and conceptual work, like Rainer's dance practice and Johnston's writing, make a radically democratic point: *everything corresponds to everything*. This move to denaturalize aesthetic value is one that thematically and affectively binds the emergent queer postmodernism of that period.

Johnston, in an article titled "Untitled," claimed that "every genealogy is a fiction. There is no such thing. There's only one genealogy. It takes place in our dreams. Every specific genealogy is a fiction."[9] Much in the same way that postmodern dance was intended to disrupt the codes of value assigned to different movements and gestures, Johnston took swipes at objective reality. Naturalized origin stories were dismantled by Johnston's intermedia, a concept that framed various and often contradictory stories about life and aesthetics as interchangeable.

I think Ray would agree with Jill's statement about genealogies. Furthermore, he would add that since every genealogy is a fiction, one should get to the project of writing—in words, movements, images, collages, gestures, fidgets, twitches, stumbles. I trace a line from my biographical coordinates to this critical project on Johnson. Although the account I render is true, it is, of course, also a fiction. It is a queer imaging that traverses friendship and gossip, strolls through the archives on a Sunday afternoon, and so much more. The archives is a fiction. Nobody knows that better than queers—people who have had to cope with the fiction of a socially prescribed straightness. Queers make up genealogies and worlds. So let us write it down. Jill Johnston did, and so did Ray Johnson. I am following their lead and always have, even before I knew these figures. Now, through a return to these artists' work—the ephemeral shards of their previous lives—I attempt to inhabit a queer practice, a mode of being in the world that is also inventing the world. I want to assign a certain value to this move so that it resonates as something more than individual dementia. I call such a move necessarily utopian, because it is my belief that such a move is necessary in the face of the political nihilism that characterizes this present moment.

I do not wish to render a picture of utopia that is prescriptive. I want instead to connote an ideality—a desire for a thing, or a way, that is not here but is nonetheless desirable, something worth striving for. This desire does not lead to practical politics or even a practical critical practice, because pragmatism has only ever failed us. It is political pragmatism that has led us to a historical moment when the right to serve in the military and the right to participate in the suspect institution of marriage have become the gay movement's major issue. Thus, I return to the Johnston of *Marmalade*

Me and not the Johnston of *Lesbian Nation*—not because *Lesbian Nation* is not an admirable text and not because it is not important. The moment that Jill Johnston named herself and her sexual identity was important for the history of queer politics and thinking. Yet if we read that move alongside Johnston's refusal to name in *Marmalade Me*, we are faced with her salient question, "What does it mean to name something? Where do we get off giving everything a legal identity?"[10] The reader is warned that to accept this naming is to agree to "a real or pseudo-etymological exercise"[11] in which one can "uncover the hoax of a frozen legal identity which finds its way into that mausoleum called the dictionary."[12] Johnston claims that the dictionary is one of her favorite books. But how can a mausoleum be one of her favorite books? I suggest that Johnston is a Hollywood voodoo queen in the mausoleum of the dictionary, where she routinely raises the dead, calling attention to its status as fixed and frozen and magically reanimating it. This again is a queer practice worth calling attention to.

The fictional relationality of the genealogy that is a dream is performed beautifully in the work of Ray Johnson. In a typed mailing Johnson unfurls the narrative of one of the NYCS's meetings. The text reads,

> The N.Y.C.S. attacked itself and strangled itself, mutilated itself, tried to kill itself, tried to kill itself off but returns! The fetish has to be fed. The non-profit organization without a Girl Friday konked out under the weight of the fantastic network of previous structures. Very encouraging was the response from England who even came up with the London Correspondance School. David Bourdon was dropped whose valentine in part read "don't send me your emotional blackmail." Bici Henbricks told me stories about how Xenia Cage asked to be take off *her* list. Years ago, Jeanne Raynal expressed distaste at the "mailing" saying it had all been done before. Michael Malce has not been heard from in quite a while. Is he dead?[13]

That is the first paragraph of the document. The NYCS lives, or so it is announced (later Johnson wrote and submitted various obituaries announcing the death of the school). Although the school, in this report, lives, it has also apparently "konked out" under the "fantastic weight of the network of previous structures." One can therefore begin to arrive at a definition of the relational chain of the NYCS as a structure, or a network of structures. It is a structure that must resist the weight, gravity, or pull of previous structures that attempt to fatigue, challenge, and compromise the

NYCS. If the NYCS is a social formation, it is therefore one responding to previous social structures, or relational orderings, other ways of being in the world. Membership in the NYCS is like a queer kinship, an alternate chain of belonging, of knowing the other and being in the world. Some characters, such as Xenia Cage, wish to be taken off the list and therefore opt not to belong to these different relational networks. Perhaps she prefers traditional genealogies and systems of belonging.

The NYCS is not held by the same truth claims that organized previous networks or social structures. One might wonder if Johnson's reportage is based in objective reality. Did these meetings actually happen? Although the quoted statement may, in fact, be an account of some reality—many of the people did receive letters and mail art from Johnson—it is not something that can be described as objective reality. Instead it represents a queerly subjective account of the world. The narrative spun by Johnson is part of an artwork that insists on a revisionary framing of friendship, kinship, and belonging. If we consider Michel Foucault's charge that we must always be in the process of "becoming homosexual and not be obstinate in recognizing that we are" and that the homosexual must "invent from A to Z a relationship that is formless," we can begin to understand the rejection of "objective" reality proposed in the work of these queer utopian artists and writers.[14] This is a mode of objectivity to which Jill Johnston could respond. Indeed she is included in the mailed seating assignment for a proposed 1968 meeting of the group. Johnston can be found in the first column of the seventh row of a grid that included seventy-eight boxes. In these bohemian squares some of the names are still recognizable as art-world celebrities, whereas other square occupants, such as Nancy Dowd (column 1, row 3), my friend Luke's mother, was a friend of Johnson's but not a known art-world celebrity.

One way of looking at this organizing of names is in contrast with Andy Warhol's Factory and the Warholian elevation of freaks, weirdos, and social oddities to superstar status. Later, in the 1967 document, it is reported that "Andy Warhol has never been a superstar in the NYCS but Billy Linich recently received two personailty [sic] posters of Peter Fonda."[15] In this instance Johnson is pitting his NYCS map of the world against the Warhol Factory cosmology. Yet Warhol starlet Ultra Violet is included on the 1968 grid mailing alongside the young man favored with two Peter Fonda personality poster mailings, Billy Linich, also known as Billy Name. The first thing we can infer from this is that Johnson was no great fan of Warhol. The same kind of resentment or distaste toward Warhol is also articulated

Meeting-Seating

DIANE ARBUS	DORE ASHTON	BETSY BAKER	MARY BAUERMEISTER	LAURA BENSON	CAROL BERGE
PAMELA BIANCO	HELEN GURLEY BROWN	RHETT BROWN	JEAN-CLAUDE CHRISTO	SUZANNE DE MARIA	VICKI DOUGAN
NANCY DOWD	LOTTE DREW-BEAR	VIRGINIA DWAN	SUSAN ELIAS	SANDRA FEIGEN	SEVIM FESCI
VIRGINIA FRITZ	SUZI GABLIK	WANDA GAG	CHARLOTTE GILBERTSON	LILA GOODMAN	NANCY GRAVES
MRS. RONALD GROSS	HANNELORE HAHN	TINA HAHN	PIRI HALACZ	MRS. DAVID HARE	MARCIA HERSCOVITZ
EVA HESS	ALISON HIGGINS	HELEN IRANYI	HELEN JACOBSON	PATRICIA JOHANSON	MARGUERITE JOHNSON
JILL JOHNSTON	SACHA KOLIN	JILL KORNBLEE	CHRISTINE KOZLOV	ALICIA LEGG	RUTH LEVI
MRS. JULIEN LEVY	IRIS LEZAK	LUCY LIPPARD	POLLY MARSTERS	SYLVIA MILGRAM	MARTA MINUJIN
MITSOU	KARLA MUNGER	ALICE NEEL	BABETTE NEWBURGER	BETTY PARSONS	LIL PICARD
N. PIETKIEWICZ	VERONIKA PIETKJEWICZ	PRIMAROSA	FRANCES X. PROFUMO	ROBIN RICHMAN	BARBARA ROSE
LINDA ROSENKRANTZ	DOROTHY SIEBERLING	FLO SPISELMAN	TOBY SPISELMAN	N. STRUTZ	KAY SUSSMAN
MARCIA TUCKER	JOHANNA VANDERBEEK	MRS. JAN VAN DER MARCK	ELAYNE VARIAN	ULTRA VIOLET	DIANE WALDMAN
ELEANOR WARD	ANNE WEHRER	HANNAH WEINER	WILLIAM WILEY	MARION WILLARD	MAY WILSON

Ray Johnson 1968

Ray Johnson, *Seating Chart.* Courtesy of The Estate of Ray Johnson at Richard L. Feigen & Co.

by Jack Smith at different moments in his oeuvre. Johnson was present at the play orgy that was the filming of Smith's *Flaming Creatures.* This fact, the attendance of Johnson at Smith's cinematic orgy, enables me to visualize a network of queer cross-associations and influences. Smith's performances, like Ray Johnson's mad art, contained a utopian impulse that I associate with a larger circuit of queer intellectuals and artists in New York at that time. The list would include, but would certainly not be limited to, writers such as Frank O'Hara and LeRoi Jones (now the not-so-queer Amiri Baraka), O'Hara's tradey object of desire—the painter Larry Rivers, dance critic Edwin Denby, dancer Fred Herko (whose name appears in several of Johnson's posters and mailings), poet and fag hag Diane di Prima, science-fiction writer and theorist Samuel Delany, and columnist Jill Johnston. It would also include my friend Luke's father, John Dowd, who did not acquire the fame of the others in my list but would nonetheless make it onto the grid I would draw of that moment, from my perspective as queer archivist and theorist.

My cues for this critical endeavor, my approach to this material, come from my reading of Johnson and Johnston and what I understand as the cross-temporal performative reverberations of their work of the 1960s. In the parlance of the age, I am attempting to reflect a certain vibe, a structure of feeling that I understand as utopian. To that end, the work of Bloch is useful. Bloch's three-volume treatise on hope is incredibly instructive when one considers the rejection of the real that one encounters in Johnson's NYCS or the wildly associative flights of fancy that characterize Johnston's journalism. Bloch, in a published discussion with Theodor Adorno, remarks that the secret to utopia is an understanding that it must have multiple goals.[16] For example, utopia is not about simply achieving happiness or freedom; utopia is in fact a casting of a picture of potentiality and possibility. This casting or imaging is also an act of negation. What is negated is the present in lieu of another time or place. Thus, utopia has a positive valence, that of a projection forward, and a negative function, which is the work of critique.

Both Johnston's criticism and Johnson's art perform the negation that Adorno and Bloch ruminate about insofar as they, through associative protocols, chip away at the fabric of reality. This chipping away in Johnston is a casting of a picture of the future that she calls intermedia. Her notion of intermedia is worth citing at length:

> Re-integration. The everything as everything. The organism as totally illegal. The legality of nothing but pleasure. In an orgy of self-reproduction (the paramecium). The end of importance. The end of politics. The end of hierarchies. The end of families. The end of groups. The end of the earth as a penal colony (Burroughs). No end to what there can be an end of in the great reintegration: the intermedia of

the cosmic village; the intermedia of the genealogy of a vast prolific dream; the intermedia of language as the gurgling of happy infants; the intermedia of hordes of artists (all the people) making sand castles and other inanities inside and outside of their heads, or doing nothing at all. Intermedia is the world before and after we chop it up into bits of pieces and stash it away in a filing cabinet labeled MINE, YOURS, THEIRS.[17]

When I consider this far-out hippie utopianism-as-stream-of-conscious-ness it is difficult not to become pessimistic about contemporary queer politics, given that the regular lesbian columnist in today's *Village Voice* is the far right's lapdog dagger Norah Vincent, who regularly denounces progressive advances in academia in her "Higher Education" column. But Vincent is not the villain of this chapter; she, like Johnston and Johnson, is merely a representative of a moment. The point of digging and digging up, and digging, Jill Johnston and Ray Johnson is not simply to conjure them as antidotes to Vincent and other gay neoconservatives who plague the present. Rather, it is important to imagine other models of queer pres-ence in the public sphere that preceded current models. The notion of the "everything as everything" that Johnston deploys is reminiscent of John-son's seating chart and the leveling effect achieved in that work. Both of these queer culture makers are interested in art-directing the real. They offer new systems of knowing and organization. The call to end groups, hierarchies, and families is a call to replace those previous systems of clas-sification with new circuits of belonging. The NYCS is meant to replace and stand in for those previous systems. In a 1972 interview with Richard Bernstein in Andy Warhol's *Interview* magazine, Johnson explained that "the whole idea of the [New York] Correspondence School is to receive and dispense with all these bits of information, because they all refer to something else. It was just a way of having a conversation or exchange, a social intercourse."[18] Intermedia is exactly this other "social intercourse." If everything refers to something else, then the relational order of conceived reality is utterly transformed. The negation that Bloch ascribes to the uto-pian function of art exists in dialectical tension with this new ordering of epistemology (what things mean) and relationality (how the other is per-ceived). A utopian transformation is performed through Johnson's mail art process. A letter's standard temporality is that of the sender's present and the receiver's future. The letter no longer has a "here to there" trajectory. It now takes on a "here to there to there and there too" trajectory, since a piece of mail art will move between a circuit of friends and acquaintances, being altered at every point in its journey. We can call this new temporality one of queer futurity, where the future is a site of infinite and immutable potentiality. This notion of queer futurity might also be useful to an understanding of the futurity envisaged through Jill Johnston's idea of intermedia.

Taken together or separately, Johnson's intermedia practices and Johnston's idea of intermedia provide contemporary critics with models for approaching artistic practices and strategies that avoid the pitfalls of conventional disciplinarity. They help us reconsider what an archive is, what counts as evidence, and the ways in which we know the object. The queerness of both Ray Johnson and Jill Johnston during the period I am referencing has very little to do with the indexing of sexual identity (which is not to say that it is not intimately related to sexual experimentation and discovery, since they fueled the utopian impulse at that historical moment; queer sex and desire challenged standardized notions of relationality and intimacy). The work under consideration performs a queering of, as I have shown, temporality, relationality, epistemology—which is what I would describe as a world-making performativity. In this methodological performance the routinization of approach is thrown out the window in favor of vibrant collage. This open-ended collaboration also challenges the most aggressive disciplining of artworks in relation to when they are finished, incomplete, or overworked. Johnson's collage includes the ephemeral and the utopian, the fact and the anecdote. It is time to return to the source, which is to say, the site where queer energies and potentialities exploded on the world as the contemporary gay and lesbian movement.

By my clock we were queer before we were lesbian and gay. This understanding may lead to a critical looking back that may be a step forward. The past, especially the way in which it circulates in terms of relation to Ray Johnson's and Jill Johnston's biographical and cultural practices, can be instructive to queer critical and political practices that will neutralize the impasse that is the queer present, opening a portal to a queer future that would be, could be, and should be.

In closing I return to the seating chart. One of my entrances into the NYCS was column 1, row 7: Jill Johnston's box. Her notion of intermedia resonates in relation to Johnson's project in a manner that I find instructive and useful as a queer scholar and thinker. But another entrance that is equally important is column 1, row 3: Nancy Dowd's box. I find my entrance to, even my membership in, the utopian world imaged by the NYCS through a queer logic of kinship and becoming. It is through friendship and bond with Luke Dowd, who introduced me to Ray Johnson, that I situate myself and take my own seat at this gathering. Luke's art, of which a few pieces hang on the walls of my New York apartment, connect me to Johnson too. Instead of the perfectly symmetrical and graphed lines of Johnson's chart, Dowd's line art shows systems that are in collapse or disrepair. Both Dowd's and Johnson's work display the ways in which systems fail. Through Johnson's work this effect is realized by punning and tongue-in-cheek exaggeration, whereas in the art of the younger artist it is signaled through the literal collapse of graphic images.

Later, Dowd's work becomes slightly more figural. Through a stenciling technique that weirdly resonates with the experimental impulse behind Johnson's Moticos, Dowd renders beautiful images of precious gems and Koi fish. Like Johnson's collages, Dowd utilizes readily available materials such as spray paint and paper to re-create the almost mythical luster of diamonds and the otherworldly beauty of the expensive fish. On common sheets of paper, painted diamonds seem to do the opulent work of the real things, reflecting and refracting light, providing glimmers of the better life promised within the system of value in which we toil. These images are not simply representations of value. Instead they are glimpses of how value is always already a fiction to which we collectively subscribe. Form and content seem weirdly at odds. Precious stones are made dirty, common, yet they seem to retain a certain allure. They are something like the ghost of diamonds, phantom projections of the real thing that let us know the thing better than real diamonds. Diamonds are doubled, multiplied, and always cut in these frames. Dowd's process is a composition of cuts that deny the viewer a whole and singular object. The cuts allow us to see something like the essence of the diamond as a choreography of lines. The quality of the cut leaves the viewer with the raw ornamental quality of the diamond. This aesthetic strategy reminds one of the Blochian understanding of the ornamental, precisely in its rejection of utility for idealism, providing an important transport for the viewer. The ornamental in art represents a certain surplus that allow the viewer a rare and important passage that is more than an escape. Dowd's use of ornamental aesthetic captures a radical potentiality.

Like the spray-painted diamonds, the silk-screened pillow images of koi fish represent ornamental icons of value. The fish were cultivated in the Chinese Qing Dynasty and the Japanese Edo period. Koi pillows represent another perspective on value and how it is made. Stones and fish through

Luke Dowd, *Throw,* acrylic screenprint on fabric, 150 × 130 cm, 2008.

history accrue a certain kind of value that is too often taken for granted, deemed as natural. But this value is bestowed not by the individual's touch but through a larger system of value. Dowd's project illuminates the ways in which value is a fiction in which we all participate. His representations nonetheless also capture that thing in the aesthetic, that surplus, that extra, that is ultimately beyond.

My favorite piece on my apartment wall represents older work by Dowd; it is a very large painting on wood of the Silver Surfer. The Silver Surfer is a famous character from the Marvel Comics pantheon of superheroes. This painting engages me on a few levels. It certainly indexes Pop Art's interest in superhero mythology—one can look at the majesty of the Surfer in flight and think of Andy Warhol's Superman silk screens. The difference is that Superman was a dominant comic during Warhol's childhood. The sickly boy of European origins lost himself in the fantasy of this Superman who was a perfect man. I too grew up reading comics such as Marvel's *The Fantastic Four. The Fantastic Four, The X-Men,* and *Spiderman* were breaks from the grand and glowing DC Comics superhero pantheon that included characters such as Superman, Wonder Woman, and Batman—characters who were Amazons, millionaires, and super aliens. The Marvel characters broke from the previous DC model because they were

Luke Dowd, *Koi.*

real people with problems. Their powers were more curses than blessings. The Fantastic Four were a dysfunctional family, the X-Men had a certain genetic difference that made them social pariahs (like theories of the gay gene that I do not buy), and Spiderman was a fucked-up teen. The Surfer was an alien exiled to Earth, always longing to return to his homeland.

For me, a Cuban who grew up in Miami, where I was always told I was living in exile from my homeland, the Surfer's mythology resonated. Dowd's painting, then, speaks of a troubled world of superheroes both in touch with reality and defying it, not the idealized sphere of Pop Art's cartoons. The Surfer is sexy too, but not in the explicit way that Superman is. His form is perfect, but his skin is pure reflective silver. The illusion of reflection that is later mastered in the diamonds and gems is first initiated in the surface of the Silver Surfer's skin. My childhood desire for him is not Warhol's desire for this alien who looks like a hunk; it is the desire for an alien who looks like an alien, who is odd and freakish, and reflects my own freakishness back at me. I thus would like to hold up my friend's beautiful shiny painting and call attention to it as my membership card in the NYCS. It signals a desire for another way of being in the world, another way of knowing the world, and this world is one gleaming with potentiality.

8

Just Like Heaven

Queer Utopian Art and the Aesthetic Dimension

MY FATHER HATES the color green. He will not dress in green, nor will he furnish his home in the color. I grew up knowing this but not really thinking about it. Once, in the midst of my self-absorbed adolescence, I bought him a green sport shirt for Father's Day, and he reacted badly. Noticing my disappointment in his reaction to the present he quickly explained that the color green reminds him of the military, and specifically of the forced agricultural labor camp to which he was sent after he applied to move with his family from Cuba to the United States. The rest of my family immigrated in 1968, a year or two after my father had worked in that camp for seven months. He never really talks about that experience except to say that it was very difficult to be separated from his family. He will also speak of his hatred of the soldiers who oversaw him, the green of their uniform, and the general world of green that stood for the Cuban revolution. My forgetfulness on that Father's Day and my father's reaction to it foreshadowed the years of arguments that followed as my burgeoning politics became avowedly leftist and, to some relational degree, as the queer way I had chosen to live my life became undeniable.

In a way similar to my father's rejection of the color green, I have always had a strong resistance to camouflage and all it represented. I had a resistance to camouflage in art that resonated with my association of camouflage with militarism and, more specifically, U.S. foreign policy. In the same way that my father rejected the color green for its ideological connotations I could not move past my association of camouflage when I saw some hipster on the street wearing camouflage pants as part of her post-punk outfit. I felt similarly about Andy Warhol's use of camouflage. I did not like it. It was not so much that I did not get it; it was, more nearly, that I simply refused to get it. In this way I am strangely like my father. He refused to see green as a color that represented quite a few things, including, most prominently, the natural world of plants and animals. And whereas his aversion to a color is rooted in what for him is a personal and historical sense of trauma, my problems with camouflage are less grounded in experience and more about my sense of self as a political person. Camouflage, like the color green, is more than its ideologically representative uses.

Upon reading an interview with Jim Hodges I began to reconsider my position on this particular aesthetic. When Hodges is asked about the use of camouflage in his work he responds by meditating on his use of the form:

> Camouflage is a rendering of nature. This is what attracted me to it and still does. It is a manmade depiction of nature by the artist Abott Thayer. He made this observation about animal concealment and goes on to render nature in this simple reduced pattern of shadows—light and dark. I enjoy working with its source, which is nature, and then the issues that have been layered on it politically and culturally. I like loaded materials.[1]

Hodges's mention of Thayer and the origins of camouflage separate it from militarism. Thayer's book, *Concealing—Coloration in the Animal Kingdom: An Exposition of the Laws of Disguise through Color and Pattern; Being a Summary of Abbot H. Thayer's Disclosures,* had a widespread influence on the use of military camouflage during World War I.[2] Hodges's invocation of artistic and naturalist origins to what later became a technology of warfare helps us consider the way in which the form is indeed "loaded." Its meaning is also related to the next question Hodges fields about a lyric from the Laura Nyro song "Emmie." The line "you ornament the earth" speaks of the relation of art to nature in much the same way that camouflage is an artistic form that attempts to approximate nature. Hodges's interest in the way in which art touches nature helps me to reconsider my initial rejection of camouflage as a form. The linkage between nature and the ornament is compelling when considering the refusal of a certain natural order.

In this chapter I am interested in outlining a queer aesthetic dimension. Intrinsic to this discussion is a discussion of camouflage and ornament as modes of a queer aesthetic dimension. To that end I call on two sources, the artistic work of Andy Warhol and Jim Hodges and a line of German idealist thought manifest in the work of Marcuse and Bloch. Both these writers were invested in the power of the aesthetic dimension and, specifically, the utopian force of aesthetics. Utopia, in the way in which Bloch and Marcuse employ the term, is decidedly different from the dismissive invocation of naive utopianism that we encounter nowadays. Utopia in the German idealist usage is a critique of a present order, and of the overarching dictate of how things are and will always be in an unyielding status quo. I then consider the work of Warhol and Hodges as glimpses of a queer utopianism, which is to say a great refusal of an overarching here and now.

Queer Aesthetics as "Great Refusal"

It is interesting to consider Marcuse's *Eros and Civilization*, a 1955 text that anticipated 1960s countercultural movements, alongside what today might be called queerness's aesthetic. Marcuse's text, almost a blueprint for sexual liberation, contains what can only be described as an antihomophobic moment that, within its historical parameters, seems somewhat startling. In the book's eighth chapter, "The Images of Narcissus and Orpheus," the Titan Prometheus is described as a representative of what Marcuse calls the "performance principle." The performance principle, in his analysis, is a formulation that describes the conditions of alienated labor that modern man endures. Prometheus, the mythological figure who is constantly under duress and replenishing himself (a punishment for having stolen fire from the Olympian gods and delivered it to man), is juxtaposed with the images of Narcissus and Orpheus. These two kin of Dionysus stand for a different reality than that which is prescribed by the exacting rationality of the performance principle.

In mythology Narcissus was a beautiful young man who spurned "normal" sexual relations and perished. In the Ovidian telling of Narcissus's tale, the angry goddess Nemesis avenges Narcissus's rejection of the wood nymph Echo by having him fall in love with his own reflection. Unable to stop looking at himself, enraptured by his own image, the young man dies. Orpheus's tale is equally tragic. After losing his wife, Eurydice, to the god of the underworld, Hades, he rejects the love of women for relations with young men. His rejection of normal loves leads him to be ripped asunder by Maenads, female devotees of Dionysus.[3] For Marcuse, Narcissus and Orpheus represent "image[s] of joy and fulfillment; the voice which does not command but sings; the gesture which offers and receives; the deed which is peace and ends the labor of conquest; the liberation from time which unites man with god, man with nature."[4]

Although both these mythological cultural heroes' stories end in trag-edy, their images—according to Marcuse—represent the potentiality of another reality. Narcissus and Orpheus are both rehabilitated from the negative connotations that have been attached to them in the age of the performance principle and the repressive order it instantiates. At the end of the chapter an important revelation is made about Orpheus and, to a lesser degree, Narcissus:

> The classical tradition associates Orpheus with the introduction of homosexuality. Like Narcissus, he rejects the normal Eros, not for an aesthetic ideal, but for a fuller Eros. Like Narcissus, he protests against the repressive order of procreative sexuality. The Orphic and narcissis-tic Eros is to the end of the negation of this order—The Great Refusal. In the world symbolized by the culture hero Prometheus, it is the end of all order; but in this negation Orpheus and Narcissus reveal a new reality, with an order of its own, governed by different principles. The Orphic Eros transforms being: he masters cruelty and death through liberation. His language is song, and his work is play. Narcissus' life is that of beauty, and his existence is contemplation. These images refer to the aesthetic dimension as the one in which their reality principle must be sought and validated.[5]

The linkage of the Orphic to homosexuality and Narcissism to nonprocre-ative sexuality aligns both mythopoetic categories with an aesthetic proto-col that I would call queerness. In this instance I am describing queerness as "The Great Refusal" that Marcuse delineates, which is a refusal of what, once again, Marcuse calls the performance principle. More concretely, this refusal that I describe as queerness is not just homosexuality but the rejec-tion of normal love that keeps a repressive social order in place.

Eros and Civilization delineates three governing principles: the plea-sure principle, which represents Eros and play; the reality principle, which stands for labor; and finally the performance principle, which dominates the contemporary moment within which we strive. A quick translation of the performance principle would cast it as the way in which a repressive social order is set in place by limiting the forms and quantity of pleasure that the human is allowed. The performance principle is the way in which the dynamism between the pleasure principle and the reality principle are ordered. It most succinctly means, "Men do not live their own lives but perform preestablished functions. While they work, they do not fulfill their own needs and faculties but live in alienation."[6] Queerness, as I am describing it here, is more than just sexuality. It is this great refusal of a performance principle that allows the human to feel and know not only our work and our pleasure but also our selves and others.

In *Eros and Civilization* the aesthetic and the surplus it provides can potentially stand against the coercive practicality of the performance principle. A queer aesthetic can potentially function like a great refusal because art manifest itself in such a way that the political imagination can spark new ways of perceiving and acting on a reality that is itself potentially changeable. I look to two artists: one whose work is located in the past or, as philosopher Ernst Bloch would call it, the "no-longer-conscious" and the other who makes work in the present. Andy Warhol and Jim Hodges thus represent two moments in queer aesthetics that represent artistic practices that I see as being associated with the mythopoetic forces of Orpheus and Narcissus. These qualities of their work represent a joyful contemplation, a turn to the ludic and a lyrical as a response to the domination of the performance principle.

The Dance of Silver Clouds

Andy Warhol's *Sliver Clouds* were first created as a set design for Merce Cunningham's *RainForest.* That dance was first staged in 1968, a year that is best known to many people as the pinnacle of political unrest and activist zeal. Cunningham's companion, the composer John Cage, was involved with the music for the piece, and Jasper Johns worked on costumes. At the time of this collaboration none of these avant-garde luminaries was "out"; some of them never came out and refused to comment on their private lives. They are all cultural producers of aesthetic projects that I nonetheless associate with Marcuse's "Great Refusal" and what, after Marcuse's theory, I am describing as queer utopian aesthetics.

The production included six dancers in ripped leotards that represent animal-like avatars of another world, and the floating clouds standing in for trees represent the forest itself. Both Warhol and Cunningham are artists known for the reappropriation and refunctioning of the commonplace. That is to say that in the same fashion that everyday movement becomes dance in Cunningham, a pillow becomes a floating silver icon in Warhol's art practice. And within the nexus of their collaboration a floating silver pillow becomes a cloud in the enchanted *RainForest.* In this way there is something both Orphic and Narcissistic about the *RainForest* and the silver pillows that compose it.

Marcuse values both the Narcissus and Orpheus experience of the world because they both negate that which sustains the alienating life models presented by the performance principle. The pleasure principle can certainly envelop gay identities—especially those that are content to ape heterosexual social conventions and modes of being in the world. But there is a certain liberation of Eros that I am describing as not only queerness but also a queer utopianism that again, though not exclusively about gay or lesbian sexuality, certainly embraces experimental modes of love, sex, and relationality. This queer utopianism is a great refusal, and it is emblematized in the figures of Narcissus and Orpheus. Marcuse writes,

> They have not become the cultural heroes of the Western World: theirs is the image of joy and fulfillment; the voice which does not command but sings; the gesture which offers and receives; the deed which is peace and ends the labor of conquest; the liberation from time which unites man with god, man with nature.[7]

Marcuse takes the image of Narcissus not from Freudian libido theory, in which he stands in for pathologic perversion, but from mythology, in which "his silence is not of dead rigidity; and when he is contemptuous of love of hunters and nymphs he rejects Eros for another. He lives by an Eros of his own, and he does not love only himself." Marcuse goes on to explain that although Narcissus loves his own image, he does not know it is himself, and that love is also mitigated by his love of nature. At myth's end, after Narcissus's death, he is transformed into a flower. Narcissus's love is an interruption in the pleasure principle. He represents what Marcuse calls a Nirvana principle, which consists of "the redemption of pleasure, the halt of time, the absorption of death; silence, sleep, night, paradise."[8] This Nirvana principle, which represents transformative life in the face of controlled and repressed life, invokes the concept of Nirvana, the highest happiness in Buddhist thought, for the purpose of describing an ideality that is akin to the utopian in German idealist thought. The aesthetic projects of Warhol and Hodges aim to envision a Nirvana principle, which is queer and utopian, and stages a great interruption.

We can thus consider Warhol's silver pillows, which are also trees in Cunningham's *RainForest*, as components in a Narcissistic scene: to gaze into the pillows' reflective surface is to participate in the modality of

Installation, Reprint 1994, *Silver Clouds* (Warhol Museum Series), 1994, refabricated for The Andy Warhol Museum in cooperation with The Andy Warhol Foundation for the Visual Arts, Inc.; and Billy Klüver, 1994, helium-filled metalized plastic film (Scotchpak), 36 × 51 in. (91.4 × 129.5 cm), Andy Warhol (artist), Billy Klüver (contributor), Manufactured by CTI Industries Corp., Barrington, IL, The Andy Warhol Museum, Pittsburgh, © 2008 The Andy Warhol Foundation for the Visual Arts/ARS, New York.

contemplation that is an interruption in the mandates to labor, toil, and sacrifice that the performance principle prescribes. Narcissism in Warhol's cosmology would also reject a strictly Freudian condemnation of the practice. Warhol's practice of portraiture was vast and expansive. His list of "portraits" includes countless celebrity portraits, such as those of Jackie Kennedy, and the screen tests of his army of superstars and friends, as well as various self-portraits, with wigs or through the screen of camouflage. I would add the silver pillows to this list of experiments in portraiture. Onstage during Cunningham's *RainForest* they represent reflective pools to all the dancers who interact with them. In a similar fashion they offer museum visitors their very own portraits of self and their own private pools of contemplation, thus allowing the audience to enter the "stage" themselves.

If we think of the silver pillows as they float in the museum space as moving pools of meditation and self-contemplation, we begin to understand that they also serve a critical function because they invite the person engaging to contemplate self and perhaps participate in a self-critique. Critique, from Kant to Marx and beyond, is described as having self-analysis as a first moment. Seeing oneself in the moving and luminous surface of the pillow is to see oneself in a different life, in a different world. It is like seeing one's imaginary reflection in a comic-book hero's silver skin or the artificial luster of painted gems that I discussed in the previous chapter.

The fact that these playful globes also take the form of pillows is worth noting. Pillows reflect rest and respite, as opposed to forced activity and work. They also represent the realm of dreams and imagination. We can then think of these silver pillows as glittering and hovering celebrations of both rest and play, of liberation from a coercive work ethic. We can also think of the kinetic nature of these pillows. They are both pools of self-contemplation and trees in a forest. In the myth of Narcissus he communes with nature to the degree that he makes the impossible happen. That dynamic is present in both the Orphic and Narcissistic, since "Eros awakens and liberates potentialities that are real in things that are animate and inanimate. In organic and inorganic nature—real but in the un-erotic reality repressed."[9] The sway of the airborne pillow thus represents the animating force of the unreality that is promised by the Narcissistic, an unreality that is most poignant for the way it promotes a poetic contemplation of the world that can see past the screen of a coercive performance principle that rigidly structures both our work and play.

We see nature animated in both Warhol's and Hodges's use of camouflage. For both artists camouflage is an aesthetic production that does more than duplicate nature's form. In their practice it is a form that addresses nature's relation to man. In its utilitarian usage this structure of address was limited to hunting and militarism. But once it moves to the realm of the aesthetic the form is reactivated and made to perform in ways that do not correspond to the coercive and pragmatic structures of the performance principle. Warhol's camouflage painting from 1987 utilizes the bold and decidedly unnatural day-glow colors associated with the countercultural moment in which the artist first became famous. In these images the natural world that is usually, to some degree, the thing being invoked by camouflage is rendered impossible or utterly unnatural. Queer aesthetics attempt to call the natural into question. The Orphic and Narcissistic represent a queer potentiality within the realm of the natural that

Paintings, 1986, *Self-Portrait*, acrylic and silkscreen ink on linen, 40 × 40 in. (101.6 × 101.6 cm), Andy Warhol (artist), The Andy Warhol Museum, Pittsburgh; Founding Collection, Contribution, The Andy Warhol Foundation for the Visual Arts, Inc., © 2008 The Andy Warhol Foundation for the Visual Arts/ARS, New York.

has been diminished by a certain ordering or perhaps even a hijacking of the natural. Warhol's camouflage attempts to bring out a radical impossibility in the world of the natural.

In Warhol's somewhat garish camouflage painting we see a desire to reproduce nature with a difference, with a desire to entertain the impossibility of another world, of a different time and place, where that natural represents a queer potentiality that is rendered unimaginable in the straight time and place of the performance principle. Jim Hodges's beautiful *Oh Great Terrain* can be seen as both a continuation of Warhol's approach to camouflage and entirely it own advancement in the aesthetic project of picturing a queer utopian "wish-landscape." This camouflage resembles what has come to be known as "urban camouflage," employing an array of blacks, whites, and various shades of gray. But Hodges's painting animates camouflage and shuttles it from the real of the pragmatic to the idealistic. The painting represents a certain kinesthesia, a swirl of movement around a centrifugal core where the components of the camouflage landscape seem to be whirling to or out of a center. The shards of blacks, whites, and grays seem to be part of a large choreography of great magnitude. The effect gives *Oh Great Terrain* a sense of perspective that is not anticipated in relation to camouflage as a mode of painting and design. The pattern becomes something else in Hodges's piece. Suddenly camouflage incorporates a sense of distance and closeness. Ernst Bloch wrote powerfully of the utopian force in painting as the rendering of what he called a wish-landscape. In Bloch's analysis he focused on more directly representational painters such as Van Eyck, Leonardo, and Rembrandt, using this notion of a wish-landscape to discuss these historical figurative painters. Provisionally, I import this concept to describe aspects of Hodges's queer utopian aesthetic practice. Bloch describes the wish-landscape in his philosophical and lyrical parlance:

> That distance, which leaves the view unobstructed, which does not hide anything, is richer in objects. Even where the painted view lies in the mists, there is not determination but, rather, a standard set particularly for the vastness. As soon as this world, instead of heaven, began to become infinite, the wish-landscape as open distance appeared in paintings. . . . The point where the lines of perspective meet lies an infinity; the lines running in the middle section go beyond a horizon. The figures enclose something new: a centrifugal space. Thus already at the middle ages vastness, a vastness of wish.[10]

In Hodges's painting the lines swirl around a centrifugal space, but they nonetheless establish both a sense of horizon and a beyond the horizon, wherein lies potentiality, hope, and utopia. A natural representational order as restrictive directive is being redeployed as dancing artifice that disrupts the tyranny of nature as a coercive mechanism. *Oh Great Terrain* offers a sense of vastness that is Orphic and Narcissistic in that the artist remakes the natural in a fashion that enables the viewer to envision a new world. Marcuse explains that "trees and animals respond to Orpheus' language; the spring and the forest respond to Narcissus' desire."[11]

Queerness as lyric and modality are thus potentially transformative of a natural order, allowing for new horizons and a vastness of potentiality. We can now look back at Cunningham's choreography for *RainForest* to consider the ways in which the drama it staged in 1968 deployed a choreography that mimicked and animated the kinesthesia of the natural world. We can also look to Warhol's shining helium-filled sculptures as akin to the beautiful swirling choreography of gesture, color, and shade in *Oh Great Terrain.*

Landscapes of Ornamentation

Hodges's take on landscape is similar to the way in which the practice of portraiture is expanded and transformed in Warhol's art practice. Camouflage is linked to the concept of landscape, and it too is, in the terms Hodges used to describe camouflage, "loaded." The Nobel Prize–winning author J. M Coetzee has described the power of landscape writing in his native South Africa to represent the elision and degradation of an African presence in the service of propping up and justifying the white settlers' colonial endeavor.[12] Landscape art depicts a natural order, but it does not do so neutrally. Landscape art represents the ways in which the world should look, feel, and be. Hodges's take on landscape is viewed most immediately in the camouflage work I described in the preceding section. But he also uses other modes to render the natural world and the human's place in it. Take, for example, a 1998 piece titled *Landscape.* This piece links conceptually recalibrated notions of both portraiture and landscape. A seemingly starched white dress shirt is laid out on a table. Upon closer inspection the white shirt's collar contains concentric circles of different fabrics of various colors and patterns. These appear to be the collars of other shirts. The piece resembles the consolidation of a wardrobe, and through that an amalgamation of shards and pieces—both material and affective—that represent a life. In this way the work is reminiscent of the work of Hodges's friend, the deceased artist Félix González-Torres. González-Torres would use a series of dates and words, painted on the walls of a room, to represent a portrait of the person he was "painting." Words and dates render a highly subjective portrait of a subject that is nonetheless historically nuanced.

Landscape could be the discarded shirts of the artist himself or of a friend or of an acquaintance or perhaps of a lover. But the piece is called *Landscape* and not *Portrait,* and thus one needs to consider that these shards of a life represented through fabric also have a spatial connotation. The painting represents a life as a landscape. The life of a tree is deciphered through an examination of the rings in a trunk or stump that becomes part of a landscape. Men's shirts touch other men's shirts, setting a tonality that is not only about the landscape of a person's inner life but also about the various intimacies connoted by the collision of one's wardrobe touching another's apparel.

Famously, González-Torres represented loss of the beloved, in both a personal and societal register, through a picture repeated on multiple billboards depicting an unmade bed and the indentation left by two absent bodies. In a similar fashion both co-presence and absence are the queer landscape rendered by Hodges's piece. Men's shirts swirl together in a landscape suggesting another world of intimacy that is akin to both the Orphic and the Narcissistic and the interruption of the "here and now" that they promise.

Hodges's mirror work, such as the piece *Great Event,* also promises another wish-landscape. Tiny pieces of mirror connect on canvas in the shape of a circle. One immediate connotation is the disco ball and the world of play, dance, and exuberance it represents. Here the world of salvation on the dance floor is conjured. But the mirrored orb also has other connotations. It can be understood as an aerial perspective of a great glittering landscape. It can appear to be something like a demographic or population-density map of a queer utopia. Oscar Wilde's famous quip, which I have previously cited, that "a map of the world that does not include Utopia is not worth glancing at"[13] is again relevant when considering all of Hodges's landscape and camouflage art. Like *Silver Clouds,* Hodges's work represents idealistic renderings of a natural world. The art functions as a manipulation of nature's vastness and thus a site of contemplation and critique.

The Orphic and the Narcissistic converge in Hodges's mirror camouflage piece *Into the Stream IV.* In that piece another exuberant whirl of lines connotes the effect of a reimagined and vibrant natural world. It is reminiscent of another piece by González-Torres, *Untitled (Orpheus Twice) 1991,* which consists of two large door-size mirrors placed next to each other. In that piece one glimpses a convergence of Narcissus's representative symbol par excellence—yet the title's parenthetical component indexes Orpheus's name. González-Torres, like Marcuse, seems to link directly both the Orphic and the Narcissistic. Along with Marcuse and Bloch, González-Torres was a thinker involved in the project of staging a great refusal. When discussing one of his famous stacks, this time a stack of white paper that audiences were encouraged to take with them, he wrote in a note to his gallerist, Andrea Rosen, on February 14, 1992,

> The other day I was still thinking about the piece and how it fulfills me now even more. You know the title: (*Passport*) is very crucial and significant—a white empty blank uninscribed piece of paper, an untouched feeling, an undiscovered experience. A passport to another place, to another life, to a new beginning, to chance; to the chance of meeting the other who makes life a moving force, a chance to alter one's life and future, an empty passport for life: to inscribe it with the best, the most painful, the most banal, the most sublime, and yet to inscribe it with life, love, memories, fears, voids and unexpected reasons for being. A simple white object against a white wall, waiting.[14]

A blank white sheet of paper may seem to be the opposite of a mirror—one depicts nothing, and the other depicts whatever catches its reflection. But the idea of a passport and transport beyond the here brings to mind the world of transport that is represented in Lewis Carroll's looking glass. The looking glass in González-Torres and Hodges is thus the threshold for a certain transport. Gazing into the reflective surface is more than just self-appreciation but also a mode of contemplation that allows the spectator to be conscious of the coercive force of the performance principle. This looking at a mirror is thus an act that works like the symbolic passport; it speaks of a critical imagination that begins with self-analysis and a vaster social critique of how the world could be and indeed should be.

Laura Nyro's voice and her song are about the need to ornament the world, an impulse that resonates in the work of Félix González-Torres, Jim Hodges, and Andy Warhol. The desire to render the world as ornamented is the desire to see past the limits of the performance principle. Marcuse explained that people suffer from a surplus repression within the performance principle. He is clear that some repression is necessary, that we would perish in a hedonist avalanche if we did not let the reality principle (the need to work, to sustain the self materially) check the pleasure principal to some degree. The performance principle is a surplus of this repression that excessively mitigates the realm of pleasure in the service of societal normalization and control.

When one looks at Warhol's early works from the 1950s one grasps a gilded world of homoerotic desire that registers the unfolding of a line of utopian thought, a desire for a place and time that was not imaginable for men who desired men. The rich accentuation of hearts and gold-leaf paint render a world of ornamentation. In one picture beautiful shoes abound, each of them named after a friend, and the dedication on the bottom of the images reads, "to all my friends." Male lovers kiss. A boy painted in gold leaf looks up provocatively—he seems to be laying on his stomach. In another piece one man's hand seems to clutch his own genitals, coyly concealing them. In still another image, a line drawing, a flower and a leaf frame a cock, balls, and pubic hair. The field of one ballpoint-pen drawing depicts rows and rows of hearts that are repeated with the initials "CL" on two hearts. One is left to speculate about who CL may be. (It was the actor Charles Lisanby.) A self-portrait of the artist's face is adorned with stars, half-moons, and birds in flight. This work, which was produced years before what is touted as gay liberation, is the ornamented and gilded world of a daydreamer.

Within the ethos of the performance principle there is no time or place for lusty and romantic imaginings of the type found in these Warhol images. That is precisely why Bloch, for instance, values daydreaming and sees it doing the work of imaging another life, another time, another place—a version of heaven on earth that is not simply denial or distraction but a communicative and collective mode of transport that helps one think of another place where our Eros is not conscripted in the fashion that civilization demands. Daydreaming, like the ornament, represents a reactivation of the erotic imaginary that is not limited to sexual fantasies, though it includes them, but is more nearly about a fuller capacity for love and relationality, a capacity that is queer in its striking insistence on a great refusal. The Orphic and Narcissistic elements that are manifest throughout the work of the young Andy Warhol are his oeuvre at its most pronounced and joyfully resonant.

Along with these images of boys and hearts in Warhol's work we also have various images of flowers. Here the story of Narcissus once again comes to mind, as we consider his eventual fate, in which he is transformed into a flower. Warhol's silk-screened flowers of 1964 are lush and beautiful as the blurring of the process gives them a nebulous quality that in some way is anticipatory of the *Silver Clouds* that followed them. There are countless flowers throughout Warhol's work of the 1950s, but one is especially interesting. That is the drawing of a flower emerging from a bottle of Coca-Cola. The bottle of Coca-Cola is repeated throughout Warhol's career and is indicative of his Campbell's Soup can strategy, in which he brings to light the aesthetic dimension of everyday commodities. But in this image the Coke bottle is not an isolated mass-produced commodity; it is touched by a flower that springs forth much in the same way that a transformed Narcissus blooms as a flower. This brings to mind the moment in Andy Warhol's Philosophy that I mention in this books' introduction, in which he identifies a radically democratic and even utopian component in the mass-produced commodity. That Warholian notion of a radical idea of democracy via commodity form, taken alongside the image of the flowering Coco-Cola bottle, a natural surplus that surges forth from the apparently sterile container, illustrates Warhol's particular version of the queer utopian impulse. The Coke bottle is the everyday material that is represented in a different frame, laying bare its aesthetic dimension and the potentiality it represents. In its everyday manifestation such an object would represent the alienated production, consumption, and labor that is the realm of the performance principle. But for Warhol, as for Cunningham, González-Torres, and Hodges, the utopian exists in the everyday, and through an aesthetic practice that I am calling queer, the aesthetic endeavor that reveals the inherent utopian possibility is always in the horizon.

Elsewhere I have discussed the ways in which Warhol and his friend and sometimes collaborator Jean-Michel Basquiat disidentified with commodity culture through the practice of Pop Art.[15] In queer utopian aesthetic practice this disidentification is in the service of a project that is critically utopian.

I began this chapter by considering my father and his aversion to a color. I described this rejection of green as having to do with the rejection of a revolution that was for some people, but not all, a failure. I have spent much of my life arguing with my father about revolutions, in relation to both politics and Eros. The Cuban revolution of 1959 signaled a utopian moment that is squarely in the past. Roughly ten years later the Stonewall rebellion became the signal of contemporary gay liberation. In much the same way that many people think the Cuban socialist revolution succumbed to totalitarianism, I consider gay liberation to have strayed from its earlier idealism. From my vantage point the contemporary gay and lesbian movement has become assimilationist and content to follow the path laid out by the performance principle. It is important not to be content to let failed revolutions be merely finite moments. Instead we should consider them to be the blueprints to a better world that queer utopian aesthetics supply. Silver clouds, swirls of camouflage, mirrors, a stack of white sheets of paper, and painted flowers are passports allowing us entry to a utopian path, a route that should lead us to heaven or, better yet, to something just like it.

9

A Jeté Out the Window

Fred Herko's Incandescent Illumination

SURPLUS VALUE IS a loaded concept. Its origins exist in Marxian political economy. Surplus value is the value of work done or commodities produced that exceeds what a worker needs. It is the source of profits for the capitalist in bourgeois society. The process of production is essentially the production of surplus value. Within capitalism surplus value becomes profit in the form of capital for the capitalist, and it is at the expense of the alienated worker. This strict economic understanding of surplus value is transformed when we consider aesthetic theory. In Ernst Bloch's work, surplus becomes that thing in the aesthetic that exceeds the functionalism of capitalist flows. This supplementary value, which is at times manifest as aesthetic excess and at other times as a sort of deviance from conventional forms, conveys other modes of being that do not conform to capitalist maps of the world. Bloch understands art as enacting a "preappearance" in the world of another mode of being that is not yet here. In this chapter I examine the work of Fred Herko, a choreographer and performer affiliated with many countercultural performance groups, primarily the Judson Memorial Church, as both a choreography of surplus and a choreography of minor movements. I do so in an effort to frame Herko's movement as utopian traces of other ways of moving within the world. In this sense the notion of surplus I am invoking is also akin to Antonio Negri's nuanced description of surplus value as an uncontrollable and potentially disruptive integer within late capitalism's formulations.[1] Thus, I write about a surplus in movement that does not simply align itself with abundance for the capitalist but instead, to borrow Andre Lepecki's useful formulation, involves kinesthetic stuttering, that represents a problem within modernity's compulsory dance steps.[2] Herko, as I show in this chapter, represents movement that not only stutters but twitches, vamps, leaps uncontrollably, and ultimately whirls out of control into the void.

Central to this underground figure's subcultural legacy is his final performance, his suicide. Herko's suicide was staged as a performance, with only one unsuspecting friend in attendance. Herko, who was then known as a major figure in New York's queer avant-garde but who was somewhat homeless, took a bath in the Cornelia Street, Greenwich Village, apartment of his friend, the Judson lighting designer Johnny Dodd. After emerging from his bath, Herko did a nude dance in front of his friend while Mozart's Coronation Mass in C Major played. The dance was described as typical of Herko's whirling excess. We can perhaps decipher "typical" to mean a highly energetic mixture between the postmodern dance that worried the divide between theatrical and quotidian movement and an excessively campy, neoromantic style. Its conclusion, his leap out the window to his death, was an exemplary theatrical act bridging camp excess and real life (or, in this case, death) movement. Years later, when Dodd was finally able to talk about the incident, he described the leap as a perfect jeté. No part of Herko's body touched the window frame.[3] This suicide took place four years after Yves Klein's famous fake "Leap into the Void" and a year after Buddhist monk Quang Duc gained fame when he was photographed setting himself on fire in a suicide protest against the Vietnam War. We cannot know how or even if these performances influenced Herko's final leap. I nonetheless invoke them as a possible backdrop to Herko's "excessive" final act.

Herko's ultimate performance is legendary in different subcultural worlds. Speed freaks throughout the world can understand Herko's dramatic gesture even if they do not know his name. His imprint lingers in queer experimental art movements. I am interested in the traces left by Herko. By traces I mean different lines of thought, aesthetics, and political reverberations trailing from this doomed young artist. To approach one's object of study in the way I write about Herko is implicitly to make the argument that the work of queer critique is often to read outside official documentation. This chapter follows three important engagements with Herko's work authored by three eminent dance scholars: Sally Banes in *Democracy's Body* (1983, reprinted 1993), Susan Leigh Foster's essay "Improvising/History" (2003), and Ramsay Burt's *Judson Dance Theater* (2006). These three leading dance scholars have understood Herko's relevance to dance history. While I draw on the performance descriptions these three books offer, I want also to align Herko with the larger pantheon of sixties countercultural and queer artists. To that end, I also draw from considerations of Herko's film work for Andy Warhol, a film by Elaine Summers that actually depicts Herko performing, and other ephemeral items such as his résumé and glossy photos that I encountered while doing research in the Downtown Collection at New York University's Fales Library. Indeed much of Herko's story is located in ephemera, archives where "another history," queerness's history, can be glimpsed.

Gay and lesbian studies is often too concerned with finding the exemplary homosexual protagonist. This investment in the "positive image," in proper upstanding sodomites, is a mistake that is all too common in many discourses on and by "the other." The time has come to turn to failed visionaries, oddballs, and freaks who remind queers that indeed they always live out of step with straight time. Thus, this drug-addled dervish should have a central role in a queer performance studies. Herko's presence in/absence from queerness's history functions as a Blochian no-longer-conscious, which is to say a place and time in which potentiality flourished and was extinguished. Yet its example nonetheless promises a return, a reanimation, in a future time and place, a not-yet-here. There is no more appropriate example of extinguished yet animating queer potentiality than the case of this neoromantic dead gay speed freak and his inscrutable aura.

It is important in presenting Herko's case to be attentive to his relationship to life, death, and art as a radical understanding of the naturalized hierarchies and epistemologies that organize these concepts. Death is often viewed in Western thought as quintessentially antiutopian because it absolutely defines the end of potentiality. But to make "death art," especially in the flamboyant manner that Herko did, is to move beyond death as finitude. Herko's final queer act helps us look at queer life and cultural labor as resonating beyond traditional notions of finitude. His suicide is the first performance I describe in this chapter, but I do not stop there. Indeed, I want to contextualize his short and colorful oeuvre in an attempt to further explicate queer utopian performance and performativity.

In *POPism: The Warhol '60s* (1980), Andy Warhol and Pat Hackett explained that the people Warhol really liked most were show-business dropouts such as Herko.[4] Herko came to New York to study piano at Julliard. He did not take up dance until he was nearly twenty years old. He met the poet Diane di Prima in Washington Square Park, becoming her muse and best friend. Di Prima edited the groundbreaking literary journal *The Floating Bear* with her then-lover LeRoi Jones. Herko and avant-garde jazz musician Cecil Taylor stapled the first few issues. Taylor was Herko's accompanist during the first Judson Memorial Church dance concert, for a duet entitled *Like Most People: For Soren*. We are left to imagine what the relationality between these queer avant-gardists looked like. Susan Leigh Foster speculates that their love of ballet and homosexuality may have trumped the racial differences that these artists might have felt in the Cage-influenced art world of modern dance. More often than not, the Judson's postmodernism is associated with work that can be described as minimalist, such as that of Yvonne Rainer. But as descriptions and commentary on Herko's dance practice indicate, there is nothing minimalist about his practice. Indeed Herko's work, work that di Prima described as neoromanticism, was excessive, campy, and in Bloch's sense of the word *ornamental*.

For Bloch the function of the ornamental surpassed the merely aesthetic. Functional form is aligned with a normalized spatial and temporal mapping of the world, whereas the expressive exuberance of the ornament promises something else—another time and place that is not hamstrung by the present. Herko wore insane outfits and performed at a very high level of faggy flamboyance that could only be understood as expressive exuberance. Herko represented a crossroads between postmodern dance and other emerging queer subcultures. Later he was also a luminary in the freaked-out amphetamine subculture of what many participants and memoirists called "the Mole People," a group of queer men and straight women who established a circuit of belonging in relation to drug use and opera.[5] Herko would also perform as part of Fluxus, playing a comb in a concert by John Cage disciple George Brecht. But it was not the minimalism of plucking the teeth of a comb onstage for which Herko was known. Herko was known for elaborate costumes, erratic and beautiful movement, and decidedly eccentric comportment.

Herko's camp theatrics are always mentioned when he is included in the history of postmodern dance.[6] In many ways he did not conform with the aesthetic codes that dominated the movements of which he was a part. His flamboyance made him something of a difficult subject for some audiences and critics of his day, as well as for today's cultural historians. I suggest that it is also his politics that render him difficult to deal with. The political valence of his work is that of cultural/aesthetic surplus of queer potentiality. Al Carmines, associate minister at Judson, described the ways in which Herko stuck out from his contemporaries at the Judson: "Fred Herko seemed to me the most 'out' of the general tempo and style of the dance theater as a whole. His work was often piquant and ironically flamboyant, with cadenzas of pure lyrical movement. His work tended to be more directly commentary-like than most of the other dancers."[7] Carmines's comment differentiates Herko's work from that of the other dancers for primarily aesthetic reasons; yet I nonetheless suggest that it was indeed the critique implicit in the work, the "commentary-like" nature of the aesthetic practice, that marked Herko. The fact that Herko invoked a style that I am describing as "ornamental," as distinct from the composed intensity of Yvonne Rainer or David Gordon (two dancers with whom Herko began dancing in choreographer James Waring's classes), does not separate him too much from the Judson Dance Theater project. Herko's ornamental style, impulsive and extravagant, denaturalizes movement, sometimes through excess and sometimes through a certain stuttering off-courseness, in a way analogous to the reframing of everyday movement performed by Rainer and Gordon. Both the more avowedly minimalist work of the majority of Judson artists and Herko's ornamental and fairy-tale-like performances denaturalize movement, theatrical and quotidian. To denaturalize the way we dwell (move) in the world is to denaturalize the world itself in favor of a utopian performativity.

Yet denaturalization is not in and of itself utopian. At the risk of seeming reductive, the differences between both styles of Judson performance are most apparent in Judson choreographer Elaine Summers's film *Fragments* (*Judson Dance*). Summers's film offers glimpses into the world of Judson Dance intercut with shots of children at play, traffic in the city, some animation, and nature scenes. Cut into the fifteen-minute experimental film are vignettes of Herko walking out the front door of an apartment building with a large oval watering can. Each time he walks out he completes the same chore of watering the garbage cans that line the front of the building. The enactment of such a quotidian act certainly jives with one aspect of the Judson project, but the absurdity of watering garbage cans locates it squarely in Herko's domain. Furthermore, Herko is sometimes costumed in an odd cape, and sometimes he is wearing nothing but skimpy briefs, leather boots, and a sort of Greek fisherman's hat. His movement itself is ordinary, as if watering the trash is exactly what one does in the morning. Herko does seem to be aware of the fact that he looks good. He preens for the camera. Each time Herko appears, he is more dressed up. By the end of the film he walks out in what must have been one of the elaborate performance outfits for which he was so noted: a large fur coat; a tight, seemingly velvet suit; and a big hat. This time when he waters the first can a large bundle of daisies pop up—thanks to the magic of in-camera film editing. Then as he waters the cans different bouquets of flowers spring out of them. Herko picks some flowers and then nonchalantly discards them. He stares at the camera as the sequence ends, just at the end of the whole film. So Herko's quotidian action yields utopian results. This queer little garden in the gutter nicely corresponds to what Bloch called "utopian wish-landscapes," animating the desire for a time and place that is not yet here.[8]

One of Herko's earlier performances, a solo included on the bill for the first Judson Memorial Church dance concert, *Once or Twice a Week I Put on Sneakers and Go Uptown,* was meant to ridicule the culture of straight proper citizens who would go slumming downtown. The piece's critique is implicit in its title, as it alludes to the reversal of a phenomenon in which slumming uptowners dress in casual footwear to go downtown to watch the bohemian freakshow. Or perhaps alternatively we might think of fey art boys going uptown to Harlem and attempting to mix in that lifeworld. If Herko's going uptown meant that uptown, echoing the drug motif in his life, then the movement might not have been scored to Cecil Taylor or Erik Satie but to the soundtrack of Lou Reed's wailing about going uptown to meet his (pusher) man.

Keeping all these potential readings of the title in play, there are a few descriptions of this legendary performance worth considering. They are all cited first by Banes in *Democracy's Body* and later by Susan Foster. This chapter is indebted to that early research by Banes and attempts to add to it a queer performance analysis for the purpose of thinking about Herko as a source of queer utopian aesthetics. Banes cites a trio of critics from the period, starting with Allen Hughes:

> Fred Herko came out dressed in multi-colored bath or beach robe with a veil of lightweight metal chains covering his head and face. . . . One's attention was riveted to his dance, which was no more than a kind of unvaried shuffling movement around the floor to the accompaniment of a piano piece by Erik Satie (Satie, incidentally, would have loved it). . . . This was "Sneakers" dance, but Mr. Herko was barefoot all the while.[9]

Jill Johnston paid attention to Herko's quotidian movement:

> Herko did a barefoot Suzie-Q in a tassel-veil head-dress, moving around the big open performance area . . . in a semi circle, doing only the barefoot Suzie-Q with sometimes a lazy arm snaking up and collapsing down . . . [and] with no alteration of pace or movement.[10]

Less approving was Herko's colleague dancer/choreographer Bill Paxton, who was not only on the same bill but was also on the program's publicity committee:

> It seemed very campy and self conscious, which wasn't at all my interest. As I remember he was a collagist with an arch performance manner. You would get some ballet movement, none of it very high energy. Maybe a few jetés every now and then. As a dancer his real forte was so very, very elegant lines. But in terms of actual movement, transitions from one well-defined place to another, he did it very nervously. Holding a position is what he did more than moving from place to place.[11]

Banes reports on all three reactions but does not take a stand in relation to these different perspectives. I, on the other hand, follow a theoretical agenda of my own making. What turned Paxton off ignites my imagination, reminding me of what Donald McDonagh describes as Herko's incandescence,[12] a word I employ in this chapter's title because it indexes my desire and investment in this lost object, this man who represents a no-longer-conscious. To describe Herko as incandescent is to regard him as a lost object that provides an anticipatory illumination of another world. Paxton's descriptions help me see Herko as close to Jack Smith's wonderfully arch, layered, and fecund performance practice.[13] Herko, according to Paxton, appears to parallel Smith's paradoxically languid and kinetic theatricalism.

I wonder if Smith ever attended a Judson show or if Herko ever went to one of Smith's legendary loft performances. Queer theater legend John Vaccaro indicated to Dominic Johnson that since Smith and Herko shared friends and acquaintances such as drag star Frances Francine and di Prima, they must have known each other. Gerard Forde, a researcher working on a Herko biography, informed me of the fact that Smith designed costumes for Frank O'Hara's *Loves Labor* (February 14–March 8, 1964) in which Herko played the role of Paris. Both artists incorporated failure into their oeuvre in compelling ways. Dominic Johnson links Herko's and Smith's work through what he calls a politics of failure: "Posing the queer thought of *a politics of failure*, these projects perform collisions between the pitiful and the stoic, the majestic and the wretched, the horrific and the laughable."[14] This point of collision in the work of both artists, queer failure as a rejection of normative protocols of canonization and value, illustrates queer performativity. As Shoshana Felman has shown, failure, or infelicity, is intrinsic to J. L. Austin's speech act theory. In *The Scandal of the Speaking Body* Felman turns to Molière's *Don Juan* to explain all the ways in which speech acts are especially predisposed to fail or, in Austin's terminology, misfire. Associating this kind of failure with the performative, we can discover a utopian kernel: "The act of failing thus opens up referentiality—or of impossible reality—not because something is missing, but because something else is done, or because something else is said: the term 'misfire' does not refer to an absence, but to an enactment of a difference."[15] The misfire, this failure, is intrinsic to how the performative illustrates the ways different courses are traveled in contrast to what heteronormativity demands. Heteronormativity speaks not just to a bias related to sexual object choice but to that dominant and overarching temporal and spatial organization of the world that I have been calling straight time. This "something else" that Felman frames may indeed be a response to a "something missing" in Bloch's sense. Queerness and the politics of failure are linked insofar as they are about doing "something else." And in both cases they may be doing something else in relation to a something that is missing in straight time's always already flawed temporality. Thus, we think about how Jack Smith is legendary for "failing" to start his loft performances on time and keeping audiences waiting for him to emerge. We think also of di Prima in *Recollections of My Life as a Woman* talking about how Herko was always late.[16] Deborah Hay recalls that he would "arrive late and trés flamboyantly always."[17]

When going through some Judson archives, I ran across a folder marked "Herko" that contained his résumé. From its last entry I surmise that he must have given it to some potential employer a year before he died. I cannot help but see it as a document of Herko's own brand of queer failure. Half of it is typed on onionskin paper. I imagine that it is the same typewriter that Diane di Prima used to type *The Floating Bear*. The other half of it is hastily scrawled in blue ink. His typed list includes all his summer-stock dance and theater experience (1958, Detroit and Flint—*Oklahoma!*, *King and I*, *Girl Crazy*), and on the bottom half of the page Herko mentions his TV work (*The Ed Sullivan Show*). On the very top of the onionskin paper in block ink letters is written, "Sorry—I'm Slow—FH." How can someone on amphetamines be slow? Drug use and queer desires led to Herko's experiencing the world differently. Certainly by the criteria of straight time a junky is a failure. Drugs are a surplus that pushes one off course, no longer able to contribute labor power at the proper tempo.

Here, again, surplus is not simply an additive; it distorts—a stuttering particularity that shoves one off course, out of straight time. I looked at Herko's frantic and messy résumé and assumed he did not get that job for which he was angling. His address, "309 East Houston Street," is crossed out in ink. So are his personal measurements—his height, weight, inseam, and so on. We are left to think about how long-term amphetamine use might transform the body. I recognized the address as the same as the one at the top of *The Floating Bear*. By the time he turned in this résumé, he no longer lived in the apartment below di Prima; he had begun his no-madic life of couch surfing in bohemia. In his last major performance at the Judson space he played the role of "The Wanderer" in *The Palace of the Dragon Prince*. By then, Herko was a local street character who walked around Greenwich Village in a black cape, playing a pipe. The local street kids called him Zorro. I surmise that by that time his body was showing the withering signs of addiction to speed—maybe that is why his mea-surements needed to be revised. His résumé qualifies him for the position of perfect mess and proto-queer icon. It is easy at this point to feel conde-scending pity for poor Freddie. Yet such moralism needs to be avoided, and instead we need to think of Herko's life and body as becoming par-ticular, to imagine the artist striving for another way, leaping away from the here and now of a stultifying straight time and attempting to reach an-other time and place, a not-here and a not-now that is utopian.

The history of actually realized utopian enclaves is, from a dominant per-spective, a history of failures. Hope and disappointment operate within a dialectical tension in this notion of queer utopia. Queerness's failure is temporal and, from this project's perspective, potentially utopian, and in-asmuch as it does not adhere to straight time, interrupting its protocols, it can be an avant-garde practice that interrupts the here and now. To perform such interruptions is not glorious or heroic work. This aspect of Herko's story speaks to the material toll that a burning queer incandes-cence takes.

Herko's fans, Warhol and Frank O'Hara most prominent among them, loved the dancer despite the "flaws" in his style that Paxton notes. Warhol famously remarked that if he had known that Herko was going to kill him-self, he would have asked to film the event. Reading that statement now, in the context of a man whose life was temporally condensed, as many gay male temporalities in the West have been in the past century, and whose quirky oeuvre concluded with a performance of death, we can better

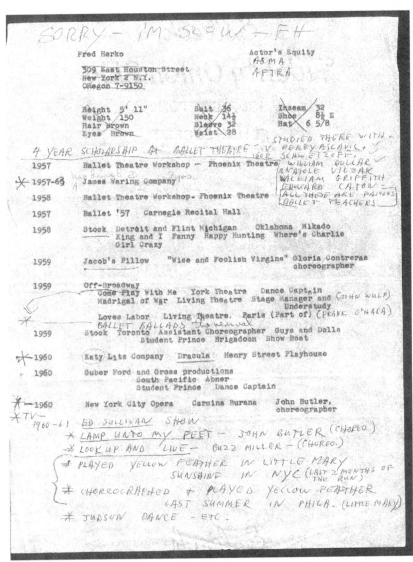

SORRY — I'M SLOW — FH

Fred Herko

309 East Houston Street
New York 2 N.Y.
ORegon 7-9150

Actor's Equity
ASMA
AFTRA

Height 5' 11"   Suit 36   Inseam 32
Weight 150   Neck 14½   Shoe 8½ E
Hair brown   Sleeve 32   Hat 6 5/8
Eyes Brown   Waist 28

4 YEAR SCHOLARSHIP AT BALLET THEATRE

STUDIED THERE WITH- V. PEREY ASLAVIC, IGOR SCHWETZOFF,

1957	Ballet Theatre Workshop — Phoenix Theatre	*WILLIAM DOLLAR*
1957-63	James Waring Company	*ANATOLE VILZAK*
		WILLIAM GRIFFITH
1958	Ballet Theatre Workshop— Phoenix Theatre	*EDWARD CATON=*
		ALL THOSE ARE FAMOUS BALLET TEACHERS
1957	Ballet '57 Carnegie Recital Hall	
1958	Stock Detroit and Flint Michigan Oklahoma Mikado	
	King and I Fanny Happy Hunting Where's Charlie Girl Crazy	
1959	Jacob's Pillow "Wise and Foolish Virgins" Gloria Contreras choreographer	
1959	Off-Broadway	
	Come Play With Me York Theatre Dance Captain	
	Madrigal of War Living Theatre Stage Manager and *(JOHN WULP)*	
	Understudy	
	Loves Labor Living Theatre. Paris (Part of) *(FRANK O'HARA)*	
	BALLET BALLADS the revival	
1959	Stock Toronto Assistant Choreographer Guys and Dolls	
	Student Prince Brigadoon Show Boat	
1960	Katy Litz Company Dracula Henry Street Playhouse	
1960	Guber Ford and Gross productions	
	South Pacific Abner	
	Student Prince Dance Captain	
1960	New York City Opera Carmina Burana John Butler, choreographer	

TV—
1960-61 ED SULLIVAN SHOW
★ LAMP UNTO MY FEET — JOHN BUTLER (CHOREO.)
★ LOOK UP AND LIVE — BUZZ MILLER — (CHOREO.)
★ PLAYED YELLOW FEATHER IN LITTLE MARY
SUNSHINE IN NYC (LAST 2 MONTHS OF THE RUN)
★ CHOREOGRAPHED + PLAYED YELLOW FEATHER
LAST SUMMER IN PHILA. (LITTLE MARY)
★ JUDSON DANCE — ETC.

Fred Herko's résumé. Image courtesy of Judson Memorial Church Archives, Fales Library,
NYU.

understand what Warhol meant. If one recalls early Warhol's interest in cinematically capturing the downtown demimonde and its weirdest denizens, at least before Valerie Solanas made her indelible mark in his life, the desire to preserve more of Herko's flickering incandescence—especially at the point of its physical and psychic transformation—strangely makes sense. Herko's nervousness and resistance to traditional movement certainly qualify as failure by Paxton's standards, yet by a different criterion, one better attuned to utopian aesthetics and their linkage with failure, we can begin to feel the dead artist's incandescence.

Carmines, with whom Herko also worked at the Judson Poets Theater, explained that Herko "always included humor and pathos and high class camp. He was an unusual actor and audiences adored him. He learned to be totally accessible to an audience."[18] We can see how the work affected other spectators in Johnston's rapt attention to Herko's Suzie-Q dance move (which Sally Banes compares to "the twist") and Hughes's parenthetical invocation of Erik Satie's loving Herko, which is certainly as much about Hughes loving Herko.

Herko was Warhol's dropout, and even his best friend, Diane di Prima, had some seemingly nasty things to say about him in her collection dedicated to the dancer, *Freddie Poems*:

> For Freddy, Fucking Again
> I think it's disgusting
> To be offcourse, in love
> Midwinter afternoons is excusable
> Especially if it rains
> But how is it you are always off course these days
> & not that much in love
> will you never grow up
> at least if you'd gone off to gather those blue flowers
> (are they called periwinkles?)
> or mussels, from the seaweed
> but no, you're off for adventures in grimy bars
> and the props not finished
> and the show is in four hours
> I think its pretty bad[19]

Di Prima worries about her friend and his "off-course" nature, but for those who read the entirety of her *Freddie Poems* it is also clear that, despite a

Fred Herko. Image courtesy of Judson Memorial Church Archives, Fales Library, NYU.

sometimes maternal fretting, di Prima loves him for his queer way of being in the world. Her mention of "off-course" behavior again speaks to the ways in which Herko's movement through the world and the performance space was always disruptive, always linked to the force of failure, the aesthetics of excess with minimalism, temporal disjointedness, madness, and a utopian surplus. In the poem di Prima worries about Herko's slutty behavior. Stephen Koch, in his account of Herko's penis-flashing star turn in Warhol's *Haircut*, describes the artist as resembling a lurid Times Square hustler.[20] He seems to mean this in a bad way. The connection here between controversial sexual comportment and aesthetic experimentation, both linked to a poetics of failure ("I think its pretty bad"), underlines the categorical entwining of slut and postmodern dancer/superstar. This connection is most compelling in Herko's Warhol collaborations.

Andy Warhol was in the audience in May 1963 when Herko did his one-skate performance, *Binghamton Birdie*. The dance was named after one of Herko's friends, part of the amphetamine-propelled coterie of gay boys who would listen to opera and shoot speed in the back of the Factory. Herko came onstage with one roller skate and a superhero-like tee-shirt with a made-up insignia that spelled out "Judson." The Judson Memorial Church's performances, as I indicated earlier, ushered in postmodern dance by making quotidian movement something worthy of staging, and Herko's appearance deconstructed the divide between art and real life—or maybe, better put, between art, life, and play. Herko was often accused of being temporarily out of joint, of being childish or infantile. Susan Foster points to moments when Herko was called childish, the most stinging perhaps being the choreographer Maxine Munt, who put it this way: "Fred Herko is indeed the enfant terrible, and his Little Gym Dance . . . shouted 'look at me, look at me'; he has yet to prove he belongs with this group."[21] The accusation of childishness reverberates alongside many dismissals of queerness as childish, disrupting straight comportment and temporality. Herko's deliberate childishness interrupted the protocols of straight time. It also challenged a conservative version of minimalism. But certainly Herko was not just excessive. At times his movements were minor and not at all the "energetic" ballet that Paxton expected. Like Ray Johnson, Herko was a collagist whose source material was, on one level, spare and, on another, deeply layered.

Following *Binghamton Birdie*, Warhol and Herko made a movie in which Herko skated around Manhattan on one skate. Like the concert, the movement in the film was dynamically "off course." That film, like a lot of

Warhol's earliest work, is lost and exists only as lore or, more nearly, queer evidence. The story indicates that Warhol filmed Herko for days, and at the end of the filming Herko's bare feet were bleeding. Herko's sacrifice both for art and for Andy anticipates the blood work of queer performers Ron Athey and Franko B.

Warhol then cast Herko in another early film, *Haircut* (1963), along with Billy Linich—a Judson artist and Factory regular who was later known as Billy Name—choreographer James Waring and John Daley. The group participated in gay male theatrics. The film reinforced Judson Dance Theater's project of making art from the quotidian while making queer bonds and sociality into art. It should go without saying that the film was extremely radical in 1963. But also the film is worth considering as an example of queer relationality, a precursor of a modality of queer ontology that had not-yet-arrived. Linich cuts the other man's hair. Herko performs a series of everyday movements, walking toward the camera and then turning around and walking away, disappearing into the shadows of Waring's apartment. He then reappears, presents a pipe to the camera, and then packs the pipe with marijuana and smokes. In the film's final sequence Herko strips for the camera, briefly exposing his penis. Throughout the film the gay men flirt with one another and rehearse a mode of queer belonging that had yet to be screened. Their comportment, though not "overtly" sexual, is sexy and signals a queer kind of becoming. Herko's performance was his own because Warhol's directing consisted mostly of setting up a scenario and letting the camera record the action. Herko bridges the Judson style with postmodern film. His insistence on public drug consumption and flagrant, ludic nudity surpasses the strictures of typical Judson minimalism. Or, again, more nearly, it keeps that modality of minimalism from being swept under a larger modernist rug. I identify this queer move as having a utopian impetus that imagined another time and place that was not yet conscious. At this historical moment, when queer politics constantly defers to the pragmatic struggles of the present, the bold and utopian experimentation of *Haircut* seems especially poignant.

Herko starred in another Warhol film, *Thirteen Most Beautiful Boys*. In that film, Warhol collects some screen tests, including Herko's. A majority of the screen-test subjects blankly stare at the screen, transforming their faces into stationary portraits. Not so with Herko, whose minor movements transform the screen test into a choreography. In *Thirteen Most Beautiful Boys* we see Herko resisting Warhol's protocols and performing instead his own drugged-out agency. A year later Herko ended his own life.

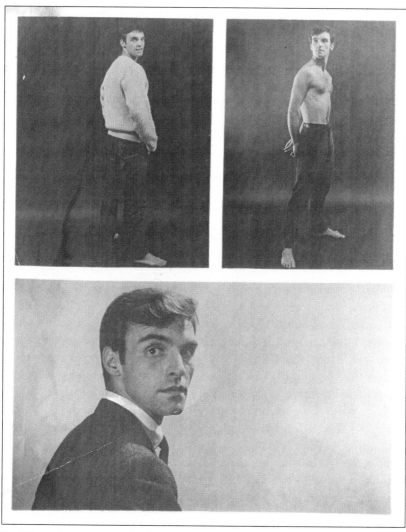

Fred Herko. Image courtesy of Judson Memorial Church Archives, Fales Library, NYU.

But in this screen test our eyes should not be content to see a drugged-out homosexual who made some underground films and danced at the Judson. What I see in this film is the artist in all his embodied cultural surplus. Twitching and moving in ways that tell us that this time and place is not enough, Herko enacts a critical impatience with the present, a dissatisfaction with the here and now. Furthermore, I see desire. Herko cruises the camera and the spectator; he flirts with it, not able to sit, wanting to display himself beyond the limits of Warhol's portraiture. Herko wants us, his future—a future he will choose not to meet—to see him as a desiring subject, in all his uneasy embodiment. Callie Angell, in her impressive catalog of *Thirteen Most Beautiful Boys*, agrees with James Stoller, who sees something tragic in Herko's performance. Stoller recalls his reaction to the portrait: it became "excruciatingly moving as I uncontrollably invested in Herko's glowering expression with meanings brought from outside the film."[22] This reading is difficult to discount, but I am arguing that there is something else available to the spectator who looks at the dancer's twitchy comportment as something more than negativity. In *Haircut* Herko is clearly and laughingly flirting with the camera. Sometimes Herko's performance in *Thirteen Most Beautiful Boys* seems just dark, and then sometimes I see it as a dark, drug-tinged cruise, purposely brooding and deliberately conveying a certain intensity that probably served Herko well in countless bars and shadowy public spaces.

Giorgio Agamben privileges gesture as a modality of movement that resists modernity's totalizing political scripts insofar as it promises a politics of a "means with out end."[23] Herko's dancing, as it exists for us in written accounts, oral histories, and films, is that of the suggestive, imperfect gesture. The gesture is utopian in that it resists the goal-oriented tautological present. The gesture is a cultural supplement that, in its incompleteness, promises another time and place. Thus, through Herko's twitch we see the gesture as the choreography of the not-yet-conscious. Randy Martin has succinctly argued for the importance of "critical moves" in a politicized dance studies. Martin makes words such as "movement" and "mobilization" do double duty as his research links theatrical dance movement with the politics of collective social movements.[24] This metaphorical link provides dance studies with a powerful materialist approach. I look at Herko's choreography of gesture and see it working alongside Martin's analysis to a point, then diverging. The divergence has to do with a politics that may not have the overarching coherency of a movement yet but may nonetheless represent a valuable interruption in the coercive choreography of a here and now that is scored to naturalize and validate dominant cultural logics such as capitalism and heterosexuality. A gesture is not a full-fledged resistance, but it is a moment when that overwhelming frame of a here and now, a spatial and temporal order that is calibrated against one, is resisted.

Herko's camp surplus, what I am calling his ornamentation, is not quite the garden-variety camp of pink flamingos or feather boas. Camp, as I have suggested elsewhere, resituates the past in the service of politics and aesthetics that often critique the present.[25] The past on which Herko called was often a distant, magical past like that of fairy tales. Di Prima meditates in her autobiography on "Freddie's groping for the allegory, the ultimate fairytale that could tell his story, could maybe save him."[26] Today we can see the allegorical utopian function of Herko's work and imagine that the fairy tale was intended to do more than simply save himself, that it was in fact interested in saving di Prima and the collectivity that she and all their friends represented. It is therefore worthwhile to consider Herko's last dance, *Palace of the Dragon Prince*—a failure according to Warhol— as Herko's invocation of a mythical past or fairy tale. Here, turning to Bloch on the utopic work of the fairy tale can help us understand Herko's performance.

> Of course the fairy tale world, especially the magical one, no longer belongs to the present. How can it mirror our wish-projections against a background that has long since disappeared? Or, to put it a better way: How can the fairy tale mirror our wish projections other than in a totally obsolete way? Real Kings no longer exists. The atavistically feudal and transcendental world from which the fairy tale stems and to which it seems to be tied has most certainly vanished. However, the mirror of the fairy tale has not become opaque, and the manner of wish-fulfillment which peers forth from it is wish-fulfillment which is not entirely without a home. It adds up to this: the fairy tale narrates a wish-fulfillment which is not bound by its own time and the apparel of its contents. In contrast to the folktale, which is always tied to a particular locale, the fairy tale remains unbound. Not only does the fairy tale remain as fresh as longing and love, but the evil demons that abound in fairy tales are still at work in the present, and the happiness of "once upon a time," which is even more abundant in the fairy tale, still affects our visions of the future.[27]

Before addressing Bloch's thesis, I want to consider the best source currently available to gather an impression of *The Palace of the Dragon Prince*, Herko's last major public performance at the church. Di Prima recounts that the performance was based on "some Russian fairy tale he'd found somewhere. It was to be huge, an epic."[28] Aesthetically it included "lots of romantic music," "flowing costumes, shmottas," and "what somebody called the "junk store aesthetic." Many people did not seem to get it, and

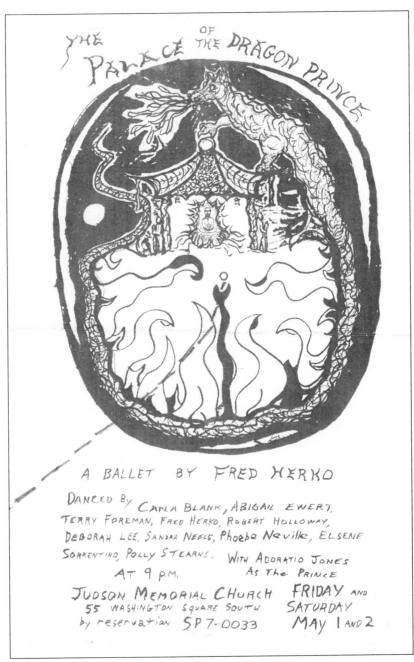

Dragon Prince poster. Image courtesy of Judson Memorial Church Archives, Fales Library, NYU.

di Prima recalls Remy Charlip, one of Herko's frequent collaborators, telling her that he thought it was "appalling." But she describes it with much greater critical generosity:

> A full-out work—I thought it was extraordinary. Oh, I could see as well as anyone the flaws, the places it needed to be cut, the technical mistakes. Or the places it got corny: too much emotion and you had to say no in self-defense. I could see all this, 'cause these were the kinds of things I'd come to recognize as necessary risks. . . . I saw the dance as extraordinarily brave.[29]

Di Prima believed in Herko's performance despite its excess, its corniness. She never hesitated to describe the artist's work as romantic vectoring on the magical. At another point, she refers to a performance memorializing the life of Sergio, an Italian friend of Herko's and di Prima's husband (and Herko's ex-boyfriend), Alan Marlowe, explaining, "When Freddie danced *For Sergio* at the New Bowery, he made a dance that was also a ritual. He magically 'did' something. Transformed something. It seems so simple now. But at that point many of us were groping our way backward to art as magick."[30] This "magically doing" speaks not only to the performative force of Herko's performance but also to how it was calibrated to provide an idea of another way of being in the world that was not allowed within an antiutopian hermeneutic. Herko's performance practice, like Bloch's fairy tale, "narrates a wish-fulfillment which is not bound by its own time and the apparel of its contents," and this "unboundness" interrupts what I have described, after Halberstam, as straight time, a naturalized temporality that is calibrated to make queer potentiality not only unrealized but also unthinkable. Indeed the present is replete with beasts that need to be vanquished, which is to say that investing in a fairy tale need not be a retreat from reality but can be a certain way of facing it.

To that end, the allegorical nature that utopian critique employs in various modes of artistic production is important to consider. Bloch preferred ballet to American jazz dance, and as in Adorno's pronouncements on jazz music, Bloch betrays a discomfort with North American vernacular art, especially African American expression. Bloch scholar Vincent Geoghegan suggests that the philosopher's investment in ballet betrays his allegiance to the Soviet Union. Nonetheless Bloch's description of ballet's performativity, what it does, speaks of the form's utopian force:

The dance allows us to move in a completely different way than the way we move in the day, at least in the everyday, it imitates something which the latter has lost or never even possessed. It paces out the wish for more beautifully moved being, fixes in the eye, ear, the whole body, just as if it already existed now.[31]

Perhaps Bloch would have been less approving of minimalist dance practices that rehearsed quotidian movement, but his interest in fairy tales and ballet seems to be aligned with the romantic experimentation and excess that characterized Herko's work. Herko is interested in pacing out a more beautifully moved being. Movement in this passage from Bloch exists at an allegorical juncture between aesthetics and political movement. Another scholar associated with the Frankfurt School, Herbert Marcuse, offered the following formulation:

The analysis of cognitive function of phantasy is thus led to aesthetics as the "science of beauty": behind the aesthetic form lies the repressed harmony of sensuousness and reason—the eternal protest against the organization of life by the logic of domination, the critique of the performance principle.[32]

The pairing of sensuousness and reason is relevant as we consider the allegorical nature of queer utopian expression. The performance principle is the cultural logic that is a manifestation of a capitalist ethos. For utopian philosophers such as Bloch and Marcuse, dance and its sensuousness exist alongside a political impulse. Movement is thus always already doubly valenced because it enables a mode of cognition that can potentially disattach itself from the performance principle and all the negation it represents.

I do not know how many steps separate my apartment from 5 Cornelia Street, the address of John Dodd's apartment, where Fred Herko took his own life. I am not patient enough to count, but let us say it is about five hundred, a few short city blocks. As I neared finishing writing this chapter, I walked to 5 Cornelia Street. This was a morbid little homage, a private performance fueled by a minor and abstract necrophilic attachment. This stroll made me think about the abstraction of writing about a suicide "as performance" and how that misses something. I did not expect to feel much, but my expectations proved wrong. I thought about a young friend who tried to take his own life and, luckily for himself and all the people who adore him, failed. I thought about another beloved person in my life and remember the shattering sadness he felt when he lost an ex-lover, who ended his life a few years ago with a leap from a bridge. But mostly I thought about my best friend from graduate school. He took his own life several years ago. I recall all the dreams I have had about him, still have about him, in which he is mysteriously still alive and living in the walls of my apartment. I discover his lingering presence in this recurring dream, and I somehow know that it is my job to get him out, to save him. I never do. I always fail. When reading all of Herko's friends' responses to his death, even Andy's wish to have filmed it, I get the impression that they too felt like they failed.

In chapter 4 I discussed Elizabeth Bishop's famous poem "One Art." As Bishop wrote, "The art of losing is not hard to master." As much as I like the sound of that line I realize that there is something artless and brutal about losing. Bishop's lover of many years, after their eventual breakup, took her own life. Was Bishop's poem about Lata? Was Bishop trying to describe the art of "losing" her lover, or was she giving her Brazilian lover instructions so she would be able to let the poet go? Was it the poet's way of reconciling that terrible loss, or a document of her failure to reconcile? Queerness and that particular modality of loss known as suicide seem linked. And to write or conjecture about suicide as a queer act, a performance of radical negativity, utopian in its negation of death as ultimate uncontrollable finitude, and not think about what it symbolizes for a larger collectivity would be remiss.

Suicide is often the end of hope, and indeed a critical and strategic notion of hope is often snuffed out for a collectivity. I have risked romanticizing Herko's loss in discussing the transhistorical relevance of his queer incandescence.[33] As I stood on the sidewalk where he ended his life I noticed a small record store in the building's bottom floor. It was cramped and seemed to be temporally "offtrack." Subterranean Records would be easy for my everyday eye to miss. I walked inside and said hello to a store clerk, who fidgeted as he sort of rocked on the stool on which he was only partially sitting. There was another potential customer in the very small store. I looked around and quickly noticed a lot of Patti Smith CDs and records, and a vinyl album I cherished when I was seventeen, The Gun Club's amazing Fire of Love. It was priced at fifty dollars. Then I imagined how Herko would have enjoyed punk if he had stayed around for another fifteen years. Along the same line of thought, I wondered how gay liberation would have affected his life. Would being gay have made his utopian and vexed queerness any easier or more painful?

10

After Jack

Queer Failure, Queer Virtuosity

JACK SMITH IS the progenitor of queer utopian aesthetics. His influence washes over this book and its desire to conjure a queer utopian sphere of potentiality. In Mary Jordan's documentary *Jack Smith and the Destruction of Atlantis* several of Smith's friends and collaborators explain that invoking the fabled lost continent of Atlantis was Smith's way of invoking the utopian. The aesthetic practice that I have previously described as disidentification focuses on the way in which dominant signs and symbols, often ones that are toxic to minoritarian subjects, can be reimagined through an engaged and animated mode of performance or spectatorship.[1] Disidentification can be a world-making project in which the limits of the here and now are traversed and transgressed. Jack Smith's version of Atlantis, glimpsed in much of his film and performance work, disidentified with the constraining and phobic limit of the present. On a material level that meant that dime-store glitter became diamond dust, and cheap polyester was transformed into silken veils. In Jack Smith's world dumpster diving became treasure hunting. Throughout this book I have attempted a sort of calculus in which queer art from the past is evoked for the purpose of better understanding work made today. Thus, the way contemporary work lines up with the historical archive helps us engage Smith's utopianism in relation to queer performance today. In this chapter the work of New York–based lesbian performance artist Dynasty Handbag and performance collective My Barbarian perform a mode of utopianism that I associate with Jack Smith's strange legacy and afterlife. I then briefly describe similarities that these two acts have with the work of drag conceptual/vocal artist Kalup Linzy. In looking at the work of all three contemporary acts, I draw on two aspects of what I describe as a queer utopian aesthetic practice: failure and virtuosity.

The version of utopia to which this book has subscribed exits somewhere between the figure of the freakish and often solitary outsider, the madwoman street preacher, and the politically engaged collectivity. I have insisted that there has always been something queer about utopia and utopian thinkers. Smith is the exemplary figure of the queer utopian artist and thinker who seeks solitariness yet calls for a queer collectivity. Dynasty Handbag, a primarily solo artist who stages acts that resemble psychotic episodes made humorous, is a clear inheritor of a performance practice that is akin to Smith's solitary loft performances. My Barbarian, a group with three primary members that sometimes expands to include friends who are musicians and performers, is reminiscent of the ragtag queer collective hysteria that Smith staged in his legendary experimental films *Flaming Creatures* and *Normal Love*. Both the lone lunatic and the crazed collective stage a desire that I have called queer utopia. Both modes of performance ask important questions of aesthetic practice, questions that attempt to visualize that which is not yet here.

To understand this desire better it is useful to return one of the sources of queer utopian longing from which I draw in this book. In Smith's well-known manifesto "Capitalism of Lotusland" he begins with a stirring meditation on art and the artist:

> Could art be useful? Ever since the glitter drifted over the burnt-out ruins of Plaster Lagoon thousands of artists have pondered and dreamed of such a thing, yet, art must not be used anymore as another elaborate means of fleeing from thinking because of the multiplying amount of information each person needs to process in order to come to any kind of decision about what kind of planet one wants to live on before business, religion, and government succeed in blowing it out of the solar system.[2]

Here Smith delineates just what is at stake in artistic production. The 1978 manifesto keenly anticipates capitalism's permutations in the age of globalization, because there are indeed "multiplying amounts[s] of information [that] each person needs to process." Smith's critiques of capitalism, or what he alternately calls "landlordism," should not be dismissed as just campy fun. Smith's virulent aversion to private property saturated his work. Through his strange and moldy mode of address Smith speaks of an economic system that is innately flawed, violently asymmetrical, and essentially exploitative. Smith's manifesto was utopian, not so much because he dreamed of Xanadu but, more nearly, because he performed alternate realities. These realities were loosely based on fantasies of glimmering lost cityscapes like Atlantis.

Queer restaging of the past helps us imagine new temporalities that interrupt straight time.[3] Smith's investment in other cultures initially appears to be nothing but Orientalist fantasy, but those renderings of the East should be considered simulacra of simulacra because they are not based on those cultures but on cheesy Hollywood fantasies of "over there" or a "not here." Smith animated these queer fairy-tale worlds not as a form of wish-fulfillment but, instead, as a challenge to the limitations of the political and aesthetic imagination. The critical work that utopian thought does, in its most concise and lucid formulation, allows us to see different worlds and realities. And this conjured reality instructs us that the "here and now" is simply not enough.

As Smith's manifesto continues he renders ideas of what a socially relevant mode of art production would look like:

> Let art continue to be entertaining, escapist, stunning, glamorous, and naturalistic—but let it be loaded with information worked into the vapid plots of, for instance, movies. Each one would be a more or less complete exposition of one subject or another. Thus you would have Tony Curtis and Janet Leigh busily making yogurt; Humphrey Bogart struggling to introduce a basic civil law course into public schools; infants being given to the old in homes for the aged by Ginger Rogers; donut-shaped dwellings with sunlight pouring into central patios for all, designed by Gary Cooper; soft, clear plastic bubble cars with hooks that attach to monorails built by Charlton Heston that pass over the Free Paradise of abandoned objects in the center of the city near where the community movie sets would also be; and where Maria Montez and Johnny Weissmüller would labour to dissolve all national boundaries and release the prisoners of Uranus. But the stairway to socialism is blocked by the Yvonne De Carlo Tabernacle Choir waving bloody palm branches and waiting to sing the "Hymn to the Sun" by Irving Berlin. This is the rented moment of the exotic landlordism of prehistoric capitialsim of tabu.[4]

This quotation needs some unpacking in relation to Smith's artistic vernacular and the unique cosmology to which he adhered. Smith imagines vapid Hollywood plots injected with redeemable social values. He looks to the Hollywood star system as a potential site of transformative potentiality. But his celebration of Hollywood is not pure festivity—he also understands obstacles in the culture industry. In Smith's universe the most hallowed saint was B-movie star Maria Montez. Montez's main competitor, Yvonne De Carlo, became the antithesis of Smith's beloved Montez. Smith described De Carlo most succinctly as a "walking career."[5] This description was meant to tag the actress with the title of a vulgar professionalist. Those of us who attempt to dream utopia within the sphere of our quotidian life must constantly overcome the disabling inertia generated by such agents of antiutopianism. De Carlo's brand of careerism was viewed by Smith as an ethos that limited the possibility of imagining a different time and place that was not organized by capitalism's injunctive to reproduce and be productive. If we apply some of Smith's irreverence to the current problem of gay and lesbian neoliberalism, we understand that the problem with groups such as the Human Rights Campaign and others that advocate the "mainstream" of queer politics is not unlike the problem of walking careerism, which is to say, then, that Yvonne De Carlo–ism dominates contemporary LGBT activism. In this book I suggest we need an idealism that is perhaps as sparkling as the hallowed iconicity of Maria Montez. Queer idealism may be the only way to usher in a new mode of radicalism that can perhaps release queer politics from its current death grip.

Smith's dream of a planet not destroyed by a savage market economy, religious fundamentalism, and mad governmentality was directly connected to his fecund fantasies of B movies that potentially offered a critique of the "here and now" in favor of a transformative "then and there." The politics of Smith's utopianism can be linked to current aesthetic projects that also imagine alternative universes that eschew the dominance of the here and now for the force and potentiality of a conjured world of fantasy and magic that is not simply a mode of fantastical escapism but, instead, a blueprint for alternative modes of being in the world. This project does not need to draw a stark distinction between escapism and radical politics. In this book I have strived to illustrate the importance of rekindling a political imagination. Furthermore, escape itself need not be a surrender but, instead, may be more like a refusal of a dominant order and its systemic violence. Queer fantasy is linked to utopian longing, and together the two can become contributing conditions of possibility for political transformation.

Utopia's rejection of pragmatism is often associated with failure. And, indeed, most profoundly, utopianism represents a failure to be normal. Throughout this book I have offered historical examples of queer aesthetic practices imbued with utopian potentiality. I have often aligned these readings of work from the past (or in Bloch's terms, the no-longer-conscious) with more contemporary queer work that displays how the radical promise of that work was part of a larger political impulse that actually exists in the present. In conclusion I turn to two examples of the aesthetic work that follows this Smithian thread, Los Angeles's My Barbarian and New York–based lesbian performer Dynasty Handbag. These artists offer a Smithian transport ignited by the force of queer utopianism. Utopia can never be prescriptive and is always destined to fail. Despite this seeming negativity, a generative politics can be potentially distilled from the aesthetics of queer failure. Within failure we can locate a kernel of potentiality. I align queer failure with a certain mode of virtuosity that helps the spectator exit from the stale and static lifeworld dominated by the alienation, exploitation, and drudgery associated with capitalism or landlordism. When I describe the ways in which Jack Smith, Dynasty Handbag, and My Barbarian perform failure, I am not claiming that they are not successful or accomplished as performers or that the performances are not strong, fulfilling, or interesting; indeed my opinion is just the opposite, as I revel in the aesthetic and political stimulation the work provides. Instead I mean to explicate the ways in which these artists thematize failure as being something like the *always already* status of queers and other minoritarian subjects in the dominant social order within which they toil. Queer failure, as I argue, is more nearly about escape and a certain kind of virtuosity.

Dynasty Handbag and the Strange Itinerant Beauty of Queer Failure

Queer failure is often deemed or understood as failure because it rejects normative ideas of value. In speech act theory it is the failure central to speech itself. It is blatantly and irrevocably antinormative. *Normal* was a despised term for Smith, and it referred to much more than sexual object choice. The normativity against which Smith argued is not Michael Warner's idea of heteronormativity, a particular mode of normativity, but, instead, a more expansive understanding of the problem of the normal.[6] This expansive understanding of the normal can tentatively be understood as the antiutopian. Smith's use of the term *normal* spoke against straight time, which is laden with temporal obstacles and challenges that ensure a certain kind of queer failure as axiomatic for the queer subject and collectivity. Within straight time the queer can only fail; thus, an aesthetic of failure can be productively occupied by the queer artist for the purpose of delineating the bias that underlies straight time's measure. The politics of failure are about doing something else, that is, doing something else in relation to a something that is missing in straight time's always already flawed temporal mapping practice. Thus, we think about how Smith is legendary for "failing" to start his loft performances on time and keeping audiences waiting for him to emerge.[7]

The work of Jibz Cameron's art persona, Dynasty Handbag, illustrates the efficacy of a certain mode of queer failure. A musician and performer, Cameron created the character of Dynasty Handbag in 2002. Dynasty Handbag can perhaps best be described as a sort of quixotic bag lady dressed in an outfit that appears to be something of an eighties fringe-laden aerobics costume. Always prepared to negotiate a threat, both real but mostly imagined, she wears a rumpled backpack filled with energy snacks. Her constant nemeses are the voices in her head. None of the Dynasty Handbag performances I have watched has been an actual failure. Indeed, they have all been far from failures inasmuch as they have left audiences of alternative music, culture, and sexuality applauding and even seemingly edified. My own experience as a spectator at those performances has been valuable precisely because of the mimetic performance of a person, a spoiled subjectivity, who is considered a loser, or rubbish, who refuses to live by an outside rule, a system of categorization that celebrates the normal, and instead insists on her own value as a countercultural heroine. Dynasty Handbag is the utopian oddball par excellence.

In the 2006 performance *Hell in a Handbag*, the character/persona Dynasty Handbag restages Dante's *Inferno*. But in this inferno the different levels of hell represent different aspects of the character's life that she finds difficult to negotiate. At one level she is confronted with visions of cookies, and she responds with a musical/dance number that is certainly saturated with a punk ethos that celebrates a certain kind of nonmastery that is failure. Dynasty Handbag's performance represents a deliberate failure to achieve melodic or choreographic conformity. Instead, on the level of movement and sound, we see a brilliant offness. This is a modality of being off script, off page, which is not so much a failure to succeed as it is a failure to participate in a system of valuation that is predicated on exploitation and conformity. The queer failure of Dynasty Handbag and countless other queer performers is a failure that is more nearly a refusal or an escape.

In *Bags*, a performance commissioned by Dance Theater Workshop in January 2009, the voices in Dynasty Handbag's head get the best of her. The

Dynasty Handbag. Photographs copyright Jibz Cameron; photographer Ves Pitts.

black stage is empty except for five small bags seemingly scattered around it. The different discarded bags begin to talk to Dynasty Handbag and dictate her movements and emotional positionality onstage. Each bag speaks to the frazzled protagonist, and the various voices play over the theater's sound system. The artist herself voices the various monologues of seduction. A brown paper bag that initially comes on sweet becomes an increasingly whiney and demanding bottom. After first seducing her, it demands more and more hand-bag penetration. She moves from that object relationship to a darker one with a black plastic bag. That entanglement starts off on a very sado-masochistic note. In the frenzy of their hand-bag intercourse a subtle boundary is crossed and the black bag violently rejects the hapless Dynasty Handbag. She is then comforted by a blue plastic bag with a cheesy fake British accent. This bag at first comforts her but then attempts to drag her into a quagmire of self-pity and nihilism. She turns away from the negative blue bag to a demanding white plastic bag that asks her to become various figures embodied in dance. Dynasty becomes a turnip, a toilet, and Mick Jagger with a dagger, and she dances her becoming in her particular style of nonmastery. She is spasmatic and slightly ridiculous in her exaggerated movements, but the audience seems to sense that she is quaking with a transformative potentiality. Being and performativity momentarily merge as the character becomes other, becoming herself, embracing her status as quixotic madwoman, oddball, and utopian. The clear plastic bag rewards her with a bite of the peanut butter sandwich that it contains. The bag tells her that it insists on preserving the flavor of the thing it surrounds, making it more natural. We see that Dynasty Handbag is now enveloped with the enabling aura of the plastic bag so that her utopian imagination is newly energized and made new. In this moment a certain kind of hopelessness and failure break momentarily and open into a new reparative moment.

Failure and hopelessness seem strange topics for a book about utopia and hope. Yet I want to see the failure and bad sentiments in Dynasty Handbag's work as active political refusal. To make this point I turn to particular moment in philosopher Paolo Virno's *A Grammar of the Multitudes,* which speaks of the emotional situation of the post-Fordist moment as characterized by a certain mode of ambivalence. This ambivalence leads to "bad sentiments." As Virno puts it, the emotional situation of the multitude today is that of these bad sentiments, which include "opportunism, cynicism, social integration, inexhaustible recanting, cheerful resignation."[8] Virno imagines the ways in which the laborer may call on restructured opportunism and cynicism as a sort of escape or exit from late capitalism's mandate to work and be productive. Negative sentiments such as cynicism, opportunism, depression, and bitchiness are often seen as solipsistic, individualistic, and anticommunal affective stances associated with an emotional tonality of hopelessness. Yet these bad sentiments can signal the capacity to transcend hopelessness. These sentiments associated with despondence contain the potentiality for new modes of collectivity, belonging in difference and dissent. The worker can potentially redirect cynicism, which may lead to a criticality that does collapse into a post-Fordist standard mode of alienation.

Virno, like other writers associated with the Italian proponents of *Operaismo* (workerism) and the Autonomia movement, makes an argument against work itself. *Operaistas* understand that capitalism is a problem not simply because workers are exploited but also because work has become the dominating condition of human life.[9] *Operaistas* do not want to take over the means of production; instead they plan on reducing it. What would it mean, on an emotional level, to make work not the defining feature of our lives? How could such a procedure be carried out?

The strategy at the center of *Operaismo* is described as exodus—a strategy of refusal or defection. This mode of resistance as refusal or escape resonates with many patterns of minoritarian resistance to structures of social command. Examples could include the trope of escapology that Daphne Brooks has recently described in her book *Bodies in Dissent*[10] or various acts of illegal border crossing. Real or symbolic "escapes" from chattel slavery and xenophobic immigration laws are examples of a certain mode of exodus, which is political action that does not automatically vector into a fixed counterdiscourse of resistance.

Cynicism, opportunism, and other bad sentiments can be responses to the current emotional situation, which many of us interested in the project of radical politics understand as hopelessness. Virno's reimagining of bad sentiments helps us understand them as something the worker can use to escape. "Bad sentiments" can be critically redeployed and function as refusals of social control mandates that become transformative behaviors.

Dynasty Handbag's queer failure is not an aesthetic failure but, instead, a political refusal. It is a going off script, and the script in this instance is the mandate that makes queer and other minoritarian cultural performers work not for themselves but for distorted cultural hierarchy.

The Anticipatory Illumination of Queer Virtuosity

The other side of the performance of failure is queer virtuosity. Failure and virtuosity are both equally important aspects of queer utopia or queerness as utopian. Queer utopia is a not just a failure to achieve normative virtuosity; it is also a virtuosity that is born in the face of failure within straight time's measure. In *A Grammar of the Multitude* Virno speaks of the potential transformation offered by virtuosity. A certain modality of virtuosity offers an escape from a systemic mandate within capitalism to labor in order to produce a product.[11] Although virtuosity can now be commodified like a traditional commodity, it nonetheless offers the potential for a certain escape or, as Virno puts it, an *exit*. Virno explains how virtuosity offers a certain defection from our current system. It, too, is a going off script. Virtuosity debunks production-based systems of value that make work and even cultural production drudgery and alienated debasement.

This modality of queer virtuosity seems especially salient in the "show-core" harmonization of My Barbarian. The spirit of Smith can be seen as an animating presence in the elaborate costumes and design of My Barbarian. The woodland frolicking of *Pagan Rights* can perhaps be seen as a contemporary version of Jack Smith's *Flaming Creatures* done as a musical. My Barbarian's interest in a mythic past, that of Arthurian legend, not unlike Jack Smith's investment in Atlantis, creates utopian deployments of the past in the service of critiquing the present for the ultimate purpose of imagining a future that is unimaginable in normative or straight time.

In the musical video *Pagan Rights* (2006) three young people are mysteriously summoned to the woods by some great mystery. After a cut, the collective emerges as naked mythological beasts. Wearing nothing but plushy masks of red, yellow, and blue synthetic fur, the group is nude from the shoulders down, conveying an almost comical vaudeville-like version of the philosophical category of the bare life. Their nude dance is a deliberate performance of studied awkwardness, the stretch, wobble, and pirouette performing an aesthetic of simultaneous failure and virtuosity. Three different bodies, two mixed-race men and one white woman, play three mythical and seemingly primal beasts. The video morphs again, with the collective turning into funky queer neohippies who literally dance around a maypole and hug trees. The interracial queer hippie collective engages in a woodland sing-along as they puff on what seems to be a marijuana cigarette. Soon there is another shift, and the larger collective marches through a tunnel holding signs that read "Our Goddess Gave Birth to Your God" and "Witch Freedom" (a phrase that sounds like "which freedom," a linguistic move that asks us to consider the various abuses of the term *freedom* in current U.S. domestic and foreign policy). As they march in this musical movement they voice a list of pagan demands that today announce a queer utopianism that counters the dead-end temporality of straight time:

1. Defy the Christians
2. Dance in a circle
3. Sacrifice with dignity
4. Anoint your body
5. Tell the future
6. Respect your mother
7. Follow your spirit

This performance imagines a time and place outside the stultifying hold of the present by calling on a mythical past where we can indeed imagine the defying of Christian totalitarianism, where we spin in concentric circles that defy linear logic, where one's own ego is sacrificed for a collective dignity, where queer bodies receive divine anointment, where the future is actively imagined, where our dying natural world can be revived, and once again, where collectively we follow our spirits.

The Golden Age is a performance by My Barbarian that the group describes as a postcolonial musical, dwelling on the history of the slave and drug trades. The past revisited in one particular musical number is devoted to the atrocity of chattel slavery. Asking the musical question "Who put the gold in the golden age?" My Barbarian illuminates the historical atrocity of the slave trade by inquiring into the economic underpinning of European imperialism. In the seventeenth and eighteenth centuries the Dutch were extremely active in the Atlantic and Indian Ocean slave trades, and for a time in the seventeenth century they dominated the Atlantic slave trade. Although some people might see the performance as making light of slavery, what is actually happening is a *revisitation* of the past. This, too, resonates with Smith's exploration of a past lifeworlds. The crucial difference at this moment is the way in which Smith revisits his mythical past with historical resonances and My Barbarian addresses an elided imperial history. To state boldly through virtuosic harmony that slavery is a foundational source of New World and European wealth is to point to the violence of imperialism's very underpinnings. Finally, to ask the audience to do the slave dance, as My Barbarian does, is to call on them to put themselves in the abjected shoes of the slave. The three core members of My Barbarian each try out virtuoso dance moves that include different old-school breakdance numbers, spinning and some locking and popping. The solos are meant to beckon the members of the Amsterdam audience to join them onstage. The performance attempts to interrupt a particular quotidian script in the imperial history of the Dutch slave trade that is often elided.

As the audience members attempt to move like the performers they are asked to join in a mimetic practice that at first might simply seem to be playful but actually demands an embodied occupation of historical memory that has been elided by the Dutch postcolonial condition.

Kalup Is Waiting

I have been charting two lines of Smithian influence through a reading of contemporary performance. A certain kind of queer failure that thematizes queer temporality has been provisionally assigned to Dynasty Handbag, and I have heuristically tagged My Barbarian with the tag of queer virtuosity. I could certainly switch the terms of analysis and describe My Barbarian's Smithian failure and Dynasty Handbag's weird Smithian utopian virtuosity. In the work of artist Kalup Linzy we can see both of these lines clearly intertwining. Linzy wears a fresh minimalist drag that often does not amount to much more than a dancer's leotard, an occasional baby doll

My Barbarian, from its performance *Golden Age* (2007). Copyright My Barbarian. Courtesy Steve Turner Contemporary, Los Angeles, and the artists.

Kalup Linzy's *Members Only* performance at Sweet Lorraine's, New Orleans. Courtesy of Art Production Fund, New York. © 2008.

dress, a wig, and a flower in her hair. The Florida-born Linzy is a tall and formidable presence but nonetheless performs a certain feminine small-ness and vulnerability that is reminiscent of drag luminaries such as Vagi-nal Davis. Like Davis, Linzy performs the vulnerable and sometimes sassy little lady. The failure in Linzy's video and performance work is evident on the level of narrative. So much of it is about tricks gone bad and lovers who treat her badly. And the virtuosity is clearly evident on the level of her powerful vocal performances. She is an excellent singer, and her mu-sic resonates beyond the register of parody. After her performances and screenings I am often left thinking, "Wow, she can really sing." A particu-larly stirring show stopper is her song "Asshole," in which she calls out a suitor who has done her wrong. On a lyrical level she perfectly describes a state of affective renunciation, but on the sonic level the song also achieves a degree of mastery that we associate with virtuosity.

Tavia Nyong'o recently presented an excellent paper that considers Lin-zy's song cycle *Sweetberry Sonnet* (2008).[12] In that paper Nyong'o suggests that we locate Linzy's work in the realm of Deleuzean masochism. Using Deleuze he describes Linzy's "constellation of masochism" as foregrounding waiting, lingering, and backwardness. The song cycle features the character of Taiwan, who has rejected a marriage proposal by her boyfriend. After this rejection she pines and moans for a sort of fulfillment that she never achieves. This wanting and waiting in Linzy is a good example of the power of longing that I have been attempting to describe throughout this book. Yes, on one level Taiwan just wants a good fuck, but when we look at this longing projected out on a screen or enacted on a stage, we see it as more; we see it collectively as a desire for the good life that we have been denied in straight time's choke hold. We are left waiting but vigilant in our desire for another time that is not yet here.

Linzy shoots most of his videos in his Brooklyn apartment, and this setting certainly reminds us of the world created by Smith in his SoHo loft. There is a transformative force in Kalup Linzy's work that is so resonant with Smith's work. In both cases, individual interior dwelling opens up and becomes a space of queer possibility and reenaction. And there is a lot of waiting in Kalup's space, just as there was waiting in Smith's loft. Waiting here means being out of time, or at least out of a linear mapping that is straight time. Smith is more the sadist who makes his audience wait, asking them to feel what waiting is like, what it is like not to have time at one's disposal. One resource for surviving waiting in Jack's loft was lighting up a joint. Drugs have often offered queers resources for negotiating our out-of-timeliness. But Linzy's waiting is definitely a masochist waiting, as Nyong'o has argued. And it also is the idealist's waiting; it is expectant and anticipatory, and here is where we might find some of the Smithian force of the work.

Near the end of Nyong'o's paper he asks a really important question that I want to take up here. He wonders, "Is there something black about waiting?" He partially answers by saying that there is certainly something familiar about waiting for black people. But from my lens I would answer my colleague's question with a resounding yes. There is something black about waiting. And there is something queer, Latino, and transgender about waiting. Furthermore, there is something disabled, Indigenous, Asian, poor, and so forth about waiting. Those who wait are those of us who are out of time in at least two ways. We have been cast out of straight time's rhythm, and we have made worlds in our temporal and spatial configurations. Certainly this would be the time of postcoloniality, but it is also crip time or, like the old joke we still use, CPT (colored people time).

It seems like the other's time is always off. Often we are the first ones there and the last to leave. The essential point here is that our temporalities are different and outside. They are practiced failure and virtuosic. In one recent video Kalup Linzy riffs on Otis Redding's "Dock of the Bay" by singing about sitting on the edge of the couch. She is sitting and waiting, but her pose is expectant, desiring, and anticipatory in the queerest utopian of ways.

The shadow of Jack Smith's hopeless hopefulness touches queer performance and performativity today. Smith was a virtuoso and a failure in the most poignant and sublime ways. Dynasty Handbag, My Barbarian, and Kalup Linzy are three queer acts that flourish at this particular historical moment of hopelessness, letting us imagine, in much the way Smith did, an escape from this world that is an insistence on another time and place that is simultaneously not yet here but able to be glimpsed in our horizon.

Conclusion

"Take Ecstasy with Me"

WE MUST VACATE the here and now for a then and there. Individual transports are insufficient. We need to engage in a collective temporal distortion. We need to step out of the rigid conceptualization that is a straight present. In this book I have argued that queerness is not yet here; thus, we must always be future bound in our desires and designs. The future is a spatial and temporal destination. It is also another place, if we believe Heidegger, who argued that the temporal is prior to the spatial. What we need to know is that queerness is not yet here but it approaches like a crashing wave of potentiality. And we must give in to its propulsion, its status as a destination. Willingly we let ourselves feel queerness's pull, knowing it as something else that we can feel, that we must feel. We must take ecstasy.

The title of this conclusion is lifted from indie pop stars the Magnetic Fields. Sung by the wonderfully languid Stephen Merritt, the band's leader, the song and its titular request could certainly be heard as a call to submit to pleasures both pharmaceutical and carnal. And let us hope that they certainly mean at least both those things. But when I listen to this song I hear something else, or more nearly, I feel something else. A wave of lush emotions washes over me, and other meanings for the word *ecstasy* are keyed. The gender-neutral song's address resonates queerly and performs a certain kind of longing for a something else. Might it be a call for a certain kind of transcendence? Or is it in fact something more? The Magnetic Fields are asking us to perform a certain "stepping out" with them. That "stepping out" would hopefully include a night on the town, but it could and maybe should be something more. Going back through religion and philosophy we might think of a stepping out of time and place, leaving the here and now of straight time for a then and a there that might be queer futurity.

Saint Theresa's ecstasy, most memorably signaled in Lorenzo Bernini's marble sculpture, has served as the visual sign of ecstasy for many

Christians. The affective transport chiseled in her face connotes a kind of rapture that has enthralled countless spectators. It represents a leaving of self for something larger in the form of divinity. Plotinus described this form of ecstasy as God's help to reach God and possess him. In Plotinus, God reaches man beyond all reason and gives him a kind of happiness that is ecstasy.[1] In seminar XX, Lacan looks to Bernini's sculpture as the most compelling example of what he calls the Other or feminine jouissance.[2] Ecstasy and jouissance thus both represent an individualistic move outside of the self. These usages resonates with the life of the term *ecstasy* in the history of philosophy. *Ekstasis,* in the ancient Greek (*exstare* in the Latin), means "to stand" or "to be out outside of oneself," *ex* meaning "out" and *stasis* meaning "stand." Generally the term has meant a mode of contemplation or consciousness that is not self-enclosed, particularly in regard to being conscious of the other. By the time we get to phenomenology, especially Heidegger, we encounter a version of being outside of oneself in time. In *Being and Time* Heidegger reflects on the activity of timeliness and its relation to *ekstatisch.*[3] Knowing ecstasy is having a sense of timeliness's motion, comprehending a temporal unity, which includes the past (having-been), the future (the not-yet), and the present (the making-present). This temporally calibrated idea of ecstasy contains the potential to help us encounter a queer temporality, a thing that is not the linearity that many of us have been calling straight time. While discussing the Montreal-based band Lesbians on Ecstasy, Halberstam points to their mobilization of queer temporality through their thought experiment of imagining lesbian history as if it were on ecstasy. Here they certainly mean the drug MDMA, but they also mean an ecstatic temporality. As Halberstam explicates, their electronic covers of earnest lesbian anthems remake the past to reimagine a new temporality.[4]

The "stepping out" that the Magnetic Fields song's title requests, this plaintive "Take Ecstasy with Me," is a request to step out of the here and now of straight time. Let us briefly consider the song's invitation, located in its lyrics. It begins with a having-been: "You used to slide down the carpeted stairs / Or down the banister / You stuttered like a Kaleidoscope / 'Cause you knew too many words / You used to make ginger bread houses / We used to have taffy pulls." After this having-been in the form of fecund romanticized childhood is rendered, we here the song's chorus, which contains this invitation to step out of time with the speaker/singer: "Take ecstasy with me, baby / Take ecstasy with me." When we first hear this invitation it seems like it is merely a beckoning to go back to this idealized having-been. But then the present (the making-present) is invoked in the song's next few lines, lines that first seem to be about further describing the mythic past but on closer listening telegraph a painful instant from the present: "You had a black snow mobile / We drove out under the northern lights / A vodka bottle gave you those raccoon eyes / We got beat up just for holding hands." Did the vodka give the song's addressee raccoon eyes? Or was it the bottle deployed in an act of violence? Certainly we know that the present being described in the song is one in which we are "beat up just for holding hands." At this point we hear the lyrical refrain differently "Take ecstasy with me, baby / Take ecstasy with me." The weird, quirky pop song takes on the affective cadence of a stirring queer anthem. (A cover of this song by the electronic dance act chk chk chk did briefly become a dance-floor anthem.) Take ecstasy with me thus becomes a request to stand out of time together, to resist the stultifying temporality and time that is not ours, that is saturated with violence both visceral and emotional, a time that is not queerness. Queerness's time is the time of ecstasy. Ecstasy is queerness's way. We know time through the field of the affective, and affect is tightly bound to temporality. But let us take ecstasy together, as the Magnetic Fields request. That means going beyond the singular shattering that a version of jouissance suggests or the transport of Christian rapture. Taking ecstasy with one another, in as many ways as possible, can perhaps be our best way of enacting a queer time that is not yet here but nonetheless always potentially dawning.

Taking ecstasy with one another is an invitation, a call, to a then-and-there, a not-yet-here. Following this book's rhythm of cross-temporal comparison, I offer lesbian poet Elizabeth Bishop's invitation to her staunch spinster mentor Marianne Moore to "come flying":

> *Invitation to Miss Marianne Moore*
> From Brooklyn, over the Brooklyn Bridge, on this fine morning,
> please come flying.
> In a cloud of fiery pale chemicals,
> please come flying,
> to the rapid rolling of thousands of small blue drums
> descending out of the mackerel sky
> over the glittering grandstand of harbor-water,
> please come flying.[5]

The next few lines describe the river that the two poets would traverse, the multitude of flags they would behold on ships. Bishop refers to Moore's signature three-cornered Paul Revere hat and her pointy black shoes, making the address all the more personal and highlighting Moore's own queer extravagance. They would "mount" the magical sky with what Bishop calls a natural heroism. Our queer dynamic duo would then fly over "the accidents, above the malignant movies, the taxicabs and injustices at large." This flight is a spectacle of queer transport made lyric. Each stanza closes with the invitation to come flying. The last two stanzas are especially poignant for my thesis:

> With dynasties of negative constructions
> darkening and dying around you,
> with grammar that suddenly turns and shines
> like flocks of sandpipers flying,
> please come flying.
>
> Come like a light in the white mackerel sky,
> come like a daytime comet
> with a long unnebulous train of words,
> from Brooklyn, over the Brooklyn Bridge, on this fine morning,
> please come flying.[6]

It is important to note that the poem's last few lines announce the flight's destination as not determinedly spatial but instead as temporal: "this fine morning." Kathryn R. Kent has written carefully about the complicated cross-generational bond between the two women that eventually led to a sort of disappointment when Moore's mother (with whom she lived) became an overarching influence in her life and overwhelmed the identificatory erotics between the two great poets.[7] (As I have maintained, disappointment is a big part of utopian longing.) Kent explains the ways in which Bishop's work signaled a queer discourse of invitation that did not subsume the other but was instead additive. Two other queer ghosts who float over the bridge are Walt Whitman and Hart Crane, both of whom wrote monumental poems about the bridge and what it represented. Bishop and Moore were both conversant about that work and the queer intertext that was being rendered. One can perhaps also decipher the living presence of writer Samuel R. Delany hovering. He is the author of "Atlantis: A Model 1924," a haunting story that meditates on his own family history as it is interlaced with Crane's biography and his relationship with the Brooklyn Bridge.[8] The point is that the poem itself is poised at a dense connective site in the North American queer imagination. The Brooklyn Bridge and crossing the river, arguably both ways, represents the possibility of queer transport, leaving the here and now for a then and there. Thus, I look at Bishop's poem as being illustrative of a queer utopianism that is by its very nature additive, like the convergence of past, present, and future that I have discussed throughout this book. This convergence is the very meaning of the ecstatic.

The poem, like the pop song, is also a unique example of the concrete utopianism for which I am calling. Bishop does not overly sugarcoat the invitation; she clearly states that there are "dynasties of negative constructions / darkening and dying around you." But this invitation, this plea, is made despite the crushing force of the dynasty of the here and now. It is an invitation to desire differently, to desire more, to desire better.

Cruising Utopia can ultimately be read as an invitation, a performative provocation. Manifesto-like and ardent, it is a call to think about our lives and times differently, to look beyond a narrow version of the here and now on which so many around us who are bent on the normative count. Utopia in this book has been about an insistence on something else, something better, something dawning. I offer this book as a resource for the political imagination. This text is meant to serve as something of a flight plan for a collective political becoming. These pages have described aesthetic and political practices that need to be seen as necessary modes of stepping out of this place and time to something fuller, vaster, more sensual, and brighter. From shared critical dissatisfaction we arrive at collective potentiality.

Notes

Notes to the Introduction

1. This brief biographical sketch of Bloch draws heavily on Vincent Geoghegan's excellent *Ernst Bloch* (New York: Routledge, 1996). Although *Cruising Utopia* employs some of Bloch's critical thinking, it nonetheless does not pretend to anything like a comprehensive introduction to Blochian theory. Indeed that book has already been written, and it is Geoghegan's.

2. Ernst Bloch, *The Principle of Hope*, 3 vols., trans. Neville Plaice, Stephen Plaice, and Paul Knight (Cambridge, MA: MIT Press, 1995).

3. Ibid.

4. Ibid., 1:146.

5. Ernst Bloch, *Literary Essays*, trans. Andrew Joron and others (Stanford, CA: Stanford University Press, 1998), 341.

6. Giorgio Agamben, *Potentialities: Collected Essays in Philosophy*, ed. and trans. Daniel Heller-Roazen (Stanford, CA: Stanford University Press, 1999).

7. Ibid., 178–181.

8. Jill Dolan, *Utopia in Performance: Finding Hope at the Theater* (Ann Arbor: University of Michigan Press, 2005).

9. Gavin Butt, *Just between You and Me: Queer Disclosures in the New York Art World, 1948–1963* (Durham, NC: Duke University Press, 2005).

10. Jennifer Doyle, *Sex Objects: Art and the Dialectics of Desire* (Minneapolis: University of Minnesota Press, 2006).

11. Fred Moten, *In the Break: The Aesthetics of the Black Radical Tradition* (Minneapolis: University of Minnesota Press, 2003).

12. See Ernst Bloch, *The Utopian Function of Art and Literature: Selected Essays*, trans. Jack Zipes and Frank Mecklenburg (Cambridge, MA: MIT Press, 1988), esp. 18–70.

13. Ibid.

14. Bloch, *Literary Essays*, 340.

15. Bloch, *Utopian Function of Art*, 71–77.

16. Frank O'Hara, "Having a Coke with You," in *The Collected Poems of Frank O'Hara*, ed. Donald Allen (Berkeley: University of California Press, 1995), 360.

17. Bloch, *Principle of Hope*, 339.

18. Bloch, *Utopian Function of Art*, 78–102.

19. Ibid.

20. Andy Warhol, *The Philosophy of Andy Warhol: From A to B and Back Again* (New York: Harcourt Brace Jovanovich, 1975), 100.

21. Agamben, *Potentialities,* 178–181.

22. Bloch, *Literary Essays,* 339–344.

23. J. L. Austin, *How to Do Things with Words* (Cambridge, MA: Harvard University Press, 1962).

24. Jean-Luc Nancy, *Being Singular Plural* (Stanford, CA: Stanford University Press, 2000).

25. Leo Bersani, *Homos* (Cambridge, MA: Harvard University Press, 1995).

26. Lee Edelman, *No Future: Queer Theory and the Death Drive* (Durham, NC: Duke University Press, 2004).

27. Lee Edelman, *Homographesis: Essays in Literary and Cultural Theory* (New York: Routledge, 1994).

28. Bloch, *Principle of Hope,* 144–178.

29. Eve Kosofsky Sedgwick, *Touching Feeling: Affect, Pedagogy, Performativity* (Durham, NC: Duke University Press, 2003).

30. Ibid.

31. Ibid.

32. Paolo Virno, *Multitude: Between Innovation and Negation,* trans. Isabella Bertoletti, James Cascaito, and Andrea Casson (New York: Semiotext(e), 2008), esp. 9–66.

33. Ibid., 18.

34. Shoshana Felman, *The Scandal of the Speaking Body: Don Juan with J. L. Austin, or Seduction in Two Languages,* trans. Catherine Porter (Stanford, CA: Stanford University Press, 2003), 104.

35. Eileen Myles, *Chelsea Girls* (New York: Black Sparrow, 1994), 274.

36. Fredric Jameson, *Archaeologies of the Future: The Desire Called Utopia and Other Science Fictions* (New York: Verso, 2005).

37. Here I am thinking of Delany's novel *The Mad Man* (New York: Kasak Books/Masquerade Books, 1994).

38. Samuel R. Delany, *Times Square Red, Times Square Blue* (New York: New York University Press, 1999). Delaney's paradigm is carefully interrogated by Ricardo Montez, in "'Trade' Marks: LA2, Keith Haring, and a Queer Economy of Collaboration," *GLQ: A Journal of Lesbian and Gay Studies* 12, no. 3 (2006): 425–440.

39. Michel Foucault, *The History of Sexuality, Volume 1: An Introduction,* trans. Robert Hurley (New York: Vintage, 1980), 15–50. Although Foucault's innovation is undeniable, the work of many historians of sexuality who have written in his wake has become rote.

40. Judith Halberstam, *In a Queer Time and Place: Transgender Bodies, Subcultural Lives* (New York: New York University Press, 2005); Carla Freccero, *Queer/Early/Modern* (Durham, NC: Duke University Press, 2005); Elizabeth Freeman,

"Packing History, Count(Er)Ing Generations," *New Literary History* 31 (2000): 727–744; Elizabeth Freeman, "Time Binds, or, Erotohistoriography," *Social Text* 84–85 (2005): 57–68; Carolyn Dinshaw, *Getting Medieval: Sexualities and Communities, Pre- and Postmodern* (Durham, NC: Duke University Press, 1999); Gayatri Gopinath, *Impossible Desires: Queer Diasporas and South Asian Public Cultures* (Durham, NC: Duke University Press, 2005); and Dolan, *Utopia in Performance*.

41. For an example of this queer-of-color critique, see the special issue of the journal *Social Text* that I edited with David and Judith Halberstam: "What's Queer about Queer Studies Now?" *Social Text* 84–85 (2005).

42. Lauren Berlant, "'68 or Something," *Critical Inquiry* 21, no. 1 (1994): 124–155. Notable publications by Berlant that followed this earlier essay include *The Queen of America Goes to Washington City: Essays on Sex and Citizenship* (Durham, NC: Duke University Press, 1997); and *The Female Complaint: The Unfinished Business of Sentimentality in American Culture* (Durham, NC: Duke University Press, 2008).

43. Along with Berlant's work, some other work that exemplifies the Public Feelings project includes Ann Cvetkovich, *An Archive of Feelings: Trauma, Sexuality, and Lesbian Public Cultures* (Durham, NC: Duke University Press, 2003); and Kathleen Stewart, *Ordinary Affects* (Durham, NC: Duke University Press, 2007).

44. See the group's website, www.feeltankchicago.net.

45. See Jonathan Flatley, *Affective Mapping* (Cambridge, MA: Harvard University Pres, 2008).

Notes to Chapter 1

1. Third World Gay Revolution, "Manifesto of the Third World Gay Revolution," in *Out of the Closets: Voices of Gay Liberation*, ed. Karla Jay and Allen Young (New York: New York University Press, 1992), 367.

2. Evan Wolfson, "All Together Now (A Blueprint for the Movement)," *Advocate*, September 11, 2001; available online at http://www.freedomtomarry.org/evan_wolfson/by/all_together_now.php (accessed February 6, 2009).

3. See Lisa Duggan, "Holy Matrimony!" *Nation*, March 15, 2004, available online at http://www.thenation.com/doc/20040315/duggan; and Lisa Duggan and Richard Kim, "Beyond Gay Marriage," *Nation*, July 18, 2005, available online at http://www.thenation.com/doc/20050718/kim.

4. Giorgio Agamben, *Potentialities: Collected Essays in Philosophy*, ed. and trans. Daniel Heller-Roazen (Stanford, CA: Stanford University Press, 1999).

5. Alain Badiou, *Being and Event* (London: Continuum, 2005).

6. Ernst Bloch, *The Principle of Hope*, trans. Neville Plaice, Stephen Plaice, and Paul Knight, 3 vols. (Cambridge, MA: MIT Press, 1995).

7. Here I draw from Judith Halberstam's notion of time and normativity that she mines from a critique of David Harvey. I see her alerting us to a normative

straight temporality that underscores heterosexual and heteronormative life and constructs straight space. My notion of time or critique of a certain modality of time is interested in the way in which a queer utopian hermeneutic wishes to interrupt the linear temporal ordering of past, present, and future. See Judith Halberstam, *In a Queer Time and Place: Transgender Bodies, Subcultural Lives* (New York: New York University Press, 2005).

8. Lee Edelman, *No Future: Queer Theory and the Death Drive* (Durham, NC: Duke University Press, 2004).

9. Edmund Husserl, *Ideas Pertaining to a Pure Phenomenology and to a Phenomenological Philosophy*, trans. R. Rojcewicz (New York: Springer, 1991).

10. Roland Barthes, *Sade, Fourier, Loyola* (New York: Hill and Wang, 1976), 23.

11. James Schuyler, *Collected Poems* (New York: Farrar, Straus and Giroux, 1993), 186–187.

12. Martin Heidegger, *Being and Time*, trans. Joan Stambaugh (Albany: State University of New York Press, 1996), 329.

13. Fredric Jameson, *Archaeologies of the Future: The Desire Called Utopia and Other Science Fictions* (New York: Verso, 2005), 10.

14. J. L. Austin, *How to Do Things with Words* (Cambridge, MA: Harvard University Press, 1962).

15. Fredric Jameson, *The Political Unconscious: Narrative as a Socially Symbolic Act* (Ithaca, NY: Cornell University Press, 1981).

16. Bloch, *Principle of Hope*, 1:141.

17. Ibid.

18. Fredric Jameson, *Marxism and Form: Twentieth-Century Dialectical Theories of Literature* (Princeton, NJ: Princeton University Press, 1972).

19. Terrence Kissack, "Freaking Fag Revolutionaries: New York's Gay Liberation Front, 1969–1971," *Radical History Review* 62 (1995): 104–135.

20. This economical summary is drawn from Michael Inwood's useful book: Michael Inwood, *Heidegger: A Very Short Introduction* (Oxford: Oxford University Press, 2000), 121.

21. Herbert Marcuse, *One-Dimensional Man: Studies in the Ideology of Advanced Industrial Society* (Boston: Beacon, 1964), 17.

22. Lisa Duggan, *The Twilight of Equality? Neoliberalism, Cultural Politics, and the Attack on Democracy* (Boston: Beacon, 2003).

23. David Harvey, *A Brief History of Neo-Liberalism* (Oxford: Oxford University Press, 2005).

24. Ibid, 46–47.

25. Halberstam, *In a Queer Time and Place*.

26. This chapter benefited from Fred Moten's thoughtful suggestions and generous attention. I am also grateful for excellent feedback from Joshua Chambers-Letson, Lisa Duggan, Anna McCarthy, Tavia Nyong'o, Shane Vogel, an audience at the University of California, Santa Cruz, and this volume's editors. John

Andrews offered me the gift of extremely generative conversations during the writing of this essay. I only partially acknowledge my gratitude by dedicating it to him.

Notes to Chapter 2

1. The talk was later published in *October*, a publication then under the editorial influence of Crimp, in which queer theory in its modern incarnations began to flourish. The essay was ultimately published in an anthology of Crimp's writings: Douglas Crimp, *Melancholia and Moralism: Essays on AIDS and Queer Politics* (Cambridge, MA: MIT Press, 2002).

2. Douglas Crimp, "Mourning and Militancy," *October* 51 (Winter 1988): 11.

3. Leo Bersani, "Is the Rectum a Grave?" in *AIDS: Cultural Analysis/Cultural Activism*, ed. Douglas Crimp and Leo Bersani (Cambridge, MA: MIT Press, 1988).

4. Leo Bersani, *Homos* (Cambridge, MA: Harvard University Press, 1995).

5. The "us" and "we" I use in this chapter are meant, in the first instance, to speak to gay men in the pandemic. But beyond that, they are intended to address people who have also been caught in the HIV/AIDS pandemic—people who have been affected by the pandemic in ways that are both direct and relational, subjects who might be women or men, queer or straight. The unifying thread of this essay's "us" and "we" is a node of commonality within a moment and space of chaos and immeasurable loss.

6. See the recent work of Lauren Berlant for a compelling reading of the political struggle currently being staged in the public sphere between "live sex acts" and "the dead citizenship of heterosexuality." Lauren Berlant, "Live Sex Acts: Parental Advisory: Explicit Material," *Feminist Studies* 21, no. 2 (1995): 379–404.

7. These myths include "Andy was asexual" or "Andy only liked to watch." For more on the degaying of Warhol, see the introduction to my coedited volume Jennifer Doyle, Jonathan Flatley, and José Esteban Muñoz, eds., *Pop Out: Queer Warhol* (Durham, NC: Duke University Press, 1996).

8. John Giorno, *You Got to Burn to Shine* (New York: High Risk Books/Serpent's Tail, 1994), 68–69.

9. Ibid., 71.

10. Ernst Bloch and Theodor W. Adorno, "Something's Missing: A Discussion between Ernst Bloch and Theodor Adorno on the Contradictions of Utopian Longing," in *The Utopian Function of Art and Literature: Selected Essays* (Cambridge, MA: MIT Press, 1988).

11. Ibid., 12.

12. Ibid.

13. Giorno, *You Got to Burn to Shine*, 72–73.

14. Ibid., 73.

15. Bloch and Adorno, "Something's Missing," 12.

16. Ibid., 13.

17. Ibid., 17.

18. Raymond Williams, *Marxism and Literature* (Oxford: Oxford University Press, 1977), 133.

19. Jacques Derrida, *Specters of Marx: The State of the Debt, the Work of Mourning, and the New International*, trans. Peggy Kamuf (New York: Routledge, 1994), 51.

20. Ibid., 63.

21. I wish to assert that Adorno's version of dialectics, and especially his emphasis on the determined aspect of the negative, complicates deconstructive protocols. Adorno's formulations show a great resistance to deconstructive challenges to dialectical materialism.

22. Ernst Bloch, *Traces,* trans. Anthony Nassar (Stanford, CA: Stanford University Press, 2006), 1.

23. Mandy Merck, "Figuring Out Warhol," in *Pop Out: Queer Warhol,* ed. Jennifer Doyle, Jonathan Flatley, and José Esteban Muñoz (Durham, NC: Duke University Press, 1996). See also Patricia White, "Female Spectator, Lesbian Specter: The Haunting," in *Inside/Out: Lesbian Theories, Gay Theories*, ed. Diana Fuss (New York: Routledge, 1991).

24. Walt Odets, *In the Shadow of the Epidemic: Being HIV-Negative in the Age of AIDS* (Durham, NC: Duke University Press, 1995).

25. Many of the ideas in this chapter were first formulated and "tried out" in a graduate seminar, "Sex in Public," that I taught in the Performance Studies program at New York University in the fall of 1995. The experience of working with those students on this topic enabled my thinking in many important ways.

Notes to Chapter 3

1. Lauren Berlant, "Live Sex Acts: Parental Advisory: Explicit Material," *Feminist Studies* 21, no. 2 (1995): 379–404.

2. C. L. R. James, *The Future in the Present: Selected Writings* (Westport, CT: Lawrence Hill, 1977).

3. Samuel R. Delany, *The Motion of Light in Water: Sex and Science Fiction Writing in the East Village* (Minneapolis: University of Minnesota Press, 2004), 179.

4. See, for example, essays by Michael Kirby, Allan Kaprow, and Richard Schechner in Mariellen R. Sandford, ed., *Happenings and Other Acts* (London: Routledge, 1995).

5. Delany, *Motion of Light in Water*, 183.

6. Ibid., 179.

7. Ibid.

8. Ibid., 202.

9. Ibid., 183.

10. Ibid., 267.

11. Joan Wallach Scott, "The Evidence of Experience," in *The Lesbian and Gay Studies Reader,* ed. Henry Abelove, Michèle Aina Barale, and David M. Halperin (New York: Routledge, 1993).

12. Lisa Duggan, *The Twilight of Equality? Neoliberalism, Cultural Politics, and the Attack on Democracy* (Boston: Beacon, 2003).

13. Delany, *Motion of Light in Water,* 266.

14. Samuel R. Delany, *Times Square Red, Times Square Blue* (New York: New York University Press, 1999), 111.

15. Duggan, *Twilight of Equality?*

16. Examples of this right-wing impulse in current gay culture include Bruce Bawer, *A Place at the Table: The Gay Individual in American Society* (New York: Poseidon, 1993); and Andrew Sullivan, *Virtually Normal: An Argument about Homosexuality* (New York: Vintage, 1996). Along with Duggan's text, two other important responses to the new gay conservatism are Phillip Brian Harper, *Private Affairs: Critical Ventures in the Culture of Social Relations* (New York: New York University Press, 1999); and Michael Warner, *The Trouble with Normal: Sex, Politics, and the Ethics of Queer Life* (New York: Free Press, 1999).

17. Theodor W. Adorno, "Sexual Taboos and Law Today," in *Critical Models: Interventions and Catchwords,* trans. Henry W. Pickford (New York: Columbia University Press, 1998), 72.

18. C. L. R. James, Grace C. Lee, and Pierre Chaulieu, *Facing Reality* (Detroit: Bewick, 1974), 137.

19. Ibid.

20. Quoted in Kent Worcester, *C. L .R. James: A Political Biography* (Albany: State University of New York Press, 1995), 141.

21. This paragraph is adapted from the last chapter of my book *Disidentifications: Queers of Color and the Performance of Politics* (Minneapolis: University of Minnesota Press, 1999).

22. José Esteban Muñoz, "Dead White: Notes on the Whiteness of the Queer Screen," *GLQ: A Journal of Gay and Lesbian Studies* 4, no. 1 (1998): 127–138.

23. For an example of such Internet sex-consumer posting, see the ATKOL Video website, http://www.atkol.com.

24. *Swallow Your Pride: A Hands-On Tool for Do-It-Yourself Activism,* independently produced activist zine, no pagination. The zine includes a return address: Ananda La Vita, 184 East 2nd Street #5F, New York, NY 10009. The zine itself is partially written as a how-to manual that gives instructions to would-be activists on how to make their own stickers and develop their own guerrilla activist projects.

25. I am grateful to Arin Mason, who participated in these stickering campaigns and who, in an excellent seminar paper, suggested the stickers' status as performative objects.

26. For these statistics and more recent ones on antigay violence, see the LAMBDA Gay and Lesbian Anti-Violence Project website at http://www.lambda.org/glnvah.htm.

27. See Ernst Bloch and Theodor W. Adorno, "Something's Missing: A Discussion between Ernst Bloch and Theodor Adorno on the Contradictions of Utopian Longing," in *The Utopian Function of Art and Literature: Selected Essays* (Cambridge, MA: MIT Press, 1988), 12.

Notes to Chapter 4

1. I am grateful to Carol Martin and Jane Desmond for advice on this chapter. Aviance has been helpful and generally divine. I appreciate Ari Gold's introducing him to me.

2. For more on the trace, see Jacques Derrida, *Of Grammatology*, trans. Gayatri Chakravorty Spivak, corrected ed. (Baltimore: Johns Hopkins University Press, 1998), 24–65.

3. Jane C. Desmond, ed., *Dancing Desires: Choreographing Sexualities on and off the Stage* (Madison: University of Wisconsin Press, 2001). The contributions to that volume that I directly engage are Paul B. Franklin, "The Terpsichorean Tramp: Unmanly Movement in the Early Films of Charlie Chaplin"; Paul Siegel, "The Right to Boogie: The First Amendment on the Dance Floor"; and Jonathan Bollen, "Queer Kinesthesia: Performativity on the Dance Floor."

4. For more on the Giuliani cabaret-license laws in relation to queer performance, see Shane Vogel, "Where Are We Now? Queer World Making and Cabaret Performance," *GLQ: A Journal of Gay and Lesbian Studies* 6, no. 1 (2000): 29–60.

5. By "historically dense queer gesture," I mean a gesture whose significance and connotative queer force is dense with antinormative meanings.

6. See Elin Diamond, *Unmaking Mimesis: Essays on Feminism and Theater* (London: Routledge, 1997).

7. That Kiki would be in her late sixties seems a bit unlikely because, according to the oral biography that Kiki and Herb recite during their performances, they began performing during the Great Depression. When I asked Bond about Kiki's age, she explained that her "official age" is sixty-six.

8. Elizabeth Bishop, "One Art," in *The Complete Poems, 1927–1979* (New York: Farrar, Straus and Giroux, 1983).

9. In some ways this idea echoes Peggy Phelan, who has famously argued that disappearance is the very ontology of something that is performed. Peggy Phelan, *Unmarked: The Politics of Performance* (London: Routledge, 1993).

10. The word *cunty* is black gay slang that describes a certain performed mode of femininity. Although its misogynist implications cannot be underemphasized,

it should be understood that the term *cunty,* unlike *cunt,* is not meant to be derogatory. A good queen strives to achieve a high level of "cuntiness."

11. For more on the process I describe at length as disidentification, see my book *Disidentifications: Queers of Color and the Performance of Politics* (Minneapolis: University of Minnesota Press, 1999).

12. The members of LaBelle were Patti LaBelle, Nona Hendrix, and Sarah Dash.

13. I take this opportunity to refer readers to Judith Halberstam's *Female Masculinity* (Durham, NC: Duke University Press, 1998).

14. I argue for the notion of resistance through dance/nightlife culture in the introduction that Celeste Fraser Delgado and I wrote for our edited volume, *Everynight Life: Culture and Dance in Latin/o America* (Durham, NC: Duke University Press, 1997).

15. Marx articulates the theory of the commodity fetish in *Capital: Volume 1,* trans. Ben Fowkes (London: Penguin, 1990).

16. See Ramsay Burt, *The Male Dancer: Bodies, Spectacle, Sexualities* (New York: Routledge, 1995).

17. See W. E. B. Du Bois, *The Souls of Black Folk* (New York: Bantam, 1989), 179–180.

18. Marcia Siegel, *At the Vanishing Point: A Critic Looks at Dance* (New York: Saturday Review Press, 1972).

Notes to Chapter 5

1. Imamu Amiri Baraka, *The Toilet* (New York: Sterling Lord Agency, 1964); hereafter cited in the text as *T.*

2. Ernst Bloch, *The Principle of Hope,* trans. Neville Plaice, Stephen Plaice, and Paul Knight, 3 vols. (Cambridge, MA: MIT Press, 1995).

3. I am covering some territory that Moten has already tread quite expertly, and I am hoping to build on his formidable analysis. See Fred Moten, *In the Break: The Aesthetics of the Black Radical Tradition* (Minneapolis: University of Minnesota Press, 2003).

4. Sally Banes, *Greenwich Village 1963: Avant-Garde Performance and the Effervescent Body* (Durham, NC: Duke University Press, 1993).

5. Moten, *In the Break,* 169.

6. Whatever currency the term *alternative* might have at this historical moment is certainly up for grabs. *Minoritized* here is meant to connote racialization in relationship to a scene dominated by whiteness, but it is also relational to the term *minoritarian,* which I often use to talk about sexual and racial minorities.

7. Gloria Anzaldúa, *Borderlands/La Frontera,* 2nd ed. (San Francisco: Aunt Lute Books, 1999).

8. Diane di Prima, *Recollections of My Life as a Woman: The New York Years: A Memoir* (New York: Viking, 2001).

9. Joe LeSueur, *Digressions on Some Poems by Frank O'Hara* (New York: Farrar, Straus and Giroux, 2003), 57.

10. Jerry Gafio Watts, *Amiri Baraka: The Politics and Art of a Black Intellectual* (New York: New York University Press, 2001).

11. Ibid., 336.

12. I do not wish simply to posit "identitarian" as always already bad. It is important to resist a knee-jerk denouncement of anything that might connote identity. Historically, identity's effects are at times both and alternatively stultifying and generative. In this project I am interested in considering moments before identity takes hold of what I describe as queer animating forces that can be deciphered at different temporal junctures.

13. Lee Edelman, *No Future: Queer Theory and the Death Drive* (Durham, NC: Duke University Press, 2004).

14. Barbara Johnson, "The Frame of Reference: Poe, Lacan, Derrida," in *Literature and Psychoanalysis*, ed. Shoshana Felman, 457–505 (Baltimore: Johns Hopkins University Press, 1977), 45.

15. Watts, *Amiri Baraka*, 129.

16. Giorgio Agamben, *Means without Ends: Notes on Politics*, trans. Vincenzo Binetti and Cesare Casarino (Minneapolis: University of Minnesota Press, 2000).

17. Ernst Bloch, *The Utopian Function of Art and Literature: Selected Essays*, trans. Jack Zipes and Frank Mecklenburg (Cambridge, MA: MIT Press, 1988), 1–17.

18. Edelman, *No Future*, 3.

19. At first glance it might seem that there are significant convergences between Agamben's privileging of a "means" at the expense of the end and Edelman's investment in the present over the future. Such an analogy would not hold because Agamben owns an investment in politics that Edelman eschews. The means when unyoked from an end can be viewed as a utopian formulation that contests the hegemony of straight time and its presentism.

20. Edelman, *No Future*, 3.

21. Watts, *Amiri Baraka*.

22. Judith Butler, "Longing for Recognition," in *Undoing Gender* (New York: Routledge, 2004), 131–151.

23. G. W. F. Hegel, *The Phenomenology of Spirit*, ed. J. N. Findlay, trans. A. V. Miller (Oxford, UK: Clarendon, 1977).

24. Butler, "Longing for Recognition," 149.

25. My invocation of woundedness is not aligned with the work of Wendy Brown and her take on "wounded attachments," with which I generally take issue, but is instead aligned with Moten's riff on fiction writer Nathaniel MacKey's notion of wounded kinship. See Wendy Brown, *States of Injury: Power and Freedom*

in Late Modernity (Princeton, NJ: Princeton University Press, 1995); Moten, *In the Break*; and Nathaniel MacKey, *Bedouin Hornbook* (Lexington, KY: Callaloo Fiction Series, 1986).

26. Leo Bersani, *Homos* (Cambridge, MA: Harvard University Press, 1995); and Leo Bersani, "Is the Rectum a Grave?" *AIDS: Cultural Analysis/Cultural Activism*, ed. Douglas Crimp and Leo Bersani (Cambridge, MA: MIT Press, 1988).

27. Cornel West and Sylvia Ann Hewitt, "A Parent's Bill of Rights," *Boston Globe*, September 18, 1998.

28. *Afrofuturism* is a term taken up by several African American writers. See the special issue edited by Alondra Nelson: "Afrofuturism," *Social Text* 20, no. 2 (2002).

Notes to Chapter 6

1. Jim Jocoy, Thurston Moore, and Exene Cervenka, *We're Desperate: The Punk Photography of Jim Jocoy* (New York: Power House Books, 2002), 270.

2. Ernst Bloch, "The Artistic Illusion and the Visible Anticipatory Illumination," in *The Utopian Function of Art and Literature: Selected Essays* (Cambridge, MA: MIT Press, 1988); Ernst Bloch, *The Principle of Hope*, trans. Neville Plaice, Stephen Plaice, and Paul Knight, 3 vols. (Cambridge, MA: MIT Press, 1995).

3. Lee Edelman, *No Future: Queer Theory and the Death Drive* (Durham, NC: Duke University Press, 2004)..

4. I am grateful to Kevin McCarty for his friendship and pictures. His project is beautifully continued on the artist's current website: imnotlikeyou.la. That site documents a youth-culture scene in LA inhabited by Latino punks. In this aspect of the artist's project, race and ethnicity are examined with the same attentiveness and care as sexuality in the Chameleon Club series.

5. Peggy Phelan, *Unmarked: The Politics of Performance* (London: Routledge, 1993).

6. Miranda Joseph, *Against the Romance of Community* (Minneapolis: University of Minnesota Press, 2002), 64.

7. Giorgio Agamben, *Potentialities: Collected Essays in Philosophy*, ed. and trans. Daniel Heller-Roazen (Stanford, CA: Stanford University Press, 1999).

8. Ernst Bloch and Theodor W. Adorno, "Something's Missing: A Discussion between Ernst Bloch and Theodor Adorno on the Contradictions of Utopian Longing," in *The Utopian Function of Art and Literature: Selected Essays* (Cambridge, MA: MIT Press, 1988), 12.

9. Giorgio Agamben, *Means without Ends: Notes on Politics,* trans. Vincenzo Binetti and Cesare Casarino (Minneapolis: University of Minnesota Press, 2000).

10. Samuel R. Delany, *The Motion of Light in Water: Sex and Science Fiction Writing in the East Village* (Minneapolis: University of Minnesota Press, 2004), 267. See also chapter 3 for further discussion of this moment in Delany's memoir.

11. Kevin McCarty, "Autobiographical Artist Statement," *GLQ: A Journal of Gay and Lesbian Studies* 11, no. 3 (2005): 427–428.

12. John Kelsey, "The Cleveland Bar Scene in the Forties," in *Lavender Culture*, ed. Karla Jay and Allen Young (New York: New York University Press, 1994), 146.

13. Ibid.

14. Ibid., 148–149.

15. Ibid., 149.

16. J. L. Austin, *How to Do Things with Words* (Cambridge, MA: Harvard University Press, 1962).

17. Shane Vogel discusses Davis and Bricktop's life and performance practices. See Shane Vogel, *The Scene of Harlem Cabaret: Race, Sexuality, Performance* (Chicago: University of Chicago Press, 2009). See also Jennifer Doyle, *Sex Objects: Art and the Dialectics of Desire* (Minneapolis: University of Minnesota Press, 2006).

18. Oscar Wilde and Linda C. Dowling, *The Soul of Man under Socialism and Selected Critical Prose* (London: Penguin, 2001), 141.

19. Brendan Mullen, Don Bolles, and Adam Parfrey, *Lexicon Devil: The Fast Times and Short Life of Darby Crash and the Germs* (Los Angeles: Feral House, 2002), 47.

Notes to Chapter 7

1. See Dick Higgins, *Horizons: Intermedia: The Poetics and Theory of the Intermedia* (Carbondale: Southern Illinois University Press, 1984).

2. See the exhibition catalog: Ray Johnson, Donna M. De Salvo, and Catherine Gudis, *Ray Johnson: Correspondences* (Columbus, OH: Wexner Center for the Arts, 1999).

3. For mention of both Ray Johnson's and Jill Johnston's involvement in that scene, see Sally Banes, *Democracy's Body: Judson Dance Theater, 1962–1964* (Durham, NC: Duke University Press, 1993).

4. The classic text on the "happening" is Michael Kirby and Jim Dine, *Happenings* (New York: Dutton, 1965).

5. Although the documentary is certainly a resource because it offers valuable footage of Johnson, his friends, and his work, it is disappointing because of the filmmaker's inability to deal with the queerness of Johnson's art and life. If this film heralds a certain canonization of the artist, then it is one that is content to keep his queerness as unknowable as possible.

6. For more on reparative criticism, see Eve Kosofsky Sedgwick, *Touching Feeling: Affect, Pedagogy, Performativity* (Durham, NC: Duke University Press, 2003).

7. Jill Johnston, *Marmalade Me*, rev. and exp. ed. (Hanover, NH: Wesleyan University Press, 1998).

8. Deborah Jowitt, introduction to *Marmalade Me*, by Jill Johnston, 12.

9. Ibid., 4.

10. Ibid.

11. Ibid.

12. Ibid., 6.

13. Johnson, De Salvo, and Gudis, *Ray Johnson: Correspondences*, 132.

14. Michel Foucault and Sylverer Lotringer, *Foucault Live: (Interviews, 1966–84)* (New York: Semiotext(e), 1989), 204.

15. Johnson, De Salvo, and Gudis, *Ray Johnson: Correspondences*, 132.

16. Ernst Bloch and Theodor W. Adorno, "Something's Missing: A Discussion between Ernst Bloch and Theodor Adorno on the Contradictions of Utopian Longing," in *The Utopian Function of Art and Literature: Selected Essays* (Cambridge, MA: MIT Press, 1988), 116–117.

17. Jowitt, introduction to *Marmalade Me*, 6.

18. Richard Bernstein, "Ray Johnson's World," *Andy Warhol's Interview*, August 1972, 40.

Notes to Chapter 8

1. "You Ornament the Earth: A Dialogue with Jim Hodges and Ian Berry," in Ian Berry and Ron Platt, *Jim Hodges* (Saratoga Springs, NY: Frances Young Tang Teaching Museum and Art Gallery at Skidmore College, 2003), 15.

2. Gerald Henderson Thayer, *Concealing—Coloration in the Animal Kingdom: An Exposition of the Laws of Disguise through Color and Pattern; Being a Summary of Abbott H. Thayer's Discoveries* (New York: Macmillan, 1909).

3. Ovid, *Metamorphoses*, trans. Rolfe Humphries (Bloomington: Indiana University Press, 1955), 162.

4. Herbert Marcuse, *Eros and Civilization: A Philosophical Inquiry into Freud* (Boston: Beacon, 1955), 171.

5. Ibid., 171.

6. Ibid., 45.

7. Ibid., 161.

8. Ibid., 164.

9. Ibid., 165.

10. Ernst Bloch, "Better Castles in the Sky," in *The Utopian Function of Art and Literature: Selected Essays*, trans. Jack Zipes and Frank Mecklenburg (Cambridge, MA: MIT Press, 1988), 283.

11. Marcuse, *Eros and Civilization*, 166.

12. J. M. Coetzee, *White Writing: On the Culture of Letters in South Africa* (New Haven, CT: Yale University Press, 1988).

13. Oscar Wilde and Linda C. Dowling, *The Soul of Man under Socialism and Selected Critical Prose* (London: Penguin, 2001), 141.

14. Quoted in Julie Ault, ed., *Félix González-Torres* (Gottingen, Germany: Steidl, 2006), 161.

15. José Esteban Muñoz, *Disidentifications: Queers of Color and the Performance of Politics* (Minneapolis: University of Minnesota Press, 1999), 37–56.

Notes to Chapter 9

1. Antonio Negri, *Marx beyond Marx: Lessons on the Grundrisse* (New York: Autonomedia, 1989).

2. Andre Lepecki, *Exhausting Dance* (London: Routledge, 2006).

3. I have run into various accounts of Herko's death while researching this chapter. The version from which I am drawing is a composite of various authors' work, including that of Sally Banes, David Bourdon, Ramsay Burt, Diane Di Prima, Andy Warhol, and Pat Hackett. I want to take this opportunity to state that I do not have the definitive account of Herko's death. Indeed, no one who was not there has any such account and the only person who was there, Johnny Dodd, died quite a few years ago. I am working with something like the legend of Fred Herko's death. We know he died after jumping out a window and we know he had spoken to various friends about planning a suicide performance. Thus we can assume that this was, at least on some level, his suicide performance. The details I'm employing here might be facts or muddled rememberances or perhaps even the elaborate projections of various parties. It is, nonetheless, the story I am working with. I cannot testify to its ultimate truth. Perhaps one day a careful, empiricially minded biographer can offer us a better account. But that is not the work I'm doing in this interpretive and theoretically oriented analysis.

4. Andy Warhol and Pat Hackett, *POPism: The Warhol '60s* (San Diego, CA: Harcourt Brace Jovanovich, 1990, a reprint of the 1980 edition).

5. See Watson, *Factory Made.*

6. To this date the greatest contribution in dance studies to remembering Herko is Sally Banes's important *Democracy's Body: Judson Dance Theater, 1962–1964* (Durham, NC: Duke University Press, 1993). More recently Susan Leigh Foster has written an excellent essay on the question of improvisation and historiography: "Improvising/History," in *Theorizing Practice: Redefining Theatre History,* ed. W. B. Worthen and Peter Holland (New York: Palgrave, 2003). Ramsay Burt has written the most thoughtful and detailed dance-historical study of Herko: *Judson Dance Theater* (London: Routledge, 2006). In queer studies Jennifer Doyle has also written a beautiful essay on friendship between gay men and women that reflects on di Prima and Herko's queer friendship, and Dominic Johnson has produced engaging work that compares Herko's work with that of the legendary Jack Smith. Jennifer Doyle, "Between Friends," in *A Companion to Lesbian, Gay, Bisexual, Transgender, and Queer Studies,* ed. George Haggerty and Molly McGarry, 325–340 (Malden, MA: Blackwell, 2007); Dominic Johnson, "Jack Smith's Rehearsals for the Destruction of Atlantis: 'Exotic' Ritual and Apocalyptic Tone," *Contemporary Theatre Review* 19, no. 2 (2009): 164–180.

7. Quoted in Banes, *Democracy's Body*, 44.

8. Ernst Bloch, *The Principle of Hope*, trans. Neville Plaice, Stephen Plaice, and Paul Knight, 3 vols. (Cambridge, MA: MIT Press, 1995).

9. Quoted in Banes, *Democracy's Body*, 43.

10. Quoted in ibid., 43.

11. Quoted in ibid., 44.

12. Donald McDonagh, "The Incandescent Innocent," *Film Culture* 45 (1968) 55–60.

13. Dominic Johnson's work elegantly compares the powerful aesthetic resonances between Smith's and Herko's work.

14. Ibid.

15. Shoshana Felman, *The Scandal of the Speaking Body: Don Juan with J. L. Austin, or Seduction in Two Languages*, trans. Catherine Porter (Stanford, CA: Stanford University Press, 2003), 57.

16. Diane di Prima, *Recollections of My Life as a Woman: The New York Years: A Memoir* (New York: Viking, 2001).

17. Quoted in Foster, "Improvising/History," 202.

18. Quote in Banes, *Democracy's Body*, 44.

19. Diane di Prima, "For Freddy, Fucking Again," in *Freddie Poems* (Point Reyes, CA: Eidolon Editions, 1974), 35.

20. Stephen Koch, *Stargazer: Andy Warhol's World and His Films*, 2nd ed. (New York: M. Boyars; distributed in the U.S. by Scribner, 1985), 53.

21. Quoted in Foster, "Improvising/History," 203.

22. Quoted in Callie Angell, *Andy Warhol Screen Tests: The Films of Andy Warhol: Catalogue Raisonnâe* (New York: H. N. Abrams/Whitney Museum of American Art, 2006), 93.

23. Giorgio Agamben, *Means without Ends: Notes on Politics*, trans. Vincenzo Binetti and Cesare Casarino (Minneapolis: University of Minnesota Press, 2000).

24. Randy Martin, *Critical Moves: Dance Studies in Theory and Politics* (Durham, NC: Duke University Press, 1998).

25. José Esteban Muñoz, *Disidentifications: Queers of Color and the Performance of Politics* (Minnesota: University of Minnesota Press, 1999).

26. Di Prima, *Recollections of My Life as a Woman*, 280.

27. Ernst Bloch, "The Fairy Tale Moves on Its Own in Time," in *Literary Essays*, trans. Andrew Joron and others (Stanford, CA: Stanford University Press, 1998), 167.

28. Di Prima, *Recollections of My Life as a Woman*, 193.

29. Ibid.

30. Ibid., 389.

31. Bloch, *Principle of Hope*, 1:394.

32. Herbert Marcuse, *Eros and Civilization: A Philosophical Inquiry into Freud* (Boston: Beacon, 1955), 144.

33. Ramsay Burt has specifically urged us not to make much of Herko's death or his drug use and instead consider his place in dance history. Although I respect Burt's scholarship, I have taken the path he warns against. I have done so to understand the difficult dialectic of failure and utopia that I see as essential if we are to counter a gay and lesbian pragmatism that currently dilutes that queer political imagination. See Burt, *Judson Dance Theater.*

Notes to Chapter 10

1. José Esteban Muñoz, *Disidentifications: Queers of Color and the Performance of Politics* (Minneapolis: University of Minnesota Press, 1999).
2. Jack Smith, "Capitalism of Lotusland," in *Wait for Me at the Bottom of the Pool: The Writings of Jack Smith,* ed. J. Hoberman and Edward Leffingwell (New York: Serpent's Tail, 1997), 11.
3. Judith Halberstam, *In a Queer Time and Place: Transgender Bodies and Subcultural Live* (New York: New York University Press, 2005), 4–7.
4. Smith, "Capitalism of Lotusland," 11.
5. Ibid.
6. Michael Warner, *The Trouble with Normal: Sex, Politics, and the Ethics of Queer Life* (New York: Free Press, 1999).
7. For an excellent account of Smith's performances, see Stefan Brecht's classic *Queer Theatre* (New York: Methuen, 1986).
8. Paolo Virno, *A Grammar of the Multitude,* trans. Isabella Bertoletti, James Cascaito, and Andrea Casson (New York: Semiotext(e), 2004), 84.
9. Ibid., 12.
10. Daphne Brooks, *Bodies in Dissent: Spectacular Performances of Race and Freedom, 1850–1910* (Durham, NC: Duke University Press, 2006).
11. Virno, *Grammar of the Multitude,* 61–62.
12. Tavia Nyong'o, "Sitting on the Edge of My Couch: Kalup Linzy's Black Queer Sublime," paper presented at the annual American Studies Association convention, Albuquerque, New Mexico, November 2008.

Notes to the Conclusion

1. Plotinus, *The Essential Plotinus: Representative Treatises from the Enneads,* trans. Elmer O'Brien (Indianapolis: Hackett, 1975).
2. Jacques Lacan, *On Feminine Sexuality, the Limits of Love and Knowledge, 1972–1973: The Seminar of Jacques Lacan, Book XX, Encore,* ed. Jacques-Alain Miller and trans. Bruce Fink (New York: Norton, 1999).
3. Martin Heidegger, *Being and Time,* trans. Joan Stambaugh (Albany: State University of New York Press, 1996), 329.

4. Judith Halberstam, "Keeping Time with Lesbians on Ecstasy," *Women and Music: A Journal of Gender and Culture* 11 (2007): 51–58.

5. Elizabeth Bishop, "Invitation to Miss Marianne Moore," in *The Complete Poems, 1927–1979* (New York: Farrar, Straus and Giroux, 1983), 82.

6. Ibid.

7. Kathryn R. Kent, *Making Girls into Women: American Women's Writing and the Rise of Lesbian Identity* (Durham, NC: Duke University Press, 2002), 187–189.

8. Samuel R. Delany, *Atlantis: Three Tales* (Hanover, NH: Wesleyan University Press, 1995).

Bibliography

Adorno, Theodor W. "Sexual Taboos and Law Today." In *Critical Models: Interventions and Catchwords.* Translated by Henry W. Pickford. New York: Columbia University Press, 1998.

Agamben, Giorgio. *Means without Ends: Notes on Politics.* Translated by Vincenzo Binetti and Cesare Casarino. Minneapolis: University of Minnesota Press, 2000.

———. *Potentialities: Collected Essays in Philosophy.* Edited and translated by Daniel Heller-Roazen. Stanford, CA: Stanford University Press, 1999.

Angell, Callie. *Andy Warhol Screen Tests: The Films of Andy Warhol: Catalogue Raisonnâe.* New York: H. N. Abrams/Whitney Museum of American Art, 2006.

Anzaldúa, Gloria. *Borderlands/La Frontera.* 2nd ed. San Francisco: Aunt Lute Books, 1999.

Ault, Julie, ed. *Félix González-Torres.* Gottingen, Germany: Steidl, 2006.

Austin, J. L. *How to Do Things with Words.* Cambridge, MA: Harvard University Press, 1962.

Badiou, Alain. *Being and Event.* London: Continuum, 2005.

Banes, Sally. *Democracy's Body: Judson Dance Theater, 1962–1964.* Durham, NC: Duke University Press, 1993.

———. *Greenwich Village 1963: Avant-Garde Performance and the Effervescent Body.* Durham, NC: Duke University Press, 1993.

Baraka, Imamu Amiri. *The Toilet.* New York: Sterling Lord Agency, 1964.

Barthes, Roland. *Sade, Fourier, Loyola.* New York: Hill and Wang, 1976.

Bawer, Bruce. *A Place at the Table: The Gay Individual in American Society.* New York: Poseidon, 1993.

Berlant, Lauren. "'68 or Something," *Critical Inquiry* 21, no. 1 (1994): 124–155.

———. *The Female Complaint: The Unfinished Business of Sentimentality in American Culture.* Durham, NC: Duke University Press, 2008.

———. "Live Sex Acts: Parental Advisory: Explicit Material." *Feminist Studies* 21, no. 2 (1995): 379–404.

———. *The Queen of America Goes to Washington City: Essays on Sex and Citizenship.* Durham, NC: Duke University Press, 1997.

Bernstein, Richard. "Ray Johnson's World." *Andy Warhol's Interview,* August 1972.

Bersani, Leo. *Homos.* Cambridge, MA: Harvard University Press, 1995.

———. "Is the Rectum a Grave?" In *AIDS: Cultural Analysis/Cultural Activism*, edited by Douglas Crimp and Leo Bersani. Cambridge, MA: MIT Press, 1988.

Bishop, Elizabeth. *The Complete Poems, 1927–1979*. New York: Farrar, Straus and Giroux, 1983.

Bloch, Ernst. "The Artistic Illusion and the Visible Anticipatory Illumination." In *The Utopian Function of Art and Literature: Selected Essays*, 141–155. Cambridge, MA: MIT Press, 1988.

———. "The Fairy Tale Moves on Its Own in Time." In *Literary Essays,* translated by Andrew Joron and others. Stanford, CA: Stanford University Press, 1998.

———. *Literary Essays*. Translated by Andrew Joron and others. Stanford, CA: Stanford University Press, 1998.

———. *The Principle of Hope*. Translated by Neville Plaice, Stephen Plaice, and Paul Knight. 3 vols. Cambridge, MA: MIT Press, 1995.

———. *The Utopian Function of Art and Literature: Selected Essays*. Translated by Jack Zipes and Frank Mecklenburg. Cambridge, MA: MIT Press, 1988.

———. *Traces*. Translated by Anthony Nassar. Stanford, CA: Stanford University Press, 2006.

Bloch, Ernst, and Theodor W. Adorno. "Something's Missing: A Discussion between Ernst Bloch and Theodor Adorno on the Contradictions of Utopian Longing." In *The Utopian Function of Art and Literature: Selected Essays*. Cambridge, MA: MIT Press, 1988.

Bollen, Jonathan. "Queer Kinesthesia: Performativity on the Dance Floor." In *Dancing Desires: Choreographing Sexualities on and off the Stage*, edited by Jane C. Desmond. Madison: University of Wisconsin Press, 2001.

Brecht, Stefan. *Queer Theatre*. New York: Methuen, 1986.

Brooks, Daphne. *Bodies in Dissent: Spectacular Performances of Race and Freedom, 1850–1910*. Durham, NC: Duke University Press, 2006.

Brown, Wendy. *States of Injury: Power and Freedom in Late Modernity*. Princeton, NJ: Princeton University Press, 1995.

Burt, Ramsay. *Judson Dance Theater*. London: Routledge, 2006.

———. *The Male Dancer: Bodies, Spectacle, and Sexuality*. New York: Routledge, 1995.

Butler, Judith. *Undoing Gender*. New York: Routledge, 2004.

Butt, Gavin. *Between You and Me: Queer Disclosures in the New York Art World, 1948–1963*. Durham, NC: Duke University Press, 2005.

Coetzee, J. M. *White Writing: On the Culture of Letters in South Africa*. New Haven, CT: Yale University Press, 1988.

Crimp, Douglas. *Melancholia and Moralism: Essays on AIDS and Queer Politics*. Cambridge, MA: MIT Press, 2002.

———. "Mourning and Militancy." *October* 51 (Winter 1988): 3–18.

Cvetkovich, Ann. *An Archive of Feelings: Trauma, Sexuality, and Lesbian Public Cultures*. Durham, NC: Duke University Press, 2003.

Delany, Samuel R. *Atlantis: Three Tales*. Hanover, NH: Wesleyan University Press, 1995.

————. *The Mad Man*. New York: Kasak Books/Masquerade Books, 1994.

————. *The Motion of Light in Water: Sex and Science Fiction Writing in the East Village*. Minneapolis: University of Minnesota Press, 2004.

————. *Times Square Red, Times Square Blue*. New York: New York University Press, 1999.

Delgado, Celeste Fraser, and José Esteban Muñoz. *Everynight Life: Culture and Dance in Latin/o America*. Durham, NC: Duke University Press, 1997.

Derrida, Jacques. *Of Grammatology*. Translated by Gayatri Chakravorty Spivak. Corrected ed. Baltimore: Johns Hopkins University Press, 1998.

————. *Specters of Marx: The State of the Debt, the Work of Mourning, and the New International*. Translated by Peggy Kamuf. New York: Routledge, 1994.

Desmond, Jane C., ed. *Dancing Desires: Choreographing Sexualities on and off the Stage*. Madison: University of Wisconsin Press, 2001.

di Prima, Diane. *Freddie Poems*. Point Reyes, CA: Eidolon Editions, 1974.

————. *Recollections of My Life as a Woman: The New York Years: A Memoir*. New York: Viking, 2001.

Diamond, Elin. *Unmaking Mimesis: Essays on Feminism and Theater*. London: Routledge, 1997.

Dinshaw, Carolyn. *Getting Medieval: Sexualities and Communities, Pre- and Postmodern*. Durham, NC: Duke University Press, 1999.

Dolan, Jill. *Utopia in Performance: Finding Hope at the Theater*. Ann Arbor: University of Michigan Press, 2005.

Doyle, Jennifer. "Between Friends." In *A Companion to Lesbian, Gay, Bisexual, Transgender, and Queer Studies*, ed. George Haggerty and Molly McGarry, 325–340. Malden, MA: Blackwell, 2007).

————. *Sex Objects: Art and the Dialectics of Desire*. Minneapolis: University of Minnesota Press, 2006.

Doyle, Jennifer, Jonathan Flatley, and José Esteban Muñoz, eds. *Pop Out: Queer Warhol*. Durham, NC: Duke University Press, 1996.

Du Bois, W. E. B. *The Souls of Black Folk*. New York: Bantam, 1989.

Duggan, Lisa. "Holy Matrimony!" *Nation*, March 15, 2004. Available online at http://www.thenation.com/doc/20040315/duggan.

————. *The Twilight of Equality? Neoliberalism, Cultural Politics, and the Attack on Democracy*. Boston: Beacon, 2003.

Duggan, Lisa, and Richard Kim. "Beyond Gay Marriage." *Nation*, July 18, 2005. Available online at http://www.thenation.com/doc/20050718/kim.

Edelman, Lee. *Homographesis: Essays in Gay Literary and Cultural Theory*. New York: Routledge, 1994.

————. *No Future: Queer Theory and the Death Drive*. Durham, NC: Duke University Press, 2004.

Felman, Shoshana. *The Scandal of the Speaking Body: Don Juan with J. L. Austin, or Seduction in Two Languages.* Translated by Catherine Porter. Stanford, CA: Stanford University Press, 2003.

Flatley, Jonathan. *Affective Mapping: Melancholia and the Politics of Modernism.* Cambridge, MA: Harvard University Press, 2008.

Foster, Susan Leigh. "Improvising/History." In *Theorizing Practice: Redefining Theatre History,* edited by W. B. Worthen and Peter Holland. New York: Palgrave, 2003.

Foucault, Michel. *The History of Sexuality, Volume 1: An Introduction.* Translated by Robert Hurley. New York: Vintage, 1980.

Foucault, Michel, and Sylverer Lotringer. *Foucault Live (Interviews, 1966–84).* New York: Semiotext(e), 1989.

Franklin, Paul B. "The Terpsichorean Tramp: Unmanly Movement in the Early Films of Charlie Chaplin." In *Dancing Desires: Choreographing Sexualities on and off the Stage,* edited by Jane C. Desmond. Madison: University of Wisconsin Press, 2001.

Freccero, Carla. *Queer/Early/Modern.* Durham, NC: Duke University Press, 2005.

Freeman, Elizabeth. "Packing History, Count(Er)Ing Generations." *New Literary History* 31 (2000): 727–744.

———. "Time Binds, or, Erotohistoriography." *Social Text* 84–85 (2005): 57–68.

Geoghegan, Vincent. *Ernst Bloch.* New York: Routledge, 1996.

Giorno, John. *You Got to Burn to Shine.* New York: High Risk Books/Serpent's Tail, 1994.

Gopinath, Gayatri. *Impossible Desires: Queer Diasporas and South Asian Public Cultures.* Durham, NC: Duke University Press, 2005.

Halberstam, Judith. *Female Masculinity.* Durham, NC: Duke University Press, 1998.

———. *In a Queer Time and Place: Transgender Bodies, Subcultural Lives.* New York: New York University Press, 2005.

———. "Keeping Time with Lesbians on Ecstasy." *Women and Music: A Journal of Gender and Culture* 11 (2007): 51–58.

Harper, Phillip Brian. *Private Affairs: Critical Ventures in the Culture of Social Relations.* New York: New York University Press, 1999.

Harvey, David. *A Brief History of Neo-Liberalism.* Oxford: Oxford University Press, 2005.

Hegel, G. W. F. *The Phenomenology of Spirit.* Edited by J. N. Findlay. Translated by A. V. Miller. Oxford, UK: Clarendon, 1977.

Heidegger, Martin. *Being and Time.* Translated by Joan Stambaugh. Albany: State University of New York Press, 1996.

Higgins, Dick. *Horizons: Intermedia: The Poetics and Theory of the Intermedia.* Carbondale: Southern Illinois University Press, 1984.

Husserl, Edmund. *Ideas Pertaining to a Pure Phenomenology and to a Phenomeno-logical Philosophy*. Translated by R. Rojcewicz. New York: Springer, 1991.

Inwood, Michael. *Heidegger: A Very Short Introduction*. Oxford: Oxford University Press, 2000.

James, C. L. R. *The Future in the Present: Selected Writings*. Westport, CT: Lawrence Hill, 1977.

James, C. L. R., Grace C. Lee, and Pierre Chaulieu. *Facing Reality*. Detroit: Bewick, 1974.

Jameson, Fredric. *Archaeologies of the Future: The Desire Called Utopia and Other Science Fictions*. New York: Verso, 2005.

———. *Marxism and Form: Twentieth-Century Dialectical Theories of Literature*. Princeton, NJ: Princeton University Press, 1972.

———. *The Political Unconscious: Narrative as a Socially Symbolic Act*. Ithaca, NY: Cornell University Press, 1981.

Jay, Karla, and Allen Young, eds. *Out of the Closets: Voices of Gay Liberation*. New York: New York University Press, 1992.

Jocoy, Jim, Thurston Moore, and Exene Cervenka. *We're Desperate: The Punk Photography of Jim Jocoy*. New York: Power House Books, 2002.

Johnson, Barbara. "The Frame of Reference: Poe, Lacan, Derrida." In *Literature and Psychoanalysis*, edited by Shoshana Felman, 457–505. Baltimore: Johns Hopkins University Press, 1977.

Johnson, Dominic. "Jack Smith's Rehearsals for the Destruction of Atlantis: 'Exotic' Ritual and Apocalyptic Tone." *Contemporary Theatre Review* 19, no. 2 (2009): 164–180.

———. "Touching the Dead: Jack Smith, Performance, Writing and Death." Ph.D. diss., Courtauld Institute of Art, 2007.

Johnson, Ray, Donna M. De Salvo, and Catherine Gudis. *Ray Johnson: Correspondences*. Columbus, OH: Wexner Center for the Arts, 1999.

Johnston, Jill. *Marmalade Me*. Rev. and exp. ed. Introduction by Deborah Jowitt. Hanover, NH: Wesleyan University Press, 1998.

Joseph, Miranda. *Against the Romance of Community*. Minneapolis: University of Minnesota Press, 2002.

Kelsey, John. "The Cleveland Bar Scene in the Forties." In *Lavender Culture*, edited by Karla Jay and Allen Young. New York: New York University Press, 1994.

Kent, Kathryn R. *Making Girls into Women: American Women's Writing and the Rise of Lesbian Identity*. Durham, NC: Duke University Press, 2002.

Kirby, Michael, and Jim Dine. *Happenings*. New York: Dutton, 1965.

Kissack, Terrence. "Freaking Fag Revolutionaries: New York's Gay Liberation Front, 1969–1971." *Radical History Review* 62 (1995):104–135 .

Koch, Stephen. *Stargazer: Andy Warhol's World and His Film*. 2nd ed. New York: M. Boyars; distributed in the U.S. by Scribner, 1985.

Lacan, Jacques. *On Feminine Sexuality, the Limits of Love and Knowledge, 1972–1973: The Seminar of Jacques Lacan, Book XX, Encore.* Edited by Jacques-Alain Miller. Translated by Bruce Fink. New York: Norton, 1999.

Lepecki, Andre. *Exhausting Dance.* London: Routledge, 2006.

LeSueur, Joe. *Digressions on Some Poems by Frank O'Hara.* New York: Farrar, Straus and Giroux, 2003.

MacKey, Nathaniel. *Bedouin Hornbook.* Lexington, KY: Callaloo Fiction Series, 1986.

Marcuse, Herbert. *Eros and Civilization: A Philosophical Inquiry into Freud.* Boston: Beacon, 1955.

———. *One-Dimensional Man: Studies in the Ideology of Advanced Industrial Society.* Boston: Beacon, 1964.

Martin, Randy. *Critical Moves: Dance Studies in Theory and Politics.* Durham, NC: Duke University Press, 1998.

Marx, Karl. *Capital: Volume 1.* Translated by Ben Fowkes. London: Penguin, 1990.

McCarty, Kevin. "Autobiographical Artist Statement." *GLQ: A Journal of Gay and Lesbian Studies* 11, no. 3 (2005): 427–428.

McDonagh, Donald. "The Incandescent Innocent." *Film Culture* 45 (1968): 55–60.

Merck, Mandy. "Figuring Out Warhol." In *Pop Out: Queer Warhol,* edited by Jennifer Doyle, Jonathan Flatley, and José Esteban Muñoz. Durham, NC: Duke University Press, 1996.

Montez, Ricardo. "'Trade' Marks: LA2, Keith Haring, and a Queer Economy of Collaboration." *GLQ: A Journal of Lesbian and Gay Studies* 12, no. 3 (2006): 425–440.

Moten, Fred. *In the Break: The Aesthetics of the Black Radical Tradition.* Minneapolis: University of Minnesota Press, 2003.

Mullen, Brendan, Don Bolles, and Adam Parfrey. *Lexicon Devil: The Fast Times and Short Life of Darby Crash and the Germs.* Los Angeles: Feral House, 2002.

Muñoz, José Esteban. "Dead White: Notes on the Whiteness of the Queer Screen." *GLQ: A Journal of Gay and Lesbian Studies* 4, no. 1 (1998): 127–138.

———. *Disidentifications: Queers of Color and the Performance of Politics.* Minneapolis: University of Minnesota Press, 1999.

Muñoz, José Esteban, David L. Eng, and Judith Halberstam, eds. "What's Queer about Queer Studies Now?" Special issue of *Social Text* 84–85 (2005).

Myles, Eileen. *Chelsea Girls.* New York: Black Sparrow, 1994.

Nancy, Jean-Luc. *Being Singular Plural.* Stanford, CA: Stanford University Press, 2000.

Negri, Antonio. *Marx beyond Marx: Lessons on the Grundrisse.* New York: Autonomedia, 1989.

Nelson, Alondra, ed. "Afrofuturism." Special issue of *Social Text* 20, no. 2 (2002).

Nyong'o, Tavia. "Sitting on the Edge of My Couch: Kalup Linzy's Black Queer Sublime." Paper presented at the annual American Studies Association convention, Albuquerque, New Mexico, November 2008.

Odets, Walt. *In the Shadow of the Epidemic: Being HIV-Negative in the Age of AIDS.* Durham, NC: Duke University Press, 1995.

O'Hara, Frank. *The Collected Poems of Frank O'Hara.* Edited by Donald Allen. Berkeley: University of California Press, 1995.

Ovid. *Metamorphoses.* Translated by Rolfe Humphries. Bloomington: Indiana University Press, 1955.

Phelan, Peggy. *Unmarked: The Politics of Performance.* London: Routledge, 1993.

Plotinus. *The Essential Plotinus: Representative Treaties from the Enneads.* Translated by Elmer O'Brien. Indianapolis: Hackett, 1975.

Sandford, Mariellen R., ed. *Happenings and Other Acts.* London: Routledge, 1995.

Schuyler, James. *Collected Poems.* New York: Farrar, Straus and Giroux, 1993.

Scott, Joan Wallach. "The Evidence of Experience." In *The Lesbian and Gay Studies Reader,* edited by Henry Abelove, Michèle Aina Barale, and David M. Halperin, 397–415. New York: Routledge, 1993.

Sedgwick, Eve Kosofsky. *Touching Feeling: Affect, Pedagogy, Performativity.* Durham, NC: Duke University Press, 2003.

Siegel, Marcia. *At the Vanishing Point: A Critic Looks at Dance.* New York: Saturday Review Press, 1972.

Siegel, Paul. "The Right to Boogie: The First Amendment on the Dance Floor." In *Dancing Desires: Choreographing Sexualities on and off the Stage,* edited by Jane C. Desmond. Madison: University of Wisconsin Press, 2001.

Smith, Jack. "Capitalism of Lotusland." In *Wait for Me at the Bottom of the Pool: The Writings of Jack Smith,* edited by J. Hoberman and Edward Leffingwell. New York: Serpent's Tail, 1997.

Stewart, Kathleen. *Ordinary Affects.* Durham, NC: Duke University Press, 2007.

Sullivan, Andrew. *Virtually Normal: An Argument about Homosexuality.* New York: Vintage, 1996.

Thayer, Gerald Henderson. *Concealing—Coloration in the Animal Kingdom: An Exposition of the Laws of Disguise through Color and Pattern; Being a Summary of Abbott H. Thayer's Discoveries.* New York: Macmillan, 1909.

Third World Gay Revolution. "Manifesto of the Third World Gay Revolution." In *Out of the Closets: Voices of Gay Liberation,* edited by Karla Jay and Allen Young. New York: New York University Press, 1992.

Virno, Paolo. *A Grammar of the Multitude.* Translated by Isabella Bertoletti, James Cascaito, and Andrea Casson. New York: Semiotext(e), 2004.

———. *Multitude: Between Innovation and Negation.* Translated by Isabella Bertoletti, James Cascaito, and Andrea Casson. New York: Semiotext(e), 2008.

Vogel, Shane. *The Scene of Harlem Cabaret: Race, Sexuality, Performance.* Chicago: University of Chicago Press, 2009.

———. "When the Little Dawn Was Gray." Ph.D. diss., New York University, 2004.

———. "Where Are We Now? Queer World Making and Cabaret Performance." *GLQ: A Journal of Gay and Lesbian Studies* 6, no. 1 (2000): 29–60.

Warhol, Andy. *The Philosophy of Andy Warhol: From A to B and Back Again.* New York: Harcourt Brace Jovanovich, 1975.

Warhol, Andy, and Pat Hackett. *POPism: The Warhol '60s.* San Diego, CA: Harcourt Brace Jovanovich, 1990, a reprint of the 1980 edition.

Warner, Michael. *The Trouble with Normal: Sex, Politics, and the Ethics of Queer Life.* New York: Free Press, 1999.

Watson, Steven. *Factory Made: Warhol and the Sixties.* New York: Pantheon, 2003.

Watts, Jerry Gafio. *Amiri Baraka: The Politics and Art of a Black Intellectual.* New York: New York University Press, 2001.

West, Cornel, and Sylvia Ann Hewitt. "A Parent's Bill of Rights." *Boston Globe,* September 18, 1998.

White, Patricia. "Female Spectator, Lesbian Specter: The Haunting." In *Inside/Out: Lesbian Theories, Gay Theories,* edited by Diana Fuss, 142–172. New York: Routledge, 1991.

Wilde, Oscar, and Linda C. Dowling. *The Soul of Man under Socialism and Selected Critical Prose.* London: Penguin, 2001.

Williams, Raymond. *Marxism and Literature.* Oxford: Oxford University Press, 1977.

Wolfson, Evan. "All Together Now (A Blueprint for the Movement)." *Advocate,* September 11, 2001. Available online at http://www.freedomtomarry.org/evan_wolfson/by/all_together_now.php (accessed February 6, 2009).

Worcester, Kent. *C. L. R. James: A Political Biography.* Albany: State University of New York Press, 1995.

Index

Adorno, Theodor, 2, 37–39, 42, 54, 64, 99, 125, 165; "casting of pictures," 38–39, 42, 73, 125
ACT-UP, 61
aesthetic dimension. *See* queer
affective, methodology, 3, 4
Agamben, Giorgio, 3, 9, 21, 90, 99–100, 162
Albers, Joseph, 119
antiutopianism, 4, 10, 12, 14, 18, 21, 26, 31, 165, 173
Anzaldúa, Gloria, 84
Aristotle, 9, 99
Athey, Ron, 160
Austin, J. L., 9, 15, 26
Aviance, Kevin, 4, 57, 65–67, 73–81

B, Franko, 160
Badiou, Alain, 21
Banes, Sally, 84, 148, 148, 157
Baraka, Amina, 95
Baraka, Shani, 94
Barthes, Roland, 22
Basquiat, Jean-Michel, 145
Bawer, Bruce, 54, 64
becoming, 15, 26; queer, 72, 112, 123
being, 159, 176; horizons of, 22; in the world, 5, 121
"belonging-in-difference," 20
Benjamin, Walter, 2, 3, 15
Berlant, Lauren, 17, 49
Bernstein, Richard, 126
Bersani, Leo, 11, 34–35, 94

binary oppositions; absence/presence, 9, 15, 46, 100; future/past, 49; HIV-positive/negative, 46–47; ideality/actuality, 43; pleasure/pain, 74; potentiality/actuality 9; truth/falsity, 9; utopianism/pragmatism, 20
Bishop, Elizabeth, 4, 70–72, 167, 187–89
Black Mountain, 119
blackness; aesthetic practices, 83–84; critiques of hyper-masculinity, 73, 77, 79, 85–86; radical tradition, 87–88, 91; vernacular tradition, 61, 165
Blake, Nayland, 118
Bloch, Ernest, 2–4, 7, 9, 12, 19, 21, 25, 27–31, 37, 40, 43, 83, 87, 90–91, 93, 97, 99, 104, 116, 125–26, 128, 132, 135, 140, 143, 147, 149–50, 152, 154, 163, 165–66, 173; anticipatory illumination, 3, 7, 15, 18, 22, 28, 49, 64, 87, 91, 99, 104, 109, 153, 177; astonishment, 5; aura-of-art, 116; "no-longer-conscious," 12, 19–21, 24, 26–31, 83–84, 87, 135, 149, 153, 160, 173; not-yet-here, 12, 46, 83, 86–90, 96, 183, 187; ornamental, 1, 7, 104, 128, 132, 143–44, 150, 162; "preappearance," 147; utopian function-of-art, 7, 37, 99; "wish landscape," 5, 140, 142, 152, 171

About the Author

JOSÉ ESTEBAN MUÑOZ is Chair of the Department of Performance Studies at New York University's Tisch School of the Arts. He is the author of *Disidentifications: Queers of Color and the Performance of Politics* and coeditor of *Pop Out: Queer Warhol,* with Jennifer Doyle and Jonathan Flatley, and *Everynight Life: Culture and Dance in Latin/o America,* with Celeste Fraser Delgado.

Lightning Source UK Ltd.
Milton Keynes UK
UKOW04f1413040216

267735UK00003B/42/P